Praise for *Master Data Management*

Few people can serve as both an academic and a practitioner. David Loshin is one of those people, and he is superbly qualified to bring sense to the topic of master data management. He has brought all his skills and experience together in this book. Anyone who is embarking on a master data management initiative will find this book a great resource, from the initial efforts to understanding the business value of master data to the methodical approach to implementation.

— Tony Fisher, President, DataFlux

It is always refreshing to get the message "straight from the shoulder." David Loshin is not trying to win a popularity contest . . . he is trying to make a contribution to humanity that will help straighten out the problems! Thank you David.

— John Zachman, Zachman International

David Loshin has a knack for getting to the bottom of the issue. By tackling the critical issues of making master data management successful, he demystifies this "black art" and helps the reader understand where the value lies; by synchronizing business practices with data management, David shows how real business value is driven not with technology, but with sound, well thought out practices that deliver time after time.

— Bill Hewitt, President and CEO, Kalido

David gives sound, practical advice for business leaders and managers planning a real implementation. His material covers the key business, operational, and technical elements of an enterprise reference data and master data program. He delivers a clear description of the functional and technical solutions that are available to business managers. David provides insights that can help business and technology managers improve strategic planning, manage organizational change, and simplify the operational integration of systems and business processes.

— Justin S. Magruder, Vice President, Enterprise Information
Strategy & Management, Freddie Mac

With his new book on MDM, David Loshin has created a comprehensive overview of a complex topic that should be one of the top 5 priorities for CIOs: to transform an enterprise through superior management of its critical business data. Much like the SOA market, MDM needs a separate category of best practices to address the hard business problems that can only be solved through better data governance. This book does a wonderful job of posing these challenges and positing some solutions. A must-have guide for those looking to understand the IT and business issues around master data management.

— Anurag Wadehra, Senior VP, Marketing
& Product Management, Siperian

D1245694

Similar to David's other books on data management, *Master Data Management* shares a deep understanding of how critical business issues are addressed through the managed integration of emerging technologies. This book provides a full-scale exposition on the benefits and the challenges of master data integration; describes approaches to justify, initiate, and design a MDM program; and guides the reader in a process to evaluate the numerous methods and solutions to determine the approach that best addresses the organization's needs. This book delivers the content in the easily read, pragmatic style that has made David Loshin one of the most popular experts for both our business and technology visitors at Business Intelligence Network (*www.B-eye-NETWORK.com*).

— Ron Powell, Editorial Director, Business Intelligence Network

Master data management is a new field of endeavor with deep roots in data quality management. As such, there is no better person than David Loshin to help data practitioners not only understand the intricacies of MDM but also implement it successfully. This how-to manual birthed from long experience is a must-read for aspiring MDM managers and developers.

— Wayne Eckerson, Director, TDWI Research

David Loshin continues the important MDM conversation by highlighting the specific technology frameworks and tactics necessary for master data management success. This book offers a spot-on look at the components of MDM—and why enterprise master data should be treated as a core corporate asset.

— Jill Dyche, Partner, Baseline Consulting and author of *Customer Data Integration: Reaching a Single Version of the Truth*

This is a very important book, and it is both necessary and timely. It helps clear up misunderstandings about master data management and offers practical help for MDM implementers. It is required reading for everyone involved in data management. The practice of MDM is essential, and this book facilitates that practice.

— Bonnie K. O'Neil, Senior Data Architect, Caridian BCT

Master Data Management

Morgan Kaufmann OMG Press

Morgan Kaufmann Publishers and the Object Management Group™ (OMG) have joined forces to publish a line of books addressing business and technical topics related to OMG's large suite of software standards.

OMG is an international, open membership, not-for-profit computer industry consortium that was founded in 1989. The OMG creates standards for software used in government and corporate environments to enable interoperability and to forge common development environments that encourage the adoption and evolution of new technology. OMG members and its board of directors consist of representatives from a majority of the organizations that shape enterprise and Internet computing today.

OMG's modeling standards, including the Unified Modeling Language™ (UML®) and Model Driven Architecture® (MDA), enable powerful visual design, execution and maintenance of software, and other processes—for example, IT Systems Modeling and Business Process Management. The middleware standards and profiles of the Object Management Group are based on the Common Object Request Broker Architecture® (CORBA) and support a wide variety of industries.

More information about OMG can be found at *http://www.omg.org/*.

Morgan Kaufmann OMG Press Titles

Database Archiving: How to Keep Lots of Data for a Very Long Time
Jack Olson

Master Data Management
David Loshin

Building the Agile Enterprise: With SOA, BPM and MBM
Fred Cummins

Business Modeling: A Practical Guide to Realizing Business Value
Dave Bridgeland and Ron Zahavi

A Practical Guide SysML: The Systems Model Language
Sanford Friedenthal, Alan Moore, and Rick Steiner

Systems Engineering with SysML/UML: Modeling, Analysis, Design
Tim Weilkiens

UML 2 Certification Guide: Fundamental and Intermediate Exams
Tim Weilkiens and Bernd Oestereich

Real-Life MDA: Solving Business Problems with Model Driven Architecture
Michael Guttman and John Parodi

Architecture Driven Modernization: A Series of Industry Case Studies
Bill Ulrich

Master Data Management

David Loshin

ELSEVIER

AMSTERDAM • BOSTON • HEIDELBERG • LONDON
NEW YORK • OXFORD • PARIS • SAN DIEGO
SAN FRANCISCO • SINGAPORE • SYDNEY • TOKYO
MORGAN KAUFMANN PUBLISHERS IS AN IMPRINT OF ELSEVIER

MORGAN KAUFMANN PUBLISHERS

Morgan Kaufmann Publishers is an imprint of Elsevier
30 Corporate Drive, Burlington, MA 01803

This book is printed on acid-free paper.

Library of Congress Cataloging-in-Publication Data
Loshin, David, 1963-
  Master data management/David Loshin.
      p. cm.
  Includes bibliographical references and index.
  ISBN 978-0-12-374225-4 (alk. paper)
  1. Management information systems. 2. Database management. 3. Data
warehousing. 4. Business intelligence. I. Title.
  T58.6.L669 2008
  658.4'038011--dc22   2008034235

For information on all Morgan Kaufmann publications, visit our
Web site at *www.mkp.com* or *www.books.elsevier.com*.

Printed in the United States
      09   10   11   12   10 9 8 7 6 5 4 3 2

Contents

Preface

A number of years ago I was working for a large company and was asked to join a team focused on improving the quality of customer name and contact information as part of a transition from an account-oriented approach to a customer-oriented approach to customer interaction and relationship management. Today, this "accounts renovation" project would be termed a Customer Data Integration (CDI) project or even a master data management (MDM) project, but at the time the driving need was to improve customer data quality and reorganize the way that the business considered its customers. Having had a number of years of experience in developing data quality and identity search and matching tools, this was yet another great opportunity to apply the pure technology to a real business.

I learned an important lesson during this project: the major challenge for integrating data from multiple sources into a transparently accessible master data asset was not about technology, or quality methods, or lofty goals such as enterprise information management—it was about people. Although one might think that acquiring tools or creating fancy centralized data hubs are critical first steps in master data management, the real first step is to understand the delicate and controversial relationships individuals form with their information. In the absence of a formal information ownership model, the default is that individuals take on an eerie form of data ownership that often prevents improvements from being made.

One particular concern was the conflicting issues that derive from the dichotomy between what is best for the organization and personal incentives. At the specific organization of which I was an employee, individuals were given bonuses based on the perceived value of their contribution to the business. However, this was most often reflected in terms of short-term tactical initiatives meant to address acute issues, requiring significant effort, with limited strategic value. Because of this perspective, no projects were allowed to exceed a 6- to 9-month time frame.

Yet the issues driving the need for master data management were fundamentally embedded within the haphazardly developed application architecture. Long-ago technical implementation decisions prevented new initiatives from properly sharing information. Multiple groups were developing applications with the same functional requirements. The information technology department did not effectively communicate its value propositions to the business clients. And poor data quality was rampant—in an industry where customer service should rule above all.

It was difficult to initiate change. A combination of the 6- to 9-month view and the tactical incentive scheme meant that addressing what was popularly seen as a nonissue over a multiyear time frame was going to be an uphill battle, one that would be difficult to manage from within the organization. And without having a core framework on which success in data quality improvement could be measured, the probability of management approval for actually solving the fundamental problems was relatively low.

So what happened? Instead of strategically introducing good information management practices into the enterprise and incrementally changing the way the company exploited its information, the senior managers adopted tactical mini-projects to treat the symptoms. Bad product pricing information being presented to the user? Hire staff to make a bunch of phone calls to get the right prices. Can't find a customer record because a name is misspelled? Create another new record (and perhaps another, and another) to make sure that the deal gets done. In essence, provide the perception that something was being done about the problem, even if those efforts were largely cosmetic.

This led to my next great revelation—the company I worked for was not unique. Every company's staff members have complex relationships with their application data sets. Most individuals are driven by incentives that are awarded based on heroism instead of ensuring predictability. Managing siloed data sets is simpler than integrating data across the entire enterprise. It is always easier to treat the symptoms and provide that cosmetic perception. Yet all of these are failure models—organizations that want to truly be competitive in the information age need to understand the value of high-quality information. But most critically: *every organization that uses data is affected by poor data management practices!* Instituting any type of enterprise data management program such as master data management is bound to improve the quality of the data and consequently lead to operational efficiencies and open opportunities for optimization.

ABOUT THE APPROACH DESCRIBED IN THIS BOOK

My reaction to this epiphany was twofold. I took on a mission to assemble a plan for strategically improving organization information quality and created a company, Knowledge Integrity, Inc. (*www.knowledge-integrity.com*), to help organizations form successful information management programs. As a way of distinguishing my effort from other consulting companies, I also instituted a few important corporate rules about the way we would do business:

1. Our mission was to develop and popularize methods for improving the management and use of enterprise data. As opposed to the craze for patenting technology, methods, and processes, we would openly publish our ideas so as to benefit anyone willing to invest the time and energy necessary to internalize the ideas we were promoting.

2. We would encourage clients to adopt our methods within their success patterns. It is a challenge (and perhaps, in a way, insulting) to walk into an organization and tell people who have done their jobs successfully that they need to drop what they are doing and change every aspect of the way they work. We believe that every organization has its own methods for success, and our job is to craft a way to integrate performance-based information quality management into the existing organizational success structure.

3. We would not establish ourselves as permanent fixtures. We believe that good data management practices should be a core competency to be managed within the organization, and our goal for each engagement is to establish the fundamental aspects of the program, transfer technology to internal resources, and then be on our way. I often say that if we do our job right, we work ourselves out of a contract.

4. We are not "selling a product," we are engaged to solve customer problems. We are less concerned about rigid compliance to a trademarked methodology than we are about making sure that the customer's core issues are resolved. That may mean adapting our methods to the success patterns inherent within the client organization, if that is the most appropriate way to solve the problem. I also like to say that we are successful when the client comes up with our ideas.

5. Effective communication is the key to change management. Articulating how good information management techniques enhance organizational effectiveness and performance is the first step in engaging business clients and ensuring their support and sponsorship. We would invest part of every engagement in establishing a strong business case accompanied by collateral information that can be socialized within and across the enterprise, yet we would derive measurable success metrics from that business case to monitor performance as the programs are put into place.

With these rules in mind, our first effort was to consolidate our ideas for semantic, rule-oriented data quality management in a book, *Enterprise Knowledge Management: The Data Quality Approach*, which was published in 2001 by Morgan Kaufmann. A number of readers have told me that the book is critical in their development of a data quality management program, and the new technical ideas proposed for rule-based data quality monitoring have, in the intervening years, been integrated into all of the major data quality vendor product suites. (Perhaps patenting might have been a good idea after all.)

Over the subsequent years, we have developed a graduate-level course on data quality for New York University as well as multiple day courses for The Data Warehousing Institute (*www.tdwi.org*), presented numerous sessions at conferences and chapter meetings for the Data Management Association (DAMA), provided quarterly columns for Robert Seiner's Data Administration Newsletter (*www.tdan.com*), written monthly columns for *DM Review* (*www. dmreview.com*), prepared a downloadable course on data quality from Better Management (*www.bettermanagement.com*), and hosted an expert channel and monthly newsletter on information value at the Business Intelligence Network (*www.b-eye-network.com*).

Since we started the company, the value of information quality management has been revealed to be one of the most important topics that senior management faces. In practices that have emerged involving the exploitation of enterprise data, such as Enterprise Resource Planning (ERP), Supply Chain Management (SCM), Customer Relationship Management (CRM), among others, there is a need for a consolidated view of high-quality representations of every critical instance of a business concept.

Increased regulatory oversight, increased need for information exchange, business performance management, and the value of service-oriented architecture are driving a greater focus on the performance-oriented management of enterprise data with respect to accessibility, consistency, currency, freshness, and usability of a common information asset. These notions coincide in the area of master data management: a concentration on relating the achievement of business objectives to high-quality data is intended to support the requirements introduced by all of these drivers.

OVERVIEW OF THE BOOK

We all agree that the kinds of data management practices embodied within a master data management program are great ideas, but how do we get started? That is where this book comes in. This book is intended to provide the knowledge necessary for getting started in MDM:

- The business value of MDM
- Stakeholder and participant involvement
- Fundamental MDM concepts
- Data governance for MDM
- The criticality of data quality
- Master data metadata
- The determination of which data to "master"
- Modeling master data
- MDM architectural styles
- Data consolidation and integration
- The synchronization of master data across the application infrastructure
- Master data services

All of this is summarized with management guidance for developing an MDM road map. Most of what we present in this book is based on our company's experiences working with clients, exploring the subtleties of each situation, and abstracting the best practices for implementing the components of master data management that address the organization's business needs.

MORE ABOUT MDM AND CONTACT INFORMATION

We are always interested in hearing about successful case studies, as well as war stories and suggestions. Although I have attempted to make the material in this book have a long shelf life, new ideas are always going to emerge. Therefore, I have set up a website at www. mdmbook.com to provide updates, new material, reviews, and more to supplement what has been published here.

We would like to hear from those of you who have the experience of assessing readiness, developing a business case, constructing a road map, preparing a strategy, designing, and implementing a master data management program. Please do not hesitate to contact me directly (e-mail me at loshin@knowledge-integrity.com) for advice—we are always happy to provide recommendations and suggestions.

Acknowledgments

What this book presents is a culmination of years of experience in projects and programs associated with master data management tools, techniques, processes, and people. A number of people were key contributors to the development of this book, and I take this opportunity to thank them for their support:

First of all, my wonderful wife, Jill, deserves the most credit for perseverance and for her encouragement in completing the book. I also must thank my children, Kira, Jonah, Brianna, Gabriella, and Emma, for their help as well.

Critical parts of this book were inspired by works that I was commissioned to assemble for DataFlux, as well as other vendors in the MDM tool space, including Identity Systems, Informatica, Initiate Systems, Siperian, Pervasive, Business Objects, Zoomix, Exeros, and Silver Creek Systems.

Folks at DataFlux provided a significant amount of input during the process: Tony Fisher (president of DataFlux), along with many key team members including Katie Fabiszak, Daniel Teachey, James Goodfellow, and Deb Procopio.

Marty Moseley, the chief technology officer at Initiate Systems, provided detailed comments to help solidify the material.

Ron Powell, Shawn Rogers, Jean Schauer, and Mary Jo Nott (to name only a few) have provided me with an excellent forum for brainstorming ideas and developing material with the data management community through the Businesss Intelligence Network (*www.b-eye-network.com*).

Bonnie O'Neil, coauthor of a great book called *Business Metadata,* was able to turn on a dime and quickly provided input as well as technical oversight.

Richard Ordowich, one of the principal consultants from Knowledge Integrity, acted as a springboard and provided critical comments too.

Colin White provided some valuable insights regarding master data services.

Cliff Longman, the chief technology officer of Kalido, reviewed the topics covered in the book and provided insight to its completeness.

Todd Goldman and Denise Sparks from Exeros, through the creation of MDM University (*www.mdmuniversity.com*), provided an additional outlet for validating material.

Jim Jarvie from Informatica provided valuable feedback regarding the use of identity-resolution techniques.

Thanks to Wilshire Conferences, presenters of the annual DAMA/Meta-Data and Data Governance conferences, The Data Warehousing Institute, and DebTech International for allowing me to develop courseware supporting the concepts in this book.

Thanks to Laura Quinter, who helped assemble the material into its final form.

I thank Mary James from Elsevier for proactively managing my progress along the way, and editor Denise Penrose who has effectively driven me to put together what I hope is perceived to be a high-quality guidebook to inform and direct practitioners and managers across the business information management community. I also want to thank Diane Cerra for her support and encouragement in getting this project started.

Most of all, I want to thank our customers, for it is that community that has trained us in what we know.

About the Author

David Loshin is president of Knowledge Integrity, Inc., a consulting company focusing on intelligent information management solutions. He is among Knowledge Integrity's experts in data quality, business intelligence, and master data management, contributing to *Intelligent Enterprise*, *DM Review*, TDAN (*www.tdan.com*), and providing ongoing analysis as a channel expert at *www.b-eye-network.com*.

His book, *Business Intelligence: The Savvy Manager's Guide* (Morgan Kaufmann, 2003), has been hailed as a resource that allows readers to "gain an understanding of business intelligence, business management disciplines, data warehousing, and how all of the pieces work together." David has created courses and tutorials on data quality and MDM for The Data Warehousing Institute (*www.tdwi.org*), DAMA/Meta-Data conferences, and various other venues, and is often called on for thought leadership for those in the information management industry.

Master Data and Master Data Management

1.1 DRIVING THE NEED FOR MASTER DATA

Our world is increasingly becoming more connected in many different ways, and as the degree of separation shrinks, the amount of information we have at our fingertips seems to have exploded. Agile organizations that can adapt to the flood of largely redundant, yet sometimes conflicting pieces of data find that a combination of information sharing and operational collaboration is a differentiating factor for organizational success. In particular, as the speed and efficiency of the underlying infrastructure improves, so does the organization's ability to control and take advantage of information assets through information sharing and collaboration. In turn, as our partners exchange and share more information, connectivity is enhanced as well—it is not just systems that work better together, but the people managing those systems forge better working relationships, leading to more effective management of the business and, ultimately, to competitive advantage.

However, the more we share information, the more we realize that years of distribution of computing power and business applications across the different lines of business has led to "islands of information coherence." Historically, business applications were designed to meet operational business needs for specific areas of focus; resources have been aligned for vertical success, and to that end, the de facto application architecture evolves organically to support the operations of each line of business, with potential repercussions at the enterprise level. In general, application architectures designed to support operational processes within each business application area required their own information technology support and its accoutrements:

data definitions, data dictionaries, table structures, and application functionality, among others, all defined from the aspect of that business application.

As a result, what we would like to refer to as the "enterprise" is often composed of many applications referring to multiple, sometimes disparate sets of data that are intended to represent the same, or similar, business concepts. Alternatively, the same or similar names are used to refer to concepts that are completely distinct. Administrative control of data still largely resides with the line-of-business management, and as long as the data are used only to fuel operations, there are probably no issues. However, the recent trends in information use tend toward projects for consolidating and transforming data into information and then into actionable knowledge, and that requires collecting the instances of the data representing the critical business concepts from across business boundaries for the purpose of the common good. In other words, a transition toward applications intended to meet enterprise-level business needs must rely on a consistent view of data drawn from many data assets.

To exploit that information for both operational and analytical processes, however, an organization must be able to clearly define those business concepts, identify the different ways that data sets represent commonly understood business concepts, integrate those data into a consistent view, and then make the consistent view available across the organization. This need has introduced a significant opportunity for organizational information integration, management, and sharing, thereby creating a truly integrated enterprise. This is the essence of the master data management (MDM) challenge—envisioning how to organize an enterprise view of the organization's key business information objects and to govern their quality, use, and synchronization to optimize the use of information to achieve the organization's operational and strategic business objectives.

This chapter explores the history of enterprise master data, describes master data and master data management, and highlights the benefits of instituting a master data management program to support enterprise information management. The chapter also looks at the characteristics of master data and provides a high-level overview of what goes into an MDM program. We will also consider some of the organizational challenges of instituting an MDM program. Finally, the chapter provides an overview of the rest of the chapters of the book.

1.2 **ORIGINS OF MASTER DATA**

Originally, there was not a master data management challenge. In the early days of computing, the groups within an organization typically relied on a single computing resource that housed all the applications and all associated data sets. Before the revolution of structured data architecture inspired relational databases, flat data files ruled the world. Of course, the absence of a concept of data normalization led to significant data redundancy, sometimes addressed via code tables, yet the business impacts related to data redundancy were largely ignored. But because applications were developed to automate the straightforward processing that could be performed in batch, data duplication within one application or synchronization of data across different applications were essentially minor issues.

The introduction of workgroup computing in the 1980s coupled with the explosion of desktop computing systems with access to their own applications ushered in an era of information management distribution. At the same time, data architecture evolved to incorporate the relational view, leading to a reengineering of many existing applications to exploit the sleekness and performance of new Relational Database Management Systems (RDBMS). Administrative control of a business application along with its required resources gave business managers a degree of freedom and agility. However, by virtue of that distribution, the managers within one line of business could dictate the processes and constraints associated with the development of their own vertical applications to run their own lines of business. The distribution of administrative control, of course, led to variance in the ways that commonly used business concepts and objects were defined.

At the same time, the increase in both power and functionality at the desktop has engendered an even finer granularity of data distribution. This allows greater freedom in describing and modeling business information. Whether it is in the mainframe files, the database server, or in the desktop spreadsheets, we start to see a confusing jumble of concepts, along with creative ways of implementing those concepts. This is the first driver for master data management—the ability to rationalize the definitions and meanings of commonly used business concepts when possible and the ability to differentiate different business terms when they do not refer to the same concept.

Interestingly, since the mid-1990s, the pendulum has swung back to centralized computing. Organizational initiatives such as those for deploying Enterprise Resource Planning (ERP), Customer Relationship Management (CRM), or Supply Chain Management (SCM) drive the development of technical infrastructure such as data warehouses and the institution of applications that help improve the business. These initiatives are launched with the intention of consolidating the organization's data into an information asset that can be mined for actionable knowledge to improve business productivity. Although the centralization of information for analysis and reporting has great promise, it has introduced a different challenge: as data sets were integrated and transformed for analysis and reporting, cleansing and corrections applied at the warehouse imply that the analysis and reports may no longer be synchronized with the data at their corresponding original sources. The differences in these reports alerted business users to qualifying the trustworthiness of the data, leading to suspicion in the correctness of the centralized system as opposed to the reporting systems on which the managers had always relied. This suggests more drivers for master data management—ensuring the quality of data that is used for analytics and maintaining consistency of the data across analytical systems as well as operational systems.

1.2.1 Example: Customer Data

Every company deals with customers, and within the company, each customer may be touched by many different business operations related to the business life cycle: marketing, sales, fulfillment, support, maintenance, customer satisfaction, billing, or service. In each of these contexts, the customer may be cast in different roles, with different aspects of the customer's attributes being particularly relevant. Consequently, every business application may value some attributes over others in relation to the business context. The telemarketer may insist on accuracy of the telephone number to avoid calling the same prospect twice; the sales representative is concerned about duplication; the shipping department craves high-quality location information.

Within each business application, there may be a customer database, each with its own critical data attributes, and all of these records may be subjected to aggregation when consolidated into a data warehouse. But you clearly want to ensure that your business processes don't fail because the customer appears multiple times in different data sets. In addition, you want to be confident that the customer's activities are accurately portrayed in management reports.

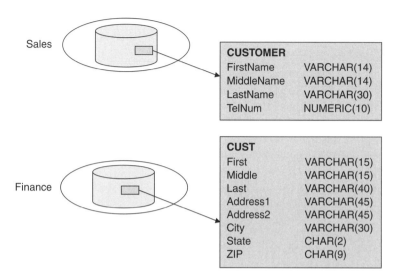

CUSTOMER

FirstName	VARCHAR(14)
MiddleName	VARCHAR(14)
LastName	VARCHAR(30)
TelNum	NUMERIC(10)

CUST

First	VARCHAR(15)
Middle	VARCHAR(15)
Last	VARCHAR(40)
Address1	VARCHAR(45)
Address2	VARCHAR(45)
City	VARCHAR(30)
State	CHAR(2)
ZIP	CHAR(9)

■ **FIGURE 1.1** Different applications may represent similar business concepts in different ways.

This example demonstrates a critical aspect of the apparent distribution of information: data sets maintain representations of business concepts (such as "customers" or "products") in different ways, even if they refer to the same real-world entities. And although different business applications record transactions or analysis regarding entities and their activities, for integration purposes it is desirable for all the business applications to agree on what those entities are, what the activities are, and whether the business terms used to describe these entities and activities truly refer to the same real-world ideas. We can summarize a number of objectives:

- When it can be determined that the entities referred to within the data sets refer to the same business concepts, integrate the multiple variations of those business entities into a unified view of uniquely identifiable data objects.
- Qualify the distinction between sets of data entities when it can be determined that they do not refer to the same business concepts.
- Provide a set of processes that enable enterprise applications to share that unified view of the business objects within the enterprise.

1.3 **WHAT IS MASTER DATA?**

In any organization, there are going to be commonly recognized concepts that are the focus of business processes, such as customers, products, suppliers, vendors, employees, finances, and policies. We have established that as line-of-business silos rely on workgroup application frameworks, disparity has crept into organizational systems, introducing duplication and distribution of variant representations of the same "things." There has been a growing desire for enterprise integration projects, such as those driven by expectations for a unified view of data as expressed by systems designed for customer relationship management (CRM), using a cleansed "product master file" and providing that all-elusive 360° view of the customer or other qualified enterprise reference repositories. In each of these instances, the underlying objective is to create a synchronized, consistent view of an organization's core business entities.

So far we have used terms such as "critical business objects," "business concepts," or "business entities" when referring to the common data themes that exist across any business, and the underlying information objects represent the organization's master data. But what characteristics define master data? Master data objects are those core business objects used in the different applications across the organization, along with their associated metadata, attributes, definitions, roles, connections, and taxonomies. Master data objects are those key "things" that matter the most—the things that are logged in our transaction systems, measured and reported on in our reporting systems, and analyzed in our analytical systems. Common examples of master data include the following:

- Customers
- Employees
- Vendors
- Suppliers
- Parts
- Products
- Locations
- Contact mechanisms
- Profiles
- Accounting items
- Contracts
- Policies

Within a master data object category there may be implicit or explicit hierarchical relationships. For example, there may be individual customer contacts within each client organization, or a product may be a shrink-wrapped collection of smaller product items. Classifications and reference tables are likely to be included as well.

Consider the following transaction: "David Loshin purchased seat 15B on flight 238 from Baltimore (BWI) to San Francisco (SFO) on July 20, 2008." Some of the master data elements in this example and their types are shown in Table 1.1.

In fact, reviewing the master data objects presented in Table 1.1 poses some new questions—for example, we have a concept of a product ("seat 15B") that in its own right has a number of attributes associated with it:

- It is nonrefundable.
- Standby is permitted, but the customer must pay the price difference.
- The fare is subject to change until the ticket is purchased.
- Limited seating, advance purchase, and other conditions may apply.

Next, consider the difference between the seat and the flight. The flight is essentially a container for seats, and the flight also has attributes associated with it, such as a departure gate, an arrival gate, an on-time departure percentage, and an on-time arrival percentage.

Also, recognize that we are using the name "Baltimore" and "BWI" interchangeably, with "Baltimore" referring to the airport closest to and serving the location called Baltimore. In other instances, though, "Baltimore" refers to a different concept (such as a geopolitical region located in the state of Maryland) and may (or may not) include the more specific location referred to as "BWI" (which can be determined via a lookup table to indicate Baltimore Washington International Airport). Clearly, the more one drills down into the specific meanings or what we will call "semantics" of data values—data elements, records representing data

Table 1.1 Master Data Elements

Master Data Object	Value
Customer	David Loshin
Product	Seat 15B
Product container	Flight 238
Location	BWI
Location	SFO
Location	Baltimore
Location	San Francisco

entities, data sets that are collections of data entity representations, and so on—the more data about the data (or "metadata") we discover.

Master data tend to exist in more than one business area within the organization, so the same customer may show up in the sales system as well as the billing system. Master data objects are used within transactions, but the underlying object sets tend to be static in comparison to transaction systems and do not change as frequently. Master data objects may be classified within a hierarchy. For example, we may have a master data category of "party," which in turn comprises "individuals" or "organizations." Those parties may also be classified based on their roles, such as "prospect," "customer," "supplier," "vendor," or "employee." Although we may see one natural hierarchy across one dimension, the nested ways in which we describe, characterize, and classify business concepts (commonly referred to as "taxonomies") may actually cross multiple hierarchies in different ways. For example, when we use the concept of a "party," we may simultaneously be referring to an individual, a customer, and an employee. Alternatively, a "customer" may be either an individual party or an organization.

In turn, the same master data categories and their related taxonomies are used for analysis and reporting. For example, the headers in a monthly sales report may be derived from the master data categories (e.g., sales by customer by region by time period). Enabling the transactional systems to refer to the same data objects as the subsequent reporting systems ensures that the analysis reports are consistent with the transaction systems.

A master data system comprising a master data set is a (potentially virtual) registry or index of uniquely identified entities with their critical data attributes synchronized from the contributing original data sources and made available for enterprise use. With the proper governance and oversight, the data in the master data system (or repository, or registry) can be qualified as a unified and coherent data asset that all applications can rely on for consistent, high-quality information.

1.4 **WHAT IS MASTER DATA MANAGEMENT?**

Master data management is a collection of best data management practices that orchestrate key stakeholders, participants, and business clients in incorporating the business applications, information management methods, and data management tools to implement the policies, procedures, services, and infrastructure to support the capture, integration, and subsequent shared use of accurate, timely, consistent, and complete master data.

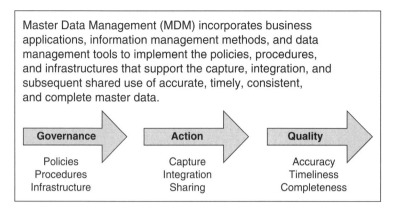

Master Data Management (MDM) incorporates business applications, information management methods, and data management tools to implement the policies, procedures, and infrastructures that support the capture, integration, and subsequent shared use of accurate, timely, consistent, and complete master data.

Governance	Action	Quality
Policies	Capture	Accuracy
Procedures	Integration	Timeliness
Infrastructure	Sharing	Completeness

■ **FIGURE 1.2** The essentials of MDM.

In other words, an MDM program is intended to support an organization's business needs by providing access to consistent views of the uniquely identifiable master data entities across the operational application infrastructure. Master data management governs the methods, tools, information, and services for doing the items listed in the sidebar.

USING MDM TO SUPPORT BUSINESS NEEDS

- Assess the use of commonly used information objects, collections of valid data values, and explicit and implicit business rules in the range of applications across the enterprise
- Identify core information objects relevant to business success that are used in different application data sets that would benefit from centralization
- Instantiate a standardized model for integrating and managing key information objects
- Manage collected and discovered metadata as an accessible, browsable resource, and use the metadata to facilitate consolidation
- Collect data from candidate data sources, evaluate how different data instances refer to the same real-world entities, and create a unique, consolidated view of each one
- Provide methods for transparent access to the unified view of real-world data objects for both existing and newly developed business applications
- Institute the proper data stewardship and management policies and procedures at corporate and line-of-business levels to ensure a high-quality master data asset

1.5 **BENEFITS OF MASTER DATA MANAGEMENT**

Understanding the scale and scope of justifying, designing, planning, implementing, and maintaining an MDM program is itself a significant investment. Seeking executive-level championship for the tasks associated with deploying an MDM solution suggests a need for justifying the business value of master data management. However, recognize that regardless of how good the data management practices are that support MDM, master data integration and master data management are not *truly* the end objectives; rather they are the means by which other strategic and operational objectives are successfully accomplished, such as those promised by customer relationship management systems, product information management systems, enterprise resource planning systems, and the like. Although the principles that drive and support MDM reflect sound data management practices, it would be unusual (although not unheard of) that senior management would embrace and fund the MDM effort solely for the sake of establishing good practices. That being said, the business justification for MDM should be coupled with programs that will benefit from the availability of the unified view of master data. Providing a master unified view of key business information objects enables significant benefits in business productivity improvement, risk management, and cost reduction. More concretely, master data management can be justified in support of a business initiative that relies on any of the following MDM benefits:

Comprehensive customer knowledge. Organically developed application infrastructures often support the same type of customer data functionality in different ways. For example, a bank may have multiple customer banking interfaces: branch banking, automatic teller machines, bank by mail, Internet banking, telephone transactions, and even text-messaging. Customer records may be created, updated, or retired through any of these applications, but in an uncoordinated environment, there would be no way to know the number of distinct customers, how they like to bank, or how many different ways they have tried to execute transactions. A master data repository for customer data provides the single source for consolidating all customer activity, which can then be used to support both operational and analytical applications in a consistent manner.

Improved customer service. A unified view of master data objects enables improvements in meeting customer expectations with respect to availability, accuracy, and responsiveness to their orders, inquiries, as well as providing transparency and governance in managing and protecting customer data.

Consistent reporting. Absent governance, duplication, and complex transformations applied differently at different places in the information processing flow introduce differences into the resulting generated reports. Reliance on end-user applications to digest intermittent system data extracts leads to questions regarding inconsistency from one report to another. Reliance on the reports generated from governed processes using master data reduces the inconsistencies experienced.

Improved competitiveness. The need to react to new business opportunities rapidly with limited resources challenges organizations to produce new business capabilities faster. MDM reduces the complexity of integrating new data and systems into the organization, thereby increasing agility and improving competitiveness.

Improved risk management. At a low degree of granularity, the more data points that applications must touch, the greater the potential for duplication, inconsistencies, or missing information to skew calculated risk assessment, either at the customer level or across lines of business. More trustworthy and consistent financial information improves the business's ability to manage enterprise risk.

Improved operational efficiency and reduced costs. Replication of the same data often is linked to replication of activities associated with managing those data sets, ranging from typical data management routines (backups, maintenance), to licensing costs for infrastructure (such as RDBMS or Extract/Transform/Load (ETL) product license and maintenance costs), to specialized applicationware or services (such as data enhancement or geo/demographic appends). Formulating a unified view of the data enables the organization to reduce operating costs and tasks.

Improved decision making. Inconsistency across business intelligence activities often occur because of replication or duplication in the underlying data used to drive the decision-making process. Questions regarding the consistency of reports can stymie management decision making, leading to missed business opportunities. The information consistency provided by MDM across applications reduces data variability, which in turn minimizes organizational data mistrust and allows for clearer (and faster) business decisions.

Better spend analysis and planning. Master data associated with product, supplier, and vendor data improve the ability to aggregate purchasing activities, coordinate competitive sourcing, be more predictable about future spend, and generally improve vendor and supplier management.

Regulatory compliance. As one of the major enterprise areas of risk, compliance drives the need for quality data and data governance, and MDM addresses both of these needs. Information auditing is simplified across a consistent master view of enterprise data, enabling more effective information controls that facilitate compliance with regulations such as Sarbanes-Oxley, as well as other more industry-focused regulations such as these that apply in the United States: 21 CFR Part 11, the U.S. Patriot Act, Bank Secrecy Act, Basel II, antikickback statutes, and Graham-Leach-Bliley, among others.

Increased information quality. Collecting metadata made up of standardized models, value domains, and business rules enables organizations to more effectively monitor conformance to information quality expectations across vertical applications, which reduces information scrap and rework.

Quicker results. A standardized view of the information asset reduces the delays associated with extraction and transformation of data, speeding the implementation of application migrations, modernization projects, and data warehouse/data mart construction.

Improved business productivity. Master data help organizations understand how the same data objects are represented, manipulated, or exchanged across applications within the enterprise and how those objects relate to business process workflows. This understanding gives enterprise architects the opportunity to explore how effective the organization is in automating its business processes by exploiting the information asset.

Simplified application development. The consolidation activities of MDM are not limited to the data; when the multiple master data objects are consolidated into a master repository, there is a corresponding opportunity to consolidate the application functionality associated with the data life cycle. For example, there may be many applications that create new product entries into various product databases. Consolidating those product systems into a single resource allows us provide a single functional service for the creation of a new product entry to which the different applications can subscribe. Introducing a technical service layer for data life cycle functionality provides the type of abstraction necessary for deploying a service-oriented architecture (SOA).

1.6 ALPHABET SOUP: WHAT ABOUT CRM/SCM/ERP/BI (AND OTHERS)?

Since the mid-1990s, data quality and data integration tools have matured in concert with a recognized desire on behalf of senior managers to aggregate and consolidate replicated or duplicated copies of common or shared data objects that are peppered across disparate or distributed enterprise systems. In fact, MDM initiatives are largely aligned with the need to establish governance and quality across enterprise systems. So what differentiates today's master data management initiatives from previous attempts at enterprise data consolidation? One might question whether there is any significant difference at all, which suggests that MDM may be destined for the same fate the earlier projects faced.

On the surface, MDM appears to be yet another attempt at consolidating data into a single "system of record" or "single version of the truth." But consider customer data integration, product data integration, and enterprise dimension analysis. These ideas have been introduced within the context of data warehousing, business intelligence, sales force automation, customer relationship management, and so on. Yet, to some extent, the promise of many technical applications (such as CRM) has not been realized, and over time there has been growing skepticism as to their success. For example, many have been critical of the inability to effectively exploit a CRM system for its intended benefits. The reasons for this may not lie in the technologies per se but perhaps are influenced by four factors:

1. Despite the recognition of their expected business value, to some extent many of the aspects of these earlier projects were technology driven, and the technical challenges often eclipsed the original business need, creating an environment that was information technology centric. IT-driven projects had characteristics that suggest impending doom: large budgets, little oversight, long schedules, and few early business deliverables.

2. MDM's focus is not necessarily to create yet another silo consisting of copies of enterprise data (which would then itself be subject to inconsistency) but rather to integrate methods for managed access to a consistent, unified view of enterprise data objects.

3. These systems are seen as independent applications that address a particular stand-alone solution, with limited ability to embed the technologies within a set of business processes guided by policies for data governance, data quality, and information sharing.

4. An analytical application's results are only as good as the organization's ability both to take action on discovered knowledge and to measure performance improvements attributable to those decisions. Most of these early projects did not properly prepare the organization along these lines.

These kinds of projects focus on integrating data from multiple sources into a single core repository, and each reflects some aspects of a master data management project. However, what differentiates MDM from previous enterprise integration efforts is that rather than having primarily a technology focus, MDM initiatives typically have a business focus, concentrating on the process of entity identification and validation with the business clients. Whereas MDM uses tools and technology, the combination of that technology with sound business and data management practices is what provides hope for a resounding success.

The intention of an MDM program is to create a single repository of high-quality master data that subsequently feeds applications across the organization with a synchronized, consistent view of enterprise data. The most critical aspects of a successful MDM solution require high-quality integration of master data instances from across the enterprise, and this relies heavily on the following:

- Inventory of data objects used throughout the enterprise
- Methods for identification of key data objects that are candidates for integration into a master data asset
- Resolution of the definitions, usage scenarios and intentions, and the meanings and semantics for these entities, as well as hierarchies and object relationships
- The ability to seamlessly facilitate standardized information extraction, sharing, and delivery
- A quality-directed migration process coupled with data survivorship rules for consolidating the "best records" for the master data asset
- An approach to transparently expose services to enterprise clients for accessing and managing the master data asset
- A governance framework for managing continued integration of enterprise data into the master data environment

Not surprisingly, the technical aspects of the tasks enumerated here depend on the traditional data quality, data integration, and data management tools and methods that most likely are already in place: database management; data profiling for discovery and analysis; parsing; standardization for data cleansing; duplicate analysis/householding and matching for identity resolution; data integration for information sharing; and data governance, stewardship, and standards oversight to ensure ongoing consistency.

In fact, many organizations that are implementing MDM programs have solutions that have evolved out of these traditional techniques.

It is common for master data integration programs to have evolved from customer data quality, product data quality, data assessment and validation, and data integration activities. Alternatively, although targeted solutions have been developed to support MDM functionality, they are often triggered by the introduction of data quality activities to support the technical infrastructure acquired for a specific purpose (e.g., enterprise resource planning or customer relationship management). Lastly, those successful evolutions occur when the ownership of the business benefits of the traditional approaches is transferred to the business side of the company, which emerges as data governance is introduced across the information sharing and collaboration context.

1.7 ORGANIZATIONAL CHALLENGES AND MASTER DATA MANAGEMENT

Numerous technologies have, in the past, been expected to address parts of this problem, providing customer master tables, industry-specific consolidated product management systems, and the like. But these applications have been criticized (perhaps unfairly) as a result of the organizational management approach to their implementation: largely IT-driven, presumed to be usable out of the box, lack of enterprise integration, and limited business acceptance. Resolving the issues pointed out by that criticism is what defines some of the considerations for implementing a successful master data management program:

- Effective technical infrastructure for collaboration
- Organizational preparedness
- "Round-trip" enterprise acceptance and integration
- Measurably high data quality
- Overseeing these (and other) processes via policies and procedures for data governance

That last point is one of the more important ones: what has emerged as a critical factor for success in growing a master data management program is establishing enterprise-wide data governance. It is important to understand how the migration of oversight and governance responsibilities from the lines of business to a centrally managed center of accountability will have impacts on the organization. Realize that years of distributing business applications into vertical lines of business has led to discrete islands of information, and the vertical alignment of IT and data management structures associated with those lines of business have erected barriers to what might be called "horizontal collaboration." This vertical alignment makes it difficult to resolve the differences in roles and responsibilities in relation to the isolated data sets as they are integrated into a master view. In addition, the politics of information ownership and management have created artificial fiefdoms overseen by individuals for whom centralization holds no incentive. Lastly, consolidating master data into a centrally managed data asset transfers the responsibility and accountability for information management from the lines of business to the organization. Therefore, some of the greatest challenges to success are not technical—they are organizational. It is largely because of these issues that MDM should be considered as a "program" and not as a project or an application. For example, these directives offer good suggestions for distinguishing a successful MDM program from one destined for failure.

Organizational preparedness. Anticipate that a rapid transition from a loosely coupled confederation of vertical silos to a more tightly coupled collaborative framework will ruffle a number of feathers. Assess the kinds of training sessions and individual incentives that must be established in order to create a smooth transition. These issues will be addressed in greater detail in Chapter 2.

Data governance. As management responsibility and accountability transition to the enterprise team, it is important to define the policies and procedures governing the oversight of master data. By distributing these policies and seeking proactive comments from across the different application teams, you have an opportunity to create the stewardship framework through consensus while preparing the organization for the transition. A comprehensive look at data governance is provided in Chapter 4.

Metadata management. All aspects of determining need, planning, migration strategy, and future state require a clarified view of the information about the data that is used within the organization—its metadata. The metadata associated with an enterprise master data set do more than just describe the size and types of each data element; rather these metadata include business definitions, valid value sets, accompanying business rules, and usage mappings, among other relevant data. A metadata registry provides a control mechanism or perhaps even a "clearing house" for unifying a master data view when possible, as well as helping to determine when that unification is not possible. The criticality of metadata to support MDM is discussed at great length in Chapter 6.

Technology integration. As is often the case, new technologies that are dependent on application packages are like the tail wagging the dog. Recognize the need to integrate technology to support the process instead of developing the process around the technology. Technology for data quality and data integration is covered in Chapters 5 and 10, with a focus on MDM solution architectures in Chapter 9.

Anticipating change. As with any paradigm shift, proper preparation and organization will subtly introduce change to the way that people think and act. The nature of a master data management program involves integrating data for competitive advantage, and this provides an opportunity for business managers to encourage individuals to begin to understand the differences between existing data replicas and a master data environment and to explore new ways to improve business productivity through the use of a master data asset.

1.8 **MDM AND DATA QUALITY**

Master data management success depends on high-quality data. Data quality can be improved through a master data management program. This codependence drives a large part of the activities that underlie the ability for the business to make use of a master data object framework:

Assessment. The ability to identify core data objects that should be incorporated into a master data repository depends on a structured process of assessment that relies on automated tools for analysis. This analysis comprises tools and techniques for empirically identifying candidate master data sets, primary keys, foreign keys, implicit relational structure, and embedded business rules before any data integration can begin.

Integration. The nature of variation associated with master data (person names, addresses, telephone numbers, product descriptions, etc.) demands that tools be used to help resolve the variation in representation of specific entities from disparate data sources. Standardization, parsing, and matching/linkage techniques have been available as part of any data cleansing tool kit, and the value of using those technologies to support new methods is abundantly clear.

Assurance. MDM is not going to be a case of "build it and they will come." Organizational stakeholders will participate in the integration and consolidation process only as long as they are able to benefit from the process, implying the need for a high degree of confidence in the high quality of master data moving forward. Auditing and monitoring compliance with defined data quality expectations coupled with effective issue response and tracking, along with strong data stewardship within a consensus-based governance model, will ensure ongoing compliance with application quality objectives.

Without a focus on managing the quality of master data, we run a risk of degenerating from an enterprise information management program to just another unsynchronized data silo. Data quality is critical to MDM success, and we will see how this theme penetrates almost all aspects of the MDM program.

1.9 TECHNOLOGY AND MASTER DATA MANAGEMENT

Although MDM should not be considered a technology project, it is clear that developing an MDM program cannot be done without leveraging tools and technology. The technical aspects of master data management rely on tools supporting data profiling, complex data analysis, metadata management, data modeling, data integration, parsing, standardization, record linkage and matching, cleansing, services-oriented architecture, access control, data federation, and data delivery, among others. However, this book is not about the tools but rather how those tools are employed to achieve the consolidated view of uniquely identifiable master data objects to support business strategy and objectives. Therefore, the descriptions of the tools and technology are presented in support of the MDM processes.

1.10 OVERVIEW OF THE BOOK

The objective of this book is to raise awareness among those tasked with developing MDM solutions of both the organizational and technical challenges and to help them develop a road map for success. To that end, the book concentrates on identifying the issues of critical importance, raises some of the questions that need to be asked and answered, and provides guidance on how to jumpstart that process within your organization. The book has 13 chapters.

- Chapter 1, Master Data and Master Data Management, introduces the historical issues that have created the need for master data management, describes both "master data" and "master data management," begins to explore what goes into an MDM program, and reviews the business value of instituting an MDM program, along with this overview of the rest of the book.

■ Chapter 2, Coordination: Stakeholders, Requirements, and Planning, describes who the MDM stakeholders are, why they are relevant to the success of an MDM program, and what their expected participation should be over the course of the program's development.

■ Every organization exhibits different levels of maturity when it comes to sharing consolidated information, and Chapter 3, MDM Components and the Maturity Model, provides a capability model against which an organization's maturity can be measured. By assessing the organization's current state, considering the level of maturity necessary to achieve the organization's objectives, and determining where the organization needs to be, one can assemble an implementation road map that enables action.

■ Master data management is an enterprise initiative, and that means an enterprise data governance program must be in place to oversee it. Governance is a critical issue for deploying MDM. In Chapter 4, Data Governance for Master Data Management, we discuss how business policies are composed of information directives, and how data rules contribute to conformance to those information directives. We'll look at what data governance is, introduce data stewardship roles and responsibilities, and propose a collaborative enterprise data governance framework for data sharing.

■ No book on MDM would be complete without a discussion of the value of data quality, and Chapter 5, Data Quality and MDM, examines the historical evolution of MDM from data quality to its reliance on high-quality information. This chapter provides a high-level view of the data quality components and methods that are used for the purposes of master data integration.

■ The key to information sharing through an MDM repository is a solid set of data standards for defining and managing enterprise data and a comprehensive business metadata management scheme for controlling the use of enterprise data. Chapter 6, Metadata Management for MDM, discusses data standards and metadata management and explores how master metadata is managed.

■ As part of the process, it is necessary to identify the master data object types and determine the data assets that make up those object types across the enterprise. In Chapter 7, Identifying Master Metadata and Master Data, we look at the process of identifying and finding the data sets that are candidates as sources for master data and how to qualify them in terms of usability.

- A core issue for MDM is creating the consolidation models to collect and aggregate master data. Chapter 8, Data Modeling for MDM, is where we will look at some of the issues associated with different source models and how to address data modeling issues for MDM.

- There are different architectural paradigms for master data management, and in Chapter 9, MDM Paradigms and Architectures, we look at existing application and information architectures and different architectural styles for MDM, how they all reflect a spectrum of implementations, and the pros and cons of each of those styles.

- Given a model and understanding the sources of master data, the next step is the actual process of data consolidation and integration, and Chapter 10, Data Consolidation and Integration, looks at collecting information from across the organization and formulating that into the integrated master data asset.

- The power of MDM increases greatly when the master data can be integrated back into the existing application environment. Chapter 11, Master Data Synchronization, discusses the needs and approaches for synchronizing data back to the existing applications.

- The value of MDM does not lie solely with the integration of data. The ability to consolidate application functionality (e.g., new customer creation) using a services layer that supplements multiple application approaches will provide additional value across the existing and future applications. The topic of a functional application services layer is covered in Chapter 12, Master Data Management and the Functional Services Layer.

- The book concludes with Chapter 13, Management Guidelines for MDM, a summary of the guidance provided throughout the preceding chapters to inform management decisions. To address the ongoing management issues, we offer some management guidelines for transitioning the project from developing the business case to maintaining a successful program.

1.11 SUMMARY

Master data management is more than just an application—it is a composition of people, tools, methods, and policies that will mold the future as organizations seek to exploit the value of the corporate information asset. The secrets to success lie in understanding how

MDM will transition your organization into one with a strong data governance framework, articulating the roles and responsibilities for data stewardship and accountability and creating a culture of proactive data quality assurance. Consider how transitioning to the different target architectures will impact the way you do business and prepare your organization for the rapid change. A successful master data management implementation will lead to a more effective integration of business and technology, as well as better organizational collaboration and productivity, and will ultimately increase your competitive advantage.

Coordination: Stakeholders, Requirements, and Planning

2.1 **INTRODUCTION**

Master data present a view into the core shared information asset within the enterprise, and as such, managing the master data asset should be considered a critical component of an enterprise information management strategy. Any initiative that spans the enterprise is bound to require significant amounts of energy for coordination: identifying the key stakeholders, gaining their support, harnessing participant collaboration, gathering requirements, and establishing the roles and responsibilities of the right set of people to make the project successful. In other words, as an enterprise initiative, master data management (MDM) requires enterprise buy-in and participation. To deploy an enterprise initiative, one must understand who the key stakeholders are within the organization; identify the individuals who will participate in the marketing, education, championing, design, implementation, and ongoing support of the program; and delineate a process for identifying their needs and requirements for the purpose of engineering a high-quality master data asset.

As a prelude to actually building and configuring the master data management environment, team members should therefore perform a number of tasks specifically intended to do the following:

- Identify the people in the organization that can benefit from MDM.
- Establish the business value of MDM and develop a business justification.
- Collect and prioritize the data requirements that will drive the design and development of the underlying MDM infrastructure.

23

- If building an application framework from scratch, design and engineer an MDM environment that supports the application infrastructure.
- Design a plan for enterprise data integration.
- Design a migration plan for the participating applications.

To do this, we must work with the many stakeholders and align their expectations so that as the master environment grows it is able to deliver value along the project life cycle. Therefore, in this chapter we look at the individual roles within the organization that are associated with master data management and examine what the responsibilities and accountabilities are for each of these roles. In addition, we examine ways to evaluate the data requirements in anticipation of designing the master repository.

2.2 COMMUNICATING BUSINESS VALUE

Interestingly, there is a difference between establishing a reasonable business case supporting the transition to MDM and communicating its value. In Chapter 1, we looked at a number of ways that a synchronized master data asset supports business productivity improvement associated with organizational initiatives and increasing the organization's ability to respond quickly to business opportunities. However, this message is typically pointed upward in the management chain to achieve senior management buy-in and championship; it does not address the value proposition for each participant and stakeholder.

This becomes particularly important at the beginning of the program when assembling the right team to do the analysis and design, because the people with the most subject matter expertise in each line of business are the same people who are likely to be affected by a transition to a new underlying information layer. Therefore, there is a need for the program champions to engage the business managers in a way that demonstrates the specific value that MDM provides to each line of business.

Therefore, as opposed to the organizational business value that was explored in Chapter 1, the value proposition for each stakeholder focuses more on improving that person's ability to get the job done effectively. This may encompass a number of different aspects of productivity improvement, including but not limited to the notions of improved data quality, reduction in need for cross-system reconciliation, reduction in operational complexity, simplification of design and implementation of applicationware, and ease of integration.

2.2.1 **Improving Data Quality**

As more inadvertent replicas of the same data instances are consolidated into a unique representation, there will be fewer opportunities for data duplication errors to occur. At the operational level, reducing the number of errors also reduces scrap and rework, the acute need to react to data failures, and the ability to focus resources on productive development and operations management instead of fire fighting. In the long term, MDM improves the trustworthiness of the data, thereby increasing businesspeople's confidence in using the data.

2.2.2 **Reducing the Need for Cross-System Reconciliation**

The ability to access organizational data sets, copy them locally on the desktop, and configure locally prepared reports is a boon to the business client. However, the proliferation of these "spread-marts" that report based on a statically copied view of the data creates a situation where there are discrepancies that are related to the time that the data was copied or how it was manipulated at the desktop. Variations in reported values must be investigated, and when the source data are pulled from different origins, there is a mad scramble to reconcile numbers, sums, accounts, and so on. Reconfiguring the report generation process to be driven off the master data asset reduces the need for cross-system reconciliation.

2.2.3 **Reducing Operational Complexity**

Whether an organization grows organically or through acquisitions, the result is that line-of-business application development will have been geared toward acutely developing applications that support the operations of the business. However, there are aspects of each business operation that must coordinate through existing systems. For example, sales transactions, no matter the system through which the system originates, must interact with the organization's order fulfillment system.

With a proliferation of applications and corresponding internal representations of each data entity, there is a great need to coordinate the many interfaces necessary to make the different applications talk to each other. MDM addresses this issue by providing a master data object model that can be used for both information persistence and application communication. Standardizing the interface into and out of the common representation significantly reduces the overhead and management complexity associated with the multitude of connectors to be put in place.

2.2.4 Simplifying Design and Implementation

There are three aspects of master data management that simplify the design and implementation of new applications and improve existing applications. First, it is less the existence of a master data asset (whether it is a single physical repository or one that provides a virtual view across enterprise data sets via a registry) than the existence of *master metadata* that simplifies application development. A master metadata repository captures the whole story associated with data element use. Instead of a glorified data dictionary, enterprise business metadata combines the knowledge derived from an intelligent analysis of enterprise data sets and the definitions and meanings assigned by subject matter experts. This integrates the semantic analysis associated with names, shapes, structures, formats, associated reference data, and, most important, definitions of data elements collected from across the organization.

The resulting metadata asset becomes an encyclopedia of knowledge of the way that data elements are used in different business purposes and how similar uses are truly distinguished. The ability to have this master metadata available reduces the effort at the beginning of the implementation in designing data models to meet defined business needs for application functionality. Master metadata is discussed at length in Chapter 6.

The second simplifying aspect is *unique identification*. Many applications frequently need to uniquely identify entities, and the approaches different application programmers use to sort through the set of records that match against identifying information are often diverse and inconsistent. Standardizing the process for unique identification reduces the need for each application developer to design the process at the application level and instead allows the developer to reuse the capability engineered into the master data environment. Tools contribute greatly to the ability to support unique identification, as we will cover in Chapter 10.

This leads to the third simplifying aspect, which is the ability to define and standardize many different kinds of *master data services*, which we will cover in Chapter 12. Clearly defining the component services at the core and the application layers provides a means for unifying the enterprise application architecture, thereby freeing the developers to focus on supporting the application business requirements.

2.2.5 **Easing Integration**

Simplifying the core representative models and standardizing metadata and access services makes it easier for applications to talk to each other. In fact, as a by-product of the aspects discussed in Sections 2.2.3 and 2.2.4, reducing complexity and harmonizing metadata and exchange interfaces will better enable applications to conform to an enterprise application architecture driven by business expectations instead of line-of-business functional needs.

2.3 **STAKEHOLDERS**

Who are the players in an MDM environment? There are many potential stakeholders across the enterprise:

- Senior management
- Business clients
- Application owners
- Information architects
- Data governance and data quality practitioners
- Metadata analysts
- System developers
- Operations staff

Here we explore who the stakeholders are and what their expected participation should be over the course of program development.

2.3.1 **Senior Management**

Clearly, without the support of the senior management, it would be difficult to execute any enterprise activity. At the senior level, managers are motivated to demonstrate that their (and their teams') performances have contributed to the organization's successful achievement of its business objectives. Transitioning to a master data environment should enable more nimbleness and agility in both ensuring the predictable behavior of existing applications and systems and rapidly developing support for new business initiatives. This core message drives senior-level engagement.

Senior management also plays a special role in ensuring that the rest of the organization remains engaged. Adopting a strategic view to oversee the long-term value of the transition and migration should trump short-term tactical business initiatives. In addition, the senior managers should also prepare the organization for the behavioral changes that will be required by the staff as responsibilities and incentives evolve from focusing on vertical business area success to how line-of-business triumphs contribute to overall organizational success.

2.3.2 **Business Clients**

For each of the defined lines of business, there are representative clients whose operations and success rely on the predictable, high availability of application data. For the most part, unless the business client is intricately involved in the underlying technology associated with the business processes, it almost doesn't matter *how* the system works, but rather *that* the system works. Presuming that the data used within the existing business applications meet the business user's expectations, incorporating the business client's data into a master repository is only relevant to the business client if the process degrades data usability.

However, the business client may derive value from improvements in data quality as a by-product of data consolidation, and future application development will be made more efficient when facilitated through a service model that supports application integration with enterprise master data services. Supporting the business client implies a number of specific actions and responsibilities, two of which are particularly relevant. First, the MDM program team must capture and document the business client's data expectations and application service-level expectations and assure the client that those expectations will be monitored and met. Second, because it is essential for the team to understand the global picture of master object use, it is important for the technical team to assess which data objects are used by the business applications and how those objects are used. Therefore, as subject matter experts, it is imperative that the business clients participate in the business process modeling and data requirements analysis process.

2.3.3 **Application Owners**

Any applications that involve the use of data objects to be consolidated within an MDM environment will need to be modified to adjust to the use of master data instead of local versions or replicas. This means that the use of the master data asset must be carefully socialized with the application owners, because they become the "gatekeepers" to MDM success. As with the business owners, each application owner will be concerned with ensuring predictable behavior of the business applications and may even see master data management as a risk to continued predictable behavior, as it involves a significant transition from one underlying (production) data asset to a potentially unproven one.

The application owner is a key stakeholder, then, as the successful continued predictable operation of the application depends on the reliability and quality of the master repository. When identifying data requirements in preparation for developing a master data model, it will be necessary to engage the application owner to ensure that operational requirements are documented and incorporated into the model (and component services) design.

2.3.4 **Information Architects**

Underlying any organizational information initiative is a need for information models in an enterprise architecture. The models for master data objects must accommodate the current needs of the existing applications while supporting the requirements for future business changes. The information architects must collaborate to address both aspects of application needs and fold those needs into the data requirements process for the underlying models and the representation framework that will be employed.

2.3.5 **Data Governance and Data Quality**

An enterprise initiative introduces new constraints on the ways that individuals create, access and use, modify, and retire data. To ensure that these constraints are not violated, the data governance and data quality staff must introduce stewardship, ownership, and management policies as well as the means to monitor observance to these policies.

A success factor for MDM is its ubiquity; the value becomes apparent to the organization as more lines of business participate, both as data suppliers and as master data consumers. This suggests that MDM needs governance to encourage collaboration and participation across the enterprise, but it also drives governance by providing a single point of truth. Ultimately, the use of the master data asset as an acknowledged high-quality resource is driven by transparent adherence to defined information policies specifying the acceptable levels of data quality for shared information. MDM programs require some layer of governance, whether that means incorporating metadata analysis and registration, developing "rules of engagement" for collaboration, defining data quality expectations and rules, monitoring and managing quality of data and changes to master data, providing stewardship to oversee automation of linkage and hierarchies, or offering processes for researching root causes and the subsequent elimination of sources of flawed data.

2.3.6 **Metadata Analysts**

Metadata represent a key component to MDM as well as the governance processes that underlie it, and managing metadata must be closely linked to information and application architecture as well as data governance. Managing all types of metadata (not just technical or structural) will provide the "glue" to connect these together. In this environment, metadata incorporate the consolidated view of the data elements and their corresponding definitions, formats, sizes, structures, data domains, patterns, and the like, and they provide an excellent platform for metadata analysts to actualize the value proposed by a comprehensive enterprise metadata repository.

2.3.7 **System Developers**

Aspects of performance and storage change as replicated data instances are absorbed into the master data system. Again, the determination of the underlying architecture approach will impact production systems as well as new development projects and will change the way that the application framework uses the underlying data asset (as is discussed in Chapters 9, 11, and 12). System analysts and developers will need to restructure their views of systemic needs as the ability to formulate system services grows at the core level, at a level targeted at the ways that conceptual data objects are used, and at the application interface level.

2.3.8 **Operations Staff**

One of the hidden risks of moving toward a common repository for master data is the fact that often, to get the job done, operations staff may need to bypass the standard protocols for data access and modification. In fact, in some organizations, this approach to bypassing standard interfaces is institutionalized, with metrics associated with the number of times that "fixes" or modifications are applied to data using direct access (e.g., updates via SQL) instead of going through the preferred channels.

Alternatively, desktop applications are employed to supplement existing applications and as a way to gather the right amount of information to complete a business process. Bypassing standard operating procedures and desktop supplements pose an interesting challenge to the successful MDM program, in absorbing what might be termed "finely grained distributed data" into the master framework as well as taming the behavior that essentially allows for leaks in the enterprise master data framework. In other words, the folks with their boots on the ground may need to change their habits as key data entities are captured and migrated into a master environment.

2.4 **DEVELOPING A PROJECT CHARTER**

As a way to focus attention on the activity, a project charter will capture the business case and value proposition for moving forward on the MDM program, as well as itemize the key individuals associated with the project, including the project sponsors, project managers, team members, and functional beneficiaries. The charter will describe the objectives of the program, the scope of the project, the acceptance and success criteria, and potential risks and mitigation strategies.

In greater detail, the project charter for MDM will contain at least sections for the following:

Business case. As described in Chapter 1 and this chapter, identify the business drivers that are used to justify the intention to create an MDM program.

Identify the key project sponsors. Of the business clients, application owners, and operations staff/managers among the potential stakeholders, it is important to identify the key project sponsors willing to subsidize the budget or provide the resources to support the program.

Description of the current state. The desire to migrate to a new environment should be triggered by issues, constraints, or problems with the current environment. To qualify what needs to be done to improve the environment, it is valuable to detail the specific issues with the current state.

Description of the desired target state. Gaps in the existing environment will be addressed through the evolution into a presumed end state. Comparing the level of maturity of the existing environment to the future state will help identify key priorities in moving the program forward.

Alternatives. To ensure that the proper approach is being selected, describe the alternatives researched as potential solutions.

Proposed solution. Describe the selected approach and why that approach was selected.

Deliverables. Detail what the project team is promising to deliver along with the expectations as directed by the project sponsors.

Budget and resource allocation. Provide high-level details about resource requirements, budgeting, and how acquired resources will be allocated and assigned.

Risks. Identify the risks associated with the project and ways to minimize or eliminate those risks.

Project plan. Provide a high-level overview of the tasks to be performed, the agreed-to dates for project milestones (or deliverables), and the key staff members to be working on those tasks.

Project oversight. Identify the principal individuals accountable for the completing the named deliverables and the processes for overseeing that completion.

2.5 PARTICIPANT COORDINATION AND KNOWING WHERE TO BEGIN

A significant challenge in coordinating participants in an MDM program is knowing where to begin. Often it is assumed that kicking off an initiative by assembling a collection of stakeholders and participants in a room is the best way to begin, but before sending out invitations, consider this: without well-defined ground rules, these meetings run the risk of turning into turf battles over whose data or definitions or application services are the "correct" ones to be mastered.

Given the diversity of stakeholders and participants and their differing requirements and expectations, how can we balance each individual's needs with the organization's drivers for master data integration? A number of techniques are available that can help in organizing the business needs in a way that can manage the initial and ongoing coordination of the participants:

- Establishing processes and procedures for collaboration before kickoff and developing ground rules for participation
- Employing a responsible, accountable, consulted, informed (RACI) model for oversight
- Using business process modeling
- Providing master metadata
- Establishing data governance

The preliminary tasks prepare the team members for the first task of establishing the feasibility of creating a master repository by evaluating the business's data requirements. These ideas are introduced in this section and are described in greater detail in subsequent chapters.

2.5.1 **Processes and Procedures for Collaboration**

There is no doubt that when assembling individuals from different business areas and different applications, there will be a difference of opinion as to the names, definitions, sources, and reasonable uses for the objects to be mastered. In fact, it is likely that there is already "corporate experience" regarding the conversations about defining common terms (e.g., "what is a customer?"). The difference between previous iterations and the one to be performed for MDM is that the objective is not to resolve all cases of the same terms and phrases into a unique definition into which all business applications must now fit their own use. On the contrary, the goal is to determine where the underlying definitions, meanings, and semantics match, as well as where they do not match, and to provide a means for qualifying the terms to ensure that the differences are respected.

This means that the rules for interaction must be changed from what might be considered a confrontational engagement (in which participants vie for definition dominance) to a collaborative engagement where the participants methodically articulate the concepts in use by their constituencies. The process should detail where there is an overlap in meaning and where there is not, properly document where the differences are, and use this as the starting point for collecting and collating master metadata. The processes and procedures for collaborating on master metadata oversee the harmonization and standardization of use where it is possible and the segregation of use where it is not possible.

2.5.2 **RACI Matrix**

We have listed a number of the participants and stakeholders associated with an MDM program. To ensure that each participant's needs are addressed and that their associated tasks are appropriately performed, there must be some delineation of specific roles, responsibilities, and accountabilities assigned to each person. One useful prototype is the RACI model; RACI is an acronym standing for *responsible, accountable, consulted,* and *informed.* A RACI model is a two-dimensional matrix listing the tasks to be performed along the rows and the roles listed along the columns. Each cell in the matrix is populated according to these participation types:

- *R* if the listed role is *responsible* for deliverables related to completing the task
- *A* if the listed role is *accountable* for delivering the task's deliverables or achieving the milestones

- *C* if the listed role is *consulted* for opinions on completing the task
- *I* if the listed role is *informed* and kept up to date on the progress of the task

There should only be one accountable role per task, meaning that each row has one and only one A. An example is shown in Table 2.1.

Developing the RACI matrix clarifies the roles and responsibilities as assigned to the individuals within particular roles. It even is used to validate that the right set of personalities has been identified for the set of processes.

2.5.3 **Modeling the Business**

Available tools, implementation constraints, and technology decisions are all factors in the ways that business applications are designed, implemented, and deployed. Application systems are intended to implement the business processes, but as the systems are built and put into production, there may be some confusion as to whether the application implements the business process or *becomes* the business process.

In other words, implementation decisions based on technology constraints may alter the way that the business process is performed within the context of the built application, and eventually the implementation is perceived as being equivalent to the business process. That being said, as an organization consolidates data into a master

Table 2.1   An Example RACI Matrix for Some MDM Tasks

	MDM Management	Business Clients	Application Owners	Information Architects	Data Governance	Metadata Analysts	System Developers	Operations Staff
Develop data harmonization processes	A	C	C	R	R	R		C
Data requirements analysis	I	C	C	A	R	R		
Metadata analysis	I	C	C	R	R	A	C	C
Master data models	I	I	I	A	C	R	C	I
...								

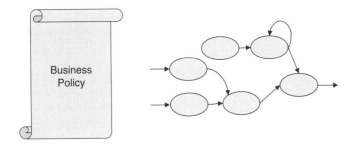

■ **FIGURE 2.1** Business policies are implemented as business processes.

environment, it creates the opportunity to truly understand what the business processes are and how they use the different data objects.

Another way of looking at this is shown in Figure 2.1, in that the business policies are translated into workflow processes to get the job done. These workflows drive the requirements for building systems to achieve the goals directed by the business policies. Ultimately, these workflows revolve around interactions with the real-world entities that facilitate business operations, such as customers, vendors, products, locations, and payment methods, and these are the same entities that emerge as our master data objects. This suggests that the exercise of modeling the business processes in isolation from the way they are currently implemented will reveal knowledge (and perhaps new opportunities) about coordination across the application horizon.

2.5.4 **Consensus Driven through Metadata**

The next means for coordination is through common semantics. The variation in use and definitions of commonly used business terms is an artifact of the distribution of work according to each line of business. In an organization committed to master data consolidation, however, there is a finer requirement for coordinating data definitions. The reason is that it is critical to ensure that data sets subjected to consolidation actually refer to the same thing. If not, the resulting master data set will be inconsistent, which violates our expectations for a collection of uniquely identifiable master data objects.

Therefore, another objective for MDM is the need for driving consensus regarding what the master data objects are and how they are defined and used. Providing a common set of processes for reaching consensus and providing a metadata catalog for publicizing the agreed-to definitions establishes the management platform for coordinating the convergence of semantics for shared data objects and data elements.

2.5.5 **Data Governance**

Data quality and data standards management are part of a larger picture with respect to oversight of master information. In the siloed environment, the responsibilities—and ultimately the accountabilities—for ensuring that the data meet the quality expectations of the client's applications lie within the management of the corresponding line of business. But for MDM, the process for master consolidation must incorporate all the data quality expectations and rules, and the resulting data quality activities must ensure that all client applications' needs are being met.

Because the resulting master data set is no longer "owned" by any one line of business, an enterprise vision for information ownership should be in place to clarify accountability for all organization data sets, and an enterprise governance program should be instantiated to ensure compliance with ownership and stewardship policies. A data governance program will encompass data quality, standards, accountability, and audit and control for reporting on policy compliance. The objective of data governance is to establish that the master data asset is a core enterprise asset for which all staff members must take accountability. Engage senior management stakeholders in creating a functional oversight hierarchy for data governance, custody, and stewardship to make sure that all stakeholder information requirements are being met and that there are procedures for remediating organizational data conflicts. The criticality of data governance is discussed in Chapter 1, and its value for a successful MDM program is so great that data governance is covered in much greater detail in Chapter 4.

2.6 **ESTABLISHING FEASIBILITY THROUGH DATA REQUIREMENTS**

Once the stakeholders and participants are aligned, the next step is to evaluate the feasibility of evolving toward a master data environment. The essential question focuses on two aspects: first, whether the business application client requirements support the use of a master repository and, second, whether the available data sources will effectively support the consolidation of the right master data objects. Therefore, the feasibility evaluation for the master data environment focuses on collecting requirements for and evaluating and defining the appropriate level of detail for data and process models in preparation for implementing master data services.

The expectation is that at the end of the process, if there is enough support for the process, there will be a proposed data model for data extraction and consolidation as well as proposed data model for persistent storage and management of master data objects and an appropriate level of detailed process design for automating the collection, management, reporting, and accessibility of master data (for more detail, see Chapter 8). To support the design process, it is important to ensure that the data requirements and characteristics for the master data objects are identified, assessed, and tested. This is accomplished by following a data requirements analysis process whose goal is to ensure the identification, suitability, and model quality of the data to meet the business requirements and provide a framework for the application components for the master data model. The process outlined in this section focuses on capturing the business requirements, business processes, and terminology used in practice along with identifying and defining the data sets and data elements that will be integrated within the master repository and ultimately defining the model for these data sets and their attribute elements.

2.6.1 **Identifying the Business Context**

This task consists of identifying the sources of information that the data analyst will use to understand and document the specific business area processes and assist in developing meaningful and relevant user interview questions. This step requires the identification of source knowledge in coordination with data analysts and the executive sponsors and stakeholders, driven by the MDM program manager. Typical documents include the business case, program charter, system scoping documents, and the business needs assessments. In turn, these artifacts should be evaluated to assess the level of integration across and relationships to existing systems.

The output of this process is to characterize and document the environmental context and essentially document enterprise impacts and constraints related to the collection and subsequent dissemination of master data. The sequence of tasks for this process includes the following:

1. **Identify relevant stakeholders.** This may involve the determination of key parties through review of documentation or directly targeted by the project manager and in discussion with other business analysts.

2. **Acquire documentation.** Capture all documents related to the scope and the goals of the MDM program, which will probably incorporate a business case, program charter, as well as other relevant artifacts such as organizational or industry standards, design constraints, current system architectures, business process flows, and so on.

3. **Document the program objectives and goals.** There are different drivers for establishing master data copies, and it is important to work with the stakeholders from the outset to establish what the objectives and goals are for the program.

4. **Summarize scope of system functional capability.** Develop this summary in concordance with the stakeholders and application/process owners and identify the high-level functions and capabilities of the target system as well as how the system supports each stakeholder.

5. **Summarize the relevant system impacts.** Do this at an appropriate level of detail to ensure compliance during final data requirements definition and logical modeling.

At the end of this process, it is reasonable to expect three aspects of the environment to be documented: a diagram documenting the environment and context, a summary of potential system impacts, and a summary of constraints that would limit master integration. A context diagram, which is developed as a result of reviewing relevant MDM program and system information, illustrates the general business process flow showing how the business applications will use the capabilities of the target system. The system impacts summary documents the way that transitioning to a master repository impacts the business environment and the associated applications, such as timeliness, quality, currency, transaction semantics, retention issues, and the types of service components necessary to support the information expectations. The systems constraints summary documents any identified constraints of the system, such as system data dependencies, inter-application processing dependencies, use of global reference data, and standards and definitions critical to business operations.

2.6.2 **Conduct Stakeholder Interviews**

Understanding the stakeholder requirements is a critical step involving collecting the line-of-business data requirements and collating and then synthesizing those requirements into an enterprise view. This process involves preparing and executing stakeholder interviews, including developing the questions, scheduling the interviews, and conducting the interviews. These sessions should be scheduled and conducted with key stakeholders including the executive sponsor(s), primary information consumers, and representatives from impacted business units. Although specific roles and responsibilities may vary by project, it is critical that the data analyst collaborate and participate with the business analyst in conducting stakeholder interviews.

Part of this task is to provide a set of questions tailored to drawing out the specific information needs of the business clients. This task relies on the constraints and impacts summaries produced during the previous stage, and it incorporates the following activities:

1. Review the general roles and responsibilities of the interview candidate to guide and focus the interview questions within the context of the system.

2. Develop focused interview questions designed to understand and document the roles, responsibilities, and needs of the information consumer in the context of the master data management system.

3. Schedule interviews with the stakeholders, starting with the executives and business clients and rounding out the interactions with the application users, developers, and managers. Information gathered as a result of interacting with the executives will provide insight for revising the business questions used in subsequent conversations.

4. Interview preparation includes reviewing the business questions ahead of each interview and ensuring that supporting material is properly prepared ahead of time. Arrange to capture tabled topics that inspire further discussion into a virtual parking lot.

5. Conduct the interviews. Provide a brief review of the system goals and objectives, and describe the data requirements gathering process. Ask the business questions that have been developed, and have a scribe capture the answers. Conclude by thanking the interviewees for their time and telling them when to expect the interview summary for review and validation.

6. Review and organize the notes from the interview including the attendee list, general notes, and answers to specific questions. Also include the business definitions that were clarified related to time, workflow, status, and so forth.

7. Identify information gaps for follow-up; summarizing the interviews will identify additional questions and highlight areas in need of greater clarity. Contact the interviewees directly for answers to additional questions.

8. Integrate, summarize, and organize the requirements in preparation for assessing and synthesizing data requirements.

2.6.3 Synthesize Requirements

This task involves reviewing, summarizing, and organizing the information obtained from the stakeholder interviews and merging that information with the business context resulting from the first task. The objective of this task is to look at the intersection between those data objects most frequently identified during the interview sessions and the data objects that are referenced in the business process tasks. The result of this task is the identification of the emergent prototypical data objects that can be tagged as candidates for mastering.

SYNTHESIS REQUIREMENTS STEPS

1. Create the reference workflow model that depicts how the business processes capture, manage, and use data objects. Use this model to identify the points within the workflow that touch critical data objects and their attributes.

2. Create a list of candidate master data objects, those data objects that emerge as the most relevant across the workflow models.

3. For each candidate master data object, document the data elements that carry the data values used for differentiating any one real-world instance from all others, also referred to as the "identifying information."

4. For each candidate master data object, document the data elements that are critical for achieving the results of the business processes transcribed in the workflow models.

5. Validate the candidate master data objects and their critical data elements with stakeholders. Present the list and walk through the workflow models with the stakeholders. Validate data requirements with the participants.

6. Identify and standardize common business terms, because early identification of the commonly used terms will ease later metadata differences. Document the source of the use of the business term. This could include design documents, policy documents, requirements-gathering sessions, application code, and user guides. Determine if the source has provided a definition for the term, and if so, capture the definition as well as any possible authoritative source for the definition.

7. Identify candidate source systems. Customer interviews will normally yield a list of candidate source systems for the relevant data objects, and this list will become the starting point for metadata analysis, data element metadata harmonization, and consensus on master data object definitions and semantics.

8. Document a glossary to capture all of the business terms associated with the business workflows, and classify the hierarchical composition of data object names and structures as used within the workflows.

2.6.4 **Establishing Feasibility and Next Steps**

At the end of these preliminary tasks, the team should be prepared to answer the question of feasibility. The data requirements process should identify whether there are common business data objects that are used in similar ways across the application infrastructure and whether there are candidate data sets that can be used to effectively populate a master view. These facts, coupled with the business value justifications, establish the feasibility of the master data management program. The next chapters focus on the steps to be taken in assembling a project road map to bring the MDM environment into the necessary level of maturity for the organization.

2.7 **SUMMARY**

Setting the stage for assembling the right team for an MDM program involves determining the best opportunities to socialize the internal value across the enterprise landscape. As this chapter has shown, this socialization is performed along a number of avenues:

- Communicating the value of presenting a centralized master data asset to the business clients, application owners, and operations staff
- Identifying the key stakeholders that will participate in the MDM program
- Carefully articulating within a project charter what will be achieved by the MDM program and how the corresponding milestones will be reached
- Providing a means for coordinating the participants to reduce conflict and encourage consensus
- Carefully detailing roles and responsibilities
- Analyzing the data requirements to establish MDM feasibility

MDM Components and the Maturity Model

3.1 INTRODUCTION

One common misconception at the highest levels of an organization is that any good idea comes ready to roll right out of the box. But make no mistake about it—there is no silver bullet for any enterprise information initiative, let alone master data management. Information professionals recognize that master information consolidation is the right thing to do, but that does not necessarily imply that there are always going to be acute business requirements that support a drastic upheaval to an information management program.

The migration to an organization that relies exclusively on master data management does not take place overnight; rather it evolves through a number of transitional information management stages. Recognizing that the process involves more than purchasing a software package or engaging outside solution vendors is the first step in achieving the MDM evolution. But it is more than that—it means understanding the essential capabilities necessary to successfully deploy MDM and the maturity of those capabilities necessary to make MDM actionable.

No functionality list completely captures the inventory of services that a specific business requires from its master data asset. However, it is worthwhile to explore a high-level enumeration of core MDM capabilities. In this chapter we provide a conceptual outline of technical MDM components. Next, we explore levels of maturity based on the ability to provide MDM services. Presenting the MDM component layers in terms of their maturity enables enterprise architects to target a desired level of MDM maturity and develop a design and implementation road map that articulates the steps to take when assembling an MDM program.

3.2 **MDM BASICS**

The proliferation of enterprise-level application expectations for shared, synchronized information drives the need for developing a single view of the key data entities in common use across the organization. At the technical level, the drivers and fundamentals of master data management can be summarized as processes for consolidating variant versions of instances of core data objects distributed across the organization into a unique representation. In turn, that unique representation is continually synchronized across the enterprise application architecture to allow master data to be available as a shared resource. The result is a master data asset of uniquely identified key data entity instances integrated through a service layer with the applications across the organization.

However, the devil is in the details. To accomplish what may seem to be a relatively straightforward set of ideas, the organization must be prepared for the technical, operational, and management challenges that will appear along the way. In fact, the deployment of an MDM solution could evolve through a number of iterations, introducing data object analysis and model consolidation for analytical purposes as an initial step, then following on with increasing levels of integration, service, and synchronization.

The end-state master data management environment presents an enterprise resource integrated with the enterprise application architecture through a collection of provided services. At the least, a mature MDM solution will encompass the capabilities and services displayed in Figure 3.1.

Although these layers represent a model of the most necessary technical, operational, and management components needed to develop an MDM capability, organizations can launch the program even with these components at various levels of maturity. The parts of this component model can be grouped into conceptual architectural levels, beginning with the architecture, then governance, management, identity management, integration services, and finally business process management. Examining the levels of maturity of these components and their relationship to the business requirements will guide the MDM program manager in developing an implementation road map. Although the architectural levels are presented from the bottom up, the maturity model will provide insight into how selected pieces of the component model can begin to add value to the organization as the implementation grows. In this chapter we review the fundamentals of each layer in this component stack, then we provide some guidance for evaluating levels of maturity.

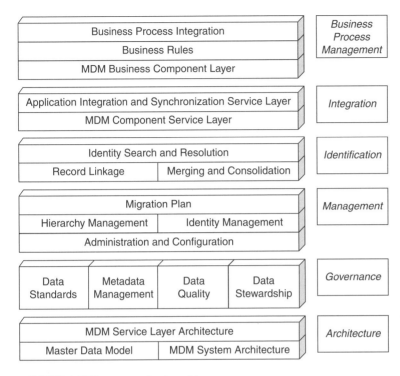

■ **FIGURE 3.1** MDM component and service model.

3.2.1 **Architecture**

Fundamentally there are three aspects to the master data management architecture, corresponding to the structure, power, and control of the environment. The structure is represented by the MDM master data models, the power reflects the MDM system architecture, and the control is encompassed by the MDM service layer.

3.2.2 **Master Data Model**

To accommodate any conceptual master data asset, all of the data elements in the various different formats and structures that exist across the enterprise need to be presented as a centralized resource that can both accommodate the differences from the existing data sources and feed the master representations back into those different representations. This implies that there must be a consolidated model for representing master data as well as models for the extraction and exchange of data as it is integrated into the master data asset.

Source metadata details can be easily captured and managed in a metadata registry, and this information can be used to develop a representative master object model for every master data object type. The representative master object model for each master data type should be resilient to the differences between existing replicated data instance models, and this suggests creating a model to support all of the data in all of the application models. In other words, the set of the data attributes of the consolidated model must be a superset of all of the important attributes from each of the application models, and the format and structures for each attribute must support all the formats and structures used for that attribute across the many variant models. This defines the fundamental challenge of the master data model: supporting variant structure and formats for both accumulating and publishing of master data objects.

3.2.3 **MDM System Architecture**

All data objects are subject to a "data life cycle," and different systems requirements are associated with and affected by each stage of that data life cycle. The MDM system architecture focuses on the aspects of that life cycle and incorporates the component methods to support them generically to higher levels of a service layer supporting applications across the enterprise. The MDM system architecture relies on a services-oriented framework, in which the functionality reflects the life cycle activities (create, access, update, retire) as they relate to the master object type.

The core functionality (e.g., create a new master record, access/update a master record) is presented as low-level component services that can be adapted or enhanced for specific master data types ("customer" or "product") or specific applications. For example, certain pieces of identifying information can be collected at different times and by different applications, but if the different applications are allowed to create a new instance, the creation service may be adapted for each application to acquire what is necessary to complete the business process.

3.2.4 **MDM Service Layer Architecture**

The MDM system architecture focuses on the core technical components to support the data life cycle. However, as the reliance of applications on the master data management environment increases, there are further requirements for data object services related to the level of service provided for application use, such as synchronization, serialization, embedded access control, integration, consolidation, and access. Business applications then are layered on top of the data object service layer by deploying or possibly reusing specific components associated with business processes.

These more comprehensive management activities for master data objects can be implemented at the system level. But because different types of applications may require different levels of service, it may be worthwhile to segregate those components with a role-based framework. For example, some applications that create new master records may have embedded timeliness requirements, such as a customer creation capability that must establish the customer record before allowing any purchase transactions. If a quick-create capability is needed within the sales organization but not necessarily within the fulfillment organization, then the quick-create can be established at the service layer along with the service level requirements (e.g., the maximum time allowed between master object creation and its availability for use).

3.3 MANIFESTING INFORMATION OVERSIGHT WITH GOVERNANCE

Because MDM is an enterprise initiative, there must be some assurance of stakeholder adherence to the rules that govern participation and information sharing. As we will discuss in great detail in the next chapter, a data governance program applied across different business-level domains will address issues of data stewardship, ownership, privacy, security, data risks, compliance, data sensitivity, and metadata management. Each of these issues focuses on integrating technical data management with oversight, ensuring organizational observance of defined information policies. The four areas of concentration for data governance include the standardization of common use at the data element level, the consolidation of metadata into enterprise management systems, managing data quality, and operational data stewardship.

3.3.1 Standardized Definitions

Whereas humans are typically adept at resolving ambiguity with words and phrases, application systems are considerably less so. People are able to overcome the barriers of missing information or potentially conflicting definitions, although at some point each individual's translation of a business term may differ slightly from other translations. This becomes an issue during integration and consolidation when data element instances that may share a name do not share a meaning, or differently named data elements are not recognized as representing the same concept. Processes for data analytics and for assessing organizational data element information and coalescing that information into business metadata provide standardized definitions that ultimately drive and control the determination of the catalog of master data objects and how they are resolved into the unique view.

3.3.2 **Consolidated Metadata Management**

A by-product of the process for identifying and clarifying data element names, definitions, and other relevant attribution is the discovery and documentation of enterprise-wide business metadata. Aside from collecting standard technical details regarding the numerous data elements that are potentially available, there is a need to determine business uses of each data element; which data element definitions refer to the same concept; the applications that refer to manifestations of that concept; how each data element and associated concepts are created, read, modified, or retired by different applications; the data quality characteristics; inspection and monitoring locations within the business process flow; and how all the uses are tied together.

Because the use of the data elements and their underlying concepts drives how the business application operates using master data, the enterprise metadata repository effectively becomes the control center driving and managing the business applications. Therefore, a critical component of an MDM environment is an enterprise business metadata management system to facilitate the desired level of control. At an even grander level, the metadata management framework supports the definition of the master data objects themselves: which data objects are managed within the MDM environment, which application data sources contribute to their consolidation and resolution, the frequency of and processes used for consolidation—everything necessary to understand the complete picture of the distributed use of master data objects across the enterprise.

It is worthwhile to note that advocating an enterprise-wide approach to metadata management does not necessarily mean purchasing an enterprise metadata management tool. Rather, the focus is on the procedures for sharing information, even if that is facilitated through less sophisticated means. The important part is reaching consensus on enterprise metadata.

3.3.3 **Data Quality**

Data quality figures into MDM at two different levels. First, the concept of the unique representation for each real-world object requires a high level of trust in the data; otherwise there would be little incentive for business clients to participate. Second, data quality tools and techniques are employed in the integration and consolidation processes.

More to the point, instituting a data quality management program will ultimately result in a change to the organization, particularly in the way that management, and in turn individual staff members, relate to and assess the information value. Instead of considering data as only the raw input to the operational running of the business, individuals grow to understand how information becomes an asset to be used in many ways for improving the business. As business practices continue to rely on master data, they will become more reliant on high-quality data. The corresponding recognition that business performance and operational productivity at the organizational as well as at the personal level depend on high-quality data becomes a core competency of any MDM program.

3.3.4 **Data Stewardship**

As more lines of business integrate with core master data object repositories, there must be some assurance of adherence to the rules that govern participation. Because MDM success relies on data governance, an operational aspect to data governance is applied across different business domains, providing economies of scale for enterprise-wide deployment. The operational aspects of governance, typically formulated as data stewardship activities, supplement the ownership models and oversight mechanisms to ensure active management and information quality.

3.4 **OPERATIONS MANAGEMENT**

By definition, a master data environment provides a unified view of the data entities dealt with by the various business applications. There is a requirement for providing the components for maintaining the special characteristics of these master data objects through the data life cycle while supporting each application's corresponding ongoing needs. This includes the unique identification of each object, and the connectivity between the replicas, instances, and usage points of each object, to say nothing of maintaining the ways that different master data objects are possibly connected, such as householded customer names. Aside from the expected administration and configuration management components, the MDM stack must provide "specialty" management services, including identity management for unique key entities, hierarchy management to track association, lineage, and relationships, and migration management as part of the transition to the MDM platform.

3.4.1 **Identity Management**

Every instance of each master data object type must represent a unique real-world object, implying the constraint that there is one, and only one, uniquely identifiable record for any specific customer (or product, employee, etc.). This means that any time a process seeks a specific individual managed within the master data asset, enough identifying information must be provided to both determine that either

- A record for that individual exists and that no more than one record for that individual exists, or
- No record exists and one can be created that can be uniquely distinguished from all others.

Identity management addresses these requirements by enabling and managing the determination of the identifying attributes necessary for unique identification, along with the search and match capabilities used to locate both exact and approximate matches as well as maintaining the master index based on the identifying attributes. This concept focuses on maintaining the right model for unique identification, and the result is the input to the Identity Search and Resolution component at the next level up. In addition, policies regarding the distinction of a unique entity across different data sources, both automatically and those instances requiring manual intervention, are *management* directives, whereas implementing those policies takes place at the *identification* layer.

3.4.2 **Hierarchy Management and Data Lineage**

The first aspect of hierarchy management essentially focuses on the lineage and process of resolving multiple records into a single representation. Because there may be records representing the unique entity in different application systems, as part of the consolidation it will be necessary to document which application data sources contribute to the master consolidation and, in certain types of MDM architectures, to provide links back from the master index to the original source records in order to materialize master information on demand. This becomes especially important as a data control in case it is determined that there are false positive matches, in which identifying information for two individual objects incorrectly resolved into a single entry, or false negatives where more than one master record exists for the same unique entity. To some extent, in this point of view, hierarchy management is more concerned with data lineage as a way to mitigate the inevitable occurrence of errors in the data integration processing streams.

The second aspect of hierarchy management for MDM revolves around the interconnectedness of master objects across multiple systems. For example, customers may be related to each other (e.g., same family, work for the same business), or different master data types may be related (e.g., the products associated with a specific supplier). These relationships are reflected in linkage hierarchies, and the hierarchy management layer also provides service components supporting the management of these connections.

3.4.3 **Migration Management**

The transition toward application integration with an MDM system is interesting to contrast with general approaches to application modernization. When either incrementally or drastically modernizing a stand-alone application, the migration plan typically will have both the version to be retired running simultaneously and the modernized version for some time period to ensure that the new version properly addresses the business requirements. But for an MDM program, one objective may be to replace the application's underlying data interactions, which would complicate the ability to have different versions operating simultaneously. Therefore, a necessary operational component is the ability to manage application migration and transition to using master data services.

3.4.4 **Administration/Configuration**

Lastly, because the framework supporting MDM may involve different architectures and frameworks, a master index of entity representations, mappings from the master index to persistent storage, and multiple application interfaces and service invocations to access and use master data, the MDM technical team will need tools and processes to configure and provide ongoing administration of various aspects of the underlying MDM framework.

3.5 **IDENTIFICATION AND CONSOLIDATION**

The wide spectrum of applications that deal with each type of master data object will eventually need to be integrated to employ the virtual master resource. That requires three capabilities: the ability to search and match for identity resolution, links to connect records within their appropriate hierarchies, and merging and consolidation of multiple records and survivorship rules applied to the attributes to formulate a single "best" version of each entity.

3.5.1 **Identity Search and Resolution**

Identity resolution refers to the ability to determine that two or more data representations can be resolved into one representation of a unique object. This is not limited to people's names or addresses, because even though the bulk of data (and consequently, the challenge) is person or business names or addresses, there is a growing need for the resolution of records associated with other kinds of data, such as product names, product codes, object descriptions, reference data, and so on.

For a given data population, identity resolution can be viewed as a two-stage process. The first stage is one of discovery and combines data profiling activities with a manual review of data. Typically, simple probabilistic models can be evolved that then feed into the second stage, which is one of similarity scoring and matching for the purpose of record linkage.

3.5.2 **Record Linkage**

Subsequent to developing the similarity scoring processes and models as part of identity resolution, the algorithms are applied to a larger population of records, taken from the different sources, to link and presumably to automatically establish (within predefined bounds) that some set of records refer to the same entity. Usually, there are some bounds to what can be deemed an automatic match, and these bounds are not just dependent on the quantification of similarity but must be defined based on the application. For example, there is a big difference between business applications that determine if the same person is being mailed two catalogs instead of one as opposed to applications that determine whether the individual boarding the plane is on the terrorist list. The record linkage component services both the identity management capability as well as the processes for merging and consolidation.

3.5.3 **Merging and Consolidation**

Enterprise data sets are reviewed using identity resolution to distinguish records representing unique entities and then are loaded into a canonical representation. Record linkage is applied to seek out similar representations, paving the way for the merging and consolidation process. Similar records are subjected to algorithms to qualify the values within each data attribute.

3.6 **INTEGRATION**

The objectives of MDM are not only achieved through data integration. Value is added when the consolidated master entity representation is integrated back into operational and analytical use by the participating applications to truly provide a single, synchronized view of the customer, product, or other master data entity.

The abstraction of the data integration layer as it relates to the development of business applications exposes two ways that master data are integrated into a services-based framework. Tactically, a services layer must be introduced to facilitate the transition of applications to use a master asset. Strategically, the abstraction of the core master entities at a data integration layer provide the foundation for establishing a hierarchical set of information services to support the rapid and efficient development of business applications. Fortunately, both of these imperatives are satisfied by a well-defined abstraction layer for services, and these concepts form the next layer of the component model.

3.6.1 **Application Integration with Master Data**

An MDM program that solely accumulates data into a consolidated repository without allowing for the use of that data is essentially worthless. One driving factor for establishing the unified view of enterprise master data objects is establishing a high-quality asset that can be shared across the enterprise. This means that information must easily be consolidated into the master view and must be easily accessible by enterprise applications. Production applications can be expected to migrate to access the master data asset as each application's data sets are consolidated within the master view. Therefore, part of the MDM framework must accommodate existing application infrastructures in ways that are minimally disruptive yet provide a standardized path for transitioning to the synchronized master.

3.6.2 **MDM Component Service Layer**

As MDM becomes more fully integrated to support business applications within the enterprise architecture, those applications can increasingly rely on the abstraction of the conceptual master data objects *and their corresponding functionality* to support newer business architecture designs. Standardizing master data object representations reduces the need for application architects to focus on traditional data-oriented issues (e.g., data access and manipulation, security and access control, or policy management) and instead can use abstracted functionality to support business requirements by relying on the lower-level data-directed services whose format and design is dictated through an MDM services layer architecture. This ability to consolidate application functionality (e.g., "creating a new customer" or "listing a new product") using a services layer that supplements multiple application approaches provides additional value across both existing and future applications by simplifying incremental development.

3.7 BUSINESS PROCESS MANAGEMENT

The highest level of abstraction, business process management, is the one at which the requirements for making application design decisions are exposed. All too often, application designs are technology driven, with implementation decisions made based on technical recommendations rather than business needs. A key (and, perhaps, ironic) goal in MDM system design is to ensure that the system is business driven. Despite the fact that MDM is largely dependent on the proper disciplines guiding the organizational use of technology, it is widely recognized that deploying the technical components without linking their functionality to a corresponding business process model is essentially pointless. At this level in the component stack, the architects incorporate business process modeling with system architecture. Clearly, MDM is differentiated from other types of technology-driven consolidation efforts because of the desire to more closely couple technology inclusion, and that is made possible through business process integration and the use of rules-based operational systems that rely on formally defined business rules.

3.7.1 Business Process Integration

All business applications should reflect the implementation of business process requirements specified, either explicitly or implicitly, as the way the business operations are performed. A *business process model* is a logical presentation that communicates the right details of a business process to the right people at the right time. It typically lists the processes involved, their inputs, aspects that control each process, the types of events or triggers that emerge as a result of each process, and the expected output of each process. The model's visual representation relies on the underlying metadata, such as activity purpose, timing attributes, operational triggers, process inputs, process duration, generated events, resources used, and the desired outputs.

As individual activities are linked, the model shows how the outputs of one activity coupled with triggered events from other activities control or influence the behavior of the enclosing application, as well as the collection of applications as a whole. In turn, these business process model descriptions are annotated with the references to the master data objects necessary to complete the procedure. This effectively integrates the business process with the MDM solution, exposing the strict and implicit data dependencies and validating the identification and selection of master data object classes.

3.7.2 **Business Rules**

Within any business process model, the logic employed for executing a particular operation combines the evaluation of the values of the shared data objects and the values expressed by defined controls. The values are examined to determine which actions to take, and that in turn will create new values and trigger new controls. There are two ways to look at a specific implementation. The first is explicit: embedding the logic within application program code to evaluate the data values and specifically executing the actions. The second, more abstract approach is to systematically use descriptive rules to examine variable values and trigger actions, all used to establish the consistency of overall system state.

The way that actors interact with the events, controls, and inputs associated with the business process model provides us with the details of the business logic that will ultimately be deployed as formal business rules. Reviewing the business process model enables the application designers to identify the key triggers for specific rules, as well as exposing the full set of conditions that need to be addressed during the business process. This review process leads to a more complete model of the system, and consequently, its corresponding master data dependencies.

3.7.3 **MDM Business Component Layer**

Underlying the definitions and requirements exposed through the business process modeling and integration component and the implementation of business rules through a rules-based system is the business component layer. It is at this layer that we begin to see the creation of more sophisticated reusable business services (as opposed to the functional services that address interaction with the master data). At the business component layer, we start to see reliance on more interesting master data objects. For example, in addition to referring to master customer records, we might also begin to integrate master customer profiles within predictive analytics embedded within operational applications. The migration toward the use of the master model will open up opportunities for creating analytics-oriented master data object types and combine their use with traditional operational applications.

3.8 **MDM MATURITY MODEL**

Our objective in defining a maturity model is not to provide a benchmark against which all MDM implementations are measured. Rather, because many organizations have already designed, coded, and deployed various versions of the described capabilities, the level of maturity describes both how the use of already deployed components and services can be exploited for the purposes of a master data management program, as well as suggesting which missing capabilities should be acquired in order to advance to more sophisticated application reliance on master data.

3.8.1 **Initial**

The *initial* level of maturity (as detailed in Table 3.1) is characterized more by the absence of capabilities than the alternative. At the initial level, there are limited possibilities for exploiting master data, but there is some degree of recognition that there are replicated copies of certain data sets that are relevant to more than one application. At the initial level, some business and technical managers are prepared to explore ways to consolidate data sets for analytical purposes.

3.8.2 **Reactive**

At the *reactive* level (detailed in Table 3.2), not only is there a recognition that the existence of replicated copies of data causes business impacts, but there are some attempts to resolve the issue. Invalid or unusable data are deemed an information technology problem. Data quality tools are purchased as a prelude to "fixing the data," although the actual business needs may lie unanalyzed while a technical team acquires tools. Initial uses of the tools satisfy some line-of-business application needs, but lessons learned are not shared, leading to a duplication of effort.

Table 3.1   The Initial Maturity Level

Component Layer	Capabilities
Architecture	Limited enterprise consolidation of representative models No master data models Collections of data dictionaries in various forms
Governance	Limited data cleansing by application/line of business, for specific purposes (e.g., address standardization) Absence of defined ownership or stewardship models Recognition of need for oversight
Management	Identity management by application when needed (e.g., customers) Some application configuration, but not coordinated through centralized management
Identification	Limited use of identity management by line of business "Tiger team" attempts at customer data consolidation as required by applications (e.g., software upgrades or transitioning of accounting applications)
Integration	Replicated copies of reference data Limited data reuse No application services reuse
Business process management	Limited or no business involvement except at highest level of requirements definition

Some attempts are made at consolidating metadata from across different applications, and tools are reviewed and purchased but still are managed as technical resources. Application needs for data sharing are attacked by vigorous and uncoordinated XML (eXtensible Markup Language) schemas and corresponding services, although there is a great need for fine-tuning the variant implementations.

Table 3.2 The Reactive Maturity Level

Component Layer	Capabilities
Architecture	Application architectures are defined for each business application Attempts to collect data dictionaries into a single repository Initial exploration into low-level application services Review of options for information sharing (e.g., enterprise information integration or enterprise application integration)
Governance	External applications used to manage metadata Introduction of data quality management for parsing, standardization, and consolidation
Management	Resources are assigned to manage the use of introduced tool sets Training for enterprise roll-out of tools and technology make capabilities available on a more widespread basis Centralized administration of metadata and master indexes
Identification	Identity search and match used to reduce duplication Identity search and match used for rudimentary record linkage for householding purposes
Integration	Initial exploration of consolidation of data for newly developed analytical (e.g., customer relationship management) applications Data warehouse used as a core repository for master data Limited or no integration back into contributing applications
Business process management	Conceptual business process models are described Analytical application integration of consolidated data Initial use of business rules embedded within applications

3.8.3 **Managed**

Once analytical applications have been created that rely on some level of consolidation, individuals within the organization can establish a value proposition for continued use and growth of consolidated master repositories. Gaining senior management buy-in enables more comprehensive enterprise modeling activities, which are supplemented by the MDM program. Whereas at the reactive level the focus may have been on a single area such as customers, at the *managed* level (detailed in Table 3.3) the ability to use master data becomes a repeatable process and can be expanded to incorporate new applications as well as

Table 3.3 The Managed Maturity Level	
Component Layer	**Capabilities**
Architecture	Defined core data model for persistence Fundamental architecture for shared master data framework Identified operational framework for low-level master data life cycle activities Defined services for integration with master data asset
Governance	Data quality tools in place Policies and procedures for data quality management Data quality issues tracking Data standards processes in place Line-of-business data stewardship
Management	Identity management centralized in master index Identity management utilized across numerous applications Identified hierarchies (households, relationships within a data class) used by analytical applications Advanced configuration and administration of application use of master data A migration plan is available for selected applications

(Continued)

Table 3.3 The Managed Maturity Level—cont'd

Component Layer	Capabilities
Identification	Identity search and match service available to all applications Record linkage integrated within the MDM service layer Rules for merging and consolidation standardized and managed under centralized control Merging and consolidation processes established and repeatable
Integration	Processes for integration back into contributing applications Definition of component services available for application integration Services for synchronization between applications and master data services
Business process management	Integration of business rules with master data operations Fundamental connectivity between business applications and core data objects Business process analysts participate in master data engineering requirements

existing applications, as the consolidation and synchronization services are available as part of the migration package.

3.8.4 **Proactive**

As organizations establish the core data models and service architectures characterized at the managed level, they become more adept at reducing individual business application dependence on its own copies of replicated data and at the *proactive* level (detailed in Table 3.4) the applications are generally integrated through the service layer with the master data environment. Synchronization for application data interactions is embedded within the component service layer, as are identity resolution, hierarchy management, and identity management. The business is able to better establish relationships at the customer/supplier/vendor level, as full profiles based on aggregated and consolidated data are managed as a core enterprise resource. Data governance is in effect across the organization with hierarchical organization down the management chain.

Table 3.4   The Proactive Maturity Level

Component Layer	Capabilities
Architecture	Master models are established Capability to move from index framework to transaction-based MDM framework SOA in place for application architecture Centralized management of business metadata
Governance	Enterprise data governance program in place Enterprise data standards and meta-data management in place Proactive monitoring for data quality control feeds into governance program
Management	Identity management fully integrated across the enterprise Unique identification of all master object instances Full-cycle hierarchy management supports both analytical and operational activities Hierarchy management enables roll-back of false positive consolidation errors
Identification	Services for data life cycle embed identity search, match, and resolution All data life cycle operations structured on top of merging and consolidation services Consolidation occurs in background
Integration	Synchronization completely embedded within life cycle services Component layer supports application integration at master object level SOA drives business application integration
Business process management	Business logic is reused Business rules are integrated within a rules engine and made available at the business process level Business analysts integral to application development Personalized customer relationships Automated business processes

3.8.5 **Strategic Performance**

MDM, coupled with a services-oriented architecture, will (at the *strategic performance* level, as detailed in Table 3.5) ultimately enable rapid development of high-quality applications that support both the operational and analytical requirements of enterprise business applications. Business analysts work closely to enumerate expectations for

Table 3.5 The Strategic Performance Level

Component Layer	Capabilities
Architecture	Complete transaction integration available to internal applications Published APIs enable straight-through processing involving master data
Governance	Cross-organization data governance assures high-quality information sharing
Management	Seamless identity management of all data objects synchronized to both internal and external representations Migration of legacy applications complete
Identification	Identity resolution services exposed externally to the organization Business performance directly tied to master dimensions
Integration	All application development is driven by business process models and their interaction with core master object models
Business process management	Businesses completely drive application design and development Applications largely integrate business rule engines Data instance profiles (customer or vendor profiles) managed within master data asset MDM enables embedded predictive analytics

outward-facing process implementations. Analytical results associated with business intelligence processes will be managed as master objects, enabling more effective and consistent predictive analytics to be embedded within customer-facing applications.

3.9 **DEVELOPING AN IMPLEMENTATION ROAD MAP**

It is relevant to note that when reviewing the capability/maturity model described in this chapter, your organization may already have a number of these capabilities in place. As an example, as part of many data warehousing projects, the process for consolidating data from multiple application data sets posed questions regarding the quality of the warehouse data. This introduced the need for data cleansing and data quality tools, along with the methods to correct warehouse data to meet analyst and reporting requirements. The availability of the tools in common practice within the organization for parsing, standardization, and cleansing demonstrates that with respect to governance, the organization has already begun to transition from the initial level to the reactive level.

On the one hand, one might expect that all organizations desire to execute at the strategic performance level. However, achieving the capabilities at this level requires a significant investment in time and resources—an investment for which interim value would be expected for delivery. Therefore, it is more reasonable to chart a road map through the different levels of maturity, detailing the business value expected as each level is attained.

This process provides three relevant benefits. First, having learned lessons in the past regarding the longevity, high cost, and limited deliverables of "big bang" projects, project managers instead may seek out the short-term tactical values achieved as the result of intermediate steps taken toward the eventual end state. This provides the business client with tangible benefits during the maturation sequence. Second, envisioning the end state and progressing there clarifies the design, development, and migration processes that will be necessary to evolve both the environment and the structural components to the point where the application and information architectures are able to rely on the master data asset. Third, the strategic view enables proper positioning, communication, and socialization of the organizational changes needed to ensure proper acceptance for the transition.

Fundamentally, the objectives of an implementation road map are to clarify the business goals for MDM, understand the set of capabilities that are necessary to achieve those business goals, determine what sets of capabilities already exist within the organization, assess the gaps, determine where the organization needs to be, and decide how to get there. More formally, we can define a conceptual process as shown in the sidebar.

IMPLEMENTATION ROAD MAP

Evaluate the business goals. Part analysis, part organizational soul-searching, this task is to develop an organizational understanding of the benefits of MDM as they reflect the current and future business objectives. This may involve reviewing the lines of business and their related business processes, evaluating where the absence of a synchronized master view impedes or prevents business processes from completing at all or introduces critical inefficiencies, and identifying key business areas that would benefit from moving to an MDM environment.

Evaluate the business needs. This step is to prioritize the business goals and determine which are most critical (of the critical goals, determine which have dependences on MDM as success criteria).

Assess current state. Here, staff members can use the maturity model to assess the current landscape of available tools, techniques, methods, and organizational readiness for MDM.

Assess the initial gap. By comparing the business needs against the evaluation of the current state, the analysts can determine the degree to which the current state is satisfactory to support business needs or alternatively determine where there are gaps that can be addressed by implementing additional MDM capabilities.

Envision the desired state. If the current capabilities are not sufficient to support the business needs, the analysts must determine the maturity level that would be satisfactory and set that as the target for the implementation.

Analyze the capability gap. The analysts determine the gaps between the current state and the desired level of maturity and identify which components and capabilities are necessary to fill the gaps.

Map the capabilites. To achieve interim benefits, the analysts seek ways to map the MDM capabilities to existing application needs to demonstrate tactical returns.

Plan the project. Having identified the capabilities, tools, and methods that need to be implemented, the "bundle" can be handed off to the project management team to assemble a project plan for the appropriate level of requirements analysis, design, development, and implementation.

In essence, we are using the maturity model as the yardstick against which the organization's MDM capabilities and readiness are measured. In turn, the maturity model is used to project an end state, which helps the business analysts to map the execution of the plan to the current application architecture and foresee the best way to reach the end state.

3.10 **SUMMARY**

The transition to MDM is viewed as a revolution, but it is more effectively developed as an evolution. We have looked at the different components necessary to implement a mature master data management program, as well as investigated levels of maturity through which organizations may grow. Although no functionality list completely captures the inventory of services that a specific business requires from a master data system, by exploring the core MDM capabilities and a conceptual outline of technical MDM components, we have provided a framework to determine where any organization's capabilities lie.

When faced with the opportunity to assemble a master data management program, one should evaluate the business requirements and then review how those requirements can be addressed at the different levels of the maturity model. The presentation of the MDM component layers in terms of their maturity enables enterprise architects to target a desired level of MDM maturity and develop a design and implementation road map that articulates the steps to take when assembling a program that effectively meets the line-of-business needs.

Chapter 4

Data Governance for Master Data Management

4.1 **INTRODUCTION**

Both external and internal pressures introduce constraints on the use of enterprise information. Financial reporting, regulatory compliance, and privacy policies are just a few examples of the kinds of pressures that prompt data management professionals and senior business managers to institute a framework for ensuring the quality and integrity of the data asset for all of its purposes. These challenges are magnified as data sets from different applications are consolidated into a master data environment. Numerous aspects of ensuring this integrity deal with the interactions between the applications, data, and individuals in the enterprise, and therefore it is worthwhile to explore the mechanics, virtues, and ongoing operations of instituting a data governance program within an organization.

At its core, the objective of data governance is predicated on the desire to assess and manage the many kinds of risks that lurk within the enterprise information portfolio and to reduce the impacts incurred by the absence of oversight. Although many data governance activities might be triggered by a concern about regulatory compliance, the controls introduced by data governance processes and protocols provide a means for quantitative metrics for assessing risk reduction as well as measuring business performance improvements. By introducing a program for defining information policies that relate to the constraints of the business and adding in management and technical oversight, the organization can realign itself around performance measures that include adherence to business policies and the information policies that support the business.

One of the major values of a master data management program is that, because it is an enterprise initiative, it facilitates the growth of an enterprise data governance program. As more lines of business integrate with core master data object repositories, there must be some assurance that the lines of business are adhering to the rules that govern participation. Although MDM success relies on data governance, a governance program can be applied across different operational domains, providing economies of scale for enterprise-wide deployment. In this chapter, we will look at the driving factors for instituting a data governance program in conjunction with master data management, setting the stage for deploying governance, critical data elements and their relation to key corporate data entities, stages for implementation, and roles and responsibilities.

One special note, though: the directive to establish data governance is a double-edged sword. An organization cannot expect to dictate into existence any type of governance framework without the perception of business value, which prevents the creation of a full-scale oversight infrastructure overnight. On the other hand, the absence of oversight will prevent success for any enterprise information initiative. This chapter, to some extent, presents an idealized view of how data governance is structured in the best of cases. However, the value of governance is linked to the value of what is being governed; incremental steps may be necessary to build of successes as a way of achieving "collateral." Continuous reassessment of the data governance program is a good way to ensure that the appropriate amount of effort is spent.

4.2 **WHAT IS DATA GOVERNANCE?**

There are different perceptions of what is meant by the term "data governance." Data governance is expected to ensure that the data meets the expectations of all the business purposes, in the context of data stewardship, ownership, compliance, privacy, security, data risks, data sensitivity, metadata management, and MDM. What is the common denominator? Each of these issues centers on ways that information management is integrated with controls for management oversight along with verification of organizational observance of information policies. In other words, each aspect of data governance relates to the specification of a set of information policies that reflect business needs and expectations, along with the processes for monitoring conformance to those information policies.

Whether we are discussing data sensitivity, financial reporting, or the way that team members execute against a sales system, each aspect of the business could be boiled down to a set of business policy requirements.

These business policies rely on the accessibility and usability of enterprise data, and the way each business policy uses data defines a set of information usage policies. Each information policy embodies a set of data rules or constraints associated with the definitions, formats, and uses of the underlying data elements.

Qualitative assertions about the quality of the data values, records, and the consistency across multiple data elements are the most granular level of governance. Together, these provide a layer of business metadata that will be employed in automating the collection and reporting of conformance to the business policies. Particularly in an age where noncompliance with external reporting requirements (e.g., Sarbanes-Oxley in the United States) can result in fines and prison sentences, the level of sensitivity to governance of information management will only continue to grow.

4.3 SETTING THE STAGE: ALIGNING INFORMATION OBJECTIVES WITH THE BUSINESS STRATEGY

Every organization has a business strategy that should reflect the business management objectives, the risk management objectives, and the compliance management objectives. Ultimately, the success of the organization depends on its ability to manage how all operations conform to that business strategy. This is true for information technology, but because of the centrality of data in the application infrastructure, it is particularly true in the area of data management.

The challenge lies in management's ability to effectively communicate the business strategy, to explain how nonconformance to the strategy impacts the business, and to engineer the oversight of information in a way that aligns the business strategy with the information architecture. This alignment is two-fold—it must demonstrate that the individuals within the organization understand how information assets are used as well as how that information asset is managed over time.

These concepts must be kept in mind when developing the policies and procedures associated with the different aspects of the MDM program. As a representation of the replicated data sets is integrated into a unified view, there is also a need to consolidate the associated information policies. The union of those policies creates a more stringent set of constraints associated with the quality of master data, requiring more comprehensive oversight and coordination among the application owners. To prepare for instituting the proper level of governance, these steps may be taken:

- Clarifying the information architecture
- Mapping information functions to business objectives
- Instituting a process framework for information policy

4.3.1 **Clarifying the Information Architecture**

Many organizational applications are created in a virtual vacuum, engineered to support functional requirements for a specific line of business without considering whether there is any overlap with other business applications. Although this tactical approach may be sufficient to support ongoing operations, it limits an enterprise's analytical capability and hampers any attempt at organizational oversight.

Before a data governance framework can be put into place, management must assess, understand, and document the de facto information architecture. A prelude to governance involves taking inventory to understand what data assets exist, how they are managed and used, and how they support the existing application architecture, and then evaluating where existing inefficiencies or redundancies create roadblocks to proper oversight.

The inventory will grow organically—initially the process involves identifying the data sets used by each application and enumerating the data attributes within each data set. As one would imagine, this process can consume a huge amount of resources. To be prudent, it is wise to focus on those data elements that have widespread, specific business relevance; the concept of the key data entity and the critical data element is treated in Sections 4.10 and 4.11.

Each data element must have a name, a structural format, and a definition, all of which must be registered within a metadata repository. Each data set models a relevant business concept, and each data element provides insight into that business concept within the context of the "owning" application. In turn, each definition must be reviewed to ensure that it is correct, defensible, and is grounded by an authoritative source.

This collection of data elements does not constitute a final architecture. A team of subject matter experts and data analysts must look at the physical components and recast them into a logical view that is consistent across the enterprise. A process called "harmonization" examines the data elements for similarity (or distinction) in meaning. Although this activity overlaps with the technical aspects of master data object analysis, its importance to governance lies in the identification and registration of the organization's critical data elements, their composed information structures, and the application functions associated with the data element life cycle.

4.3.2 **Mapping Information Functions to Business Objectives**

Every activity that creates, modifies, or retires a data element must somehow contribute to the organization's overall business objectives. In turn, the success or failure of any business activity is related to the appropriate and correct execution of all information functions that support that activity. For example, many website privacy policies specify that data about children below a specified age will not be shared without permission of the child's parent. A data element may be used to document each party's birth date and parent's permission, and there will also be functions to verify the party's age and parental permission before the information is shared with another organization.

When assessing the information architecture, one must document each information function and how it maps to achieving business objectives. In an environment where there are many instances of similar *data*, there will also be many instances of similar *functionality*, and as the data are absorbed into a master data hierarchy, the functional capabilities may likewise be consolidated into a service layer supporting the enterprise.

A standardized approach for functional description will help in assessing functional overlap, which may be subject for review as the core master data objects are identified and consolidated. However, in all situations, the application functionality essentially represents the ways that information policies are implemented across the enterprise.

4.3.3 **Instituting a Process Framework for Information Policy**

The goal of the bottom-up assessment is to understand how the information architecture and its associated functionality support the implementation of information policy. But in reality, the process should be reversed—information policy should be defined first, and then the data objects and their associated services should be designed to both implement and document compliance with that policy.

This process framework is supported by *and* supports a master data management environment. As key data entities and their associated attributes are absorbed under centralized management, the ability to map the functional service layer to the deployment of information policy also facilitates the collection and articulation of the data quality expectations associated with each data attribute, record, and data set, whether they are reviewed statically within persistent storage or in transit between two different processing stages. Clearly specified data quality expectations can be deployed as validation rules for data inspection along its "lineage," allowing for the embedding of monitoring probes (invoking enterprise services) that collectively (and reliably) report on compliance.

4.4 DATA QUALITY AND DATA GOVERNANCE

A data quality and data governance assessment clarifies how the information architecture is used to support compliance with defined information policies. It suggests that data quality and data standards management are part of a much larger picture with respect to oversight of enterprise information.

In the siloed environment, the responsibilities, and ultimately the accountability for ensuring that the data meets the quality expectations of the client applications lie within the management of the corresponding line of business. This also implies that for MDM, the concept of data ownership (which is frequently treated in a cavalier manner) must be aligned within the line of business so that ultimate accountability for the quality of data can be properly identified. But looking at the organization's need for information oversight provides a conduit for reviewing the dimensions of data quality associated with the data elements, determining their criticality to the business operations, expressing the data rules that impact compliance, defining quantitative measurements for conformance to information policies, and determining ways to integrate these all into a data governance framework.

4.5 AREAS OF RISK

What truly drives the need for governance? Although there are many drivers, a large component boils down to risk. Both business and compliance risks drive governance, and it is worthwhile to look at just a few of the areas of risk associated with master data that require information management and governance scrutiny.

4.5.1 Business and Financial

If the objective of the MDM program is to enhance productivity and thereby improve the organization's bottom line, then the first area of risk involves understanding how nonconformance with information policies puts the business's financial objectives at risk. For example, identifying errors within financial reports that have a material impact requiring restatement of results not only demonstrates instability and lack of control, it also is likely to have a negative impact on the company (and its shareholders) as a whole, often reflected in decrease in the company's value.

Absence of oversight for the quality of financial data impacts operational aspects as well. The inability to oversee a unified master view of accounts, customers, and suppliers may lead to accounting anomalies, including underbilling of customers, duplicate payments or overpayments to vendors, payments to former employees, and so on.

4.5.2 **Reporting**

Certain types of regulations (e.g., Sarbanes-Oxley for financial reporting, 21 CFR Part 11 for electronic documentation in the pharmaceutical industry, Basel II for assessing capital risk in the banking industry) require that the organization prepare documents and reports that demonstrate compliance, which establishes accurate and auditable reporting as an area of risk. Accuracy demands the existence of established practices for data validation, but the ability to conduct thorough audits requires comprehensive oversight of the processes that implement the information policies. Consequently, ensuring report consistency and accuracy requires stewardship and governance of the data sets that are used to populate (or materialize data elements for) those reports.

For example, consider that in financial reporting, determining that flawed data was used in assembling a financial statement may result in material impacts that necessitate a restatement of the financial report. Restatements may negatively affect the organization's stock price, leading to loss of shareholder value, lawsuits, significant "spin control" costs, and potentially jail time for senior executives. A governance program can help to identify opportunities for instituting data controls to reduce the risk of these kinds of situations.

4.5.3 **Entity Knowledge**

Maintaining knowledge of the parties with whom the organization does business is critical for understanding and reducing both business risks (e.g., credit rating to ensure that customers can pay their bills) and regulatory risks. Many different industries are governed by regulations that insist on customer awareness, such as the USA PATRIOT Act, the Bank Secrecy Act, and Graham-Leach-Bliley, all of which require the ability to distinguish between unique individual identities. Ensuring that the tools used to resolve identities are matching within expected levels of trust and that processes exist for remediating identity errors falls under the realm of governance and stewardship.

4.5.4 **Protection**

The flip side of entity knowledge is protection of individual potentially private information. Compliance directives that originate in regulations such as HIPAA and Graham-Leach-Bliley require that organizations protect each individual's data to limit data breaches and protect personal information. Similarly to entity knowledge, confidence in the management of protected information depends on conformance to defined privacy and data protection constraints.

4.5.5 **Limitation of Use**

Regulations and business arrangements (as codified within contractual agreements) both establish governance policies for limiting how data sets are used, how they are shared, what components may be shared, and the number of times they can be copied, as well as overseeing the determination of access rights for the data. Data lineage, provenance, and access management are all aspects of the types of information policies whose oversight is incorporated within the governance program.

4.6 **RISKS OF MASTER DATA MANAGEMENT**

If these types of risks were not enough, the deployment of a master data management program introduces organizational risks of its own. As a platform for integrating and consolidating information from across vertical lines of business into a single source of truth, MDM implies that independent corporate divisions (with their own divisional performance objectives) yield to the needs of the enterprise.

As an enterprise initiative, MDM requires agreement from the participants to ensure program success. This leads to a unique set of challenges for companies undertaking an MDM program.

4.6.1 **Establishing Consensus for Coordination and Collaboration**

The value of the master data environment is the agreement (across divisions and business units) that it represents the highest quality identifying information for enterprise master data objects. The notion of agreement implies that all application participants share their data, provide positive input into its improvement, and trust the resulting consolidated versions. The transition to using the master data asset suggests that all application groups will work in a coordinated manner to share information and resources and to make sure that the result meets the quality requirements of each participant.

4.6.2 **Data Ownership**

As an enterprise resource, master data objects should be owned by the organization, and therefore the responsibilities of ownership are assigned to an enterprise resource. There are some benefits to this approach. For example, instead of numerous agents responsible for different versions of the same objects, each is assigned to a single individual. In general, management and oversight is simplified because the number of data objects is reduced, with a corresponding reduction in resource needs (e.g., storage, backups, metadata). One major drawback to centralizing ownership is political, because the reassignment of ownership, by definition, removes responsibilities from individuals, some of whom are bound to feel threatened by the transition. The other is logistic, focusing on the process of migrating the responsibilities for data sets from a collection of individuals to a central authority.

But as any enterprise initiative like MDM or enterprise resource planning (ERP) is based on strategic drivers with the intention of adjusting the way the organization works, master data consolidation is meant to provide a high-quality, synchronized asset that can streamline application sharing of important data objects. ERP implementations reduce business complexity because the system is engineered to support the interactions *between* business applications, instead of setting up the barriers common in siloed operations. In essence, the goals of these strategic activities are to change the way that people operate, increase collaboration and transparency, and transition from being tactically driven by short-term goals into a knowledge-directed organization working toward continuous performance improvement objectives.

Therefore, any implementation or operational decisions made in deploying a strategic enterprise solution should increase collaboration and decrease distributed management. This suggests that the approach by agents for the entire organization to obtain centralized ownership of master data entities is more aligned with the strategic nature of an MDM or ERP program.

However, each line of business may have its own perception of data ownership, ranging from an information architecture owned by the business line management data that is effectively captured and embedded within an application (leading to a high level of data distribution), to undocumented perceptions of ownership on behalf of individual staff members managing the underlying data sets. As diffused application development likely occurs when there is no official data ownership policy, each business application manager may view the data owned by the group or attached to the application.

When centralizing shared master data, though, the consolidation of information into a single point of truth implies that the traditional implied data ownership model has been dissolved. This requires the definition and transference of accountability and responsibility from the line of business to the enterprise, along with its accompanying policies for governance.

4.6.3 **Semantics: Form, Function, and Meaning**

Distributed application systems designed and implemented in isolation are likely to have similar, yet perhaps slightly variant definitions, semantics, formats, and representations. The variation across applications introduces numerous risks associated with the consolidation of any business data object into a single view. For example, different understandings of what is meant by the term "customer" may be tolerated within the context of each application, but in a consolidated environment, there is much less tolerance for different counts and sums. Often these different customer counts occur because of subtleties in the definitions. For example, in the sales organization, any prospect is a "customer," but in the accounting department, only parties that have agreed to pay money in exchange for products are "customers."

An MDM migration requires establishing processes for resolving those subtle (and presumed meaningless) distinctions in meaning that can become magnified during consolidation, especially in relation to data element names, definitions, formats, and uses. This can be addressed by providing guidelines for the capture of data element metadata and its subsequent syntactic and semantic harmonization. Organizations can also establish guidelines for collaboration among the numerous stakeholders so that each is confident that using the master version of data will not impact the appropriate application. Processes for collecting enterprise metadata, harmonizing data element names, definitions, and representations are overseen by the governance program.

4.7 **MANAGING RISK THROUGH MEASURED CONFORMANCE TO INFORMATION POLICIES**

Preventing exposure to risk requires creating policies that establish the boundaries of the risk, along with an oversight process to ensure compliance with those policies. Although each set of policies may differ depending on the different related risks, all of these issues share some commonalities:

Federation. In each situation, the level of risk varies according to the way that information is captured, stored, managed, and shared among applications and individuals across multiple management or administrative boundaries. In essence, because of the diffused application architecture, to effectively address risks, all of the administrative groups must form a federation, slightly blurring their line-of-business boundaries for the sake of enterprise compliance management.

Defined policy. To overcome the challenges associated with risk exposure, policies must be defined (either externally or internally) that delineate the guidelines for risk mitigation. Although these policies reflect operational activities for compliance, they can be translated into rules that map against data elements managed within the enterprise.

Need for controls. The definition of policy is one thing, but the ability to measure conformance to that policy is characterized as a set of controls that inspect data and monitor conformance to expectations along the process information flow.

Transparent oversight. One aspect of each of the areas of risk described here is the expectation that there is some person or governing body to which policy conformance must be reported. Whether that body is a government agency overseeing regulatory compliance, an industry body that watches over industry guidelines, or public corporate shareholders, there is a need for transparency in the reporting framework.

Auditability. The need for transparency creates a need for all policy compliance to be auditable. Not only does the organization need to demonstrate compliance to the defined policies, it must be able to both show an audit trail that can be reviewed independently and show that the processes for managing compliance are transparent as well.

The upshot is that whether the objective is regulatory compliance, managing financial exposure, or overseeing organizational collaboration, centralized management will spread data governance throughout the organization. This generally happens through two techniques. First, data governance will be defined through a collection of information policies, each of which is mapped to a set of rules imposed over the life cycle of critical data elements. Second, data stewards will be assigned responsibility and accountability for both the quality of the critical data elements and the assurance of conformance to the information policies. Together these two aspects provide the technical means for monitoring data governance and provide the context to effectively manage data governance.

4.8 **KEY DATA ENTITIES**

Key data entities are the fundamental information objects that are employed by the business applications to execute the operations of the business while simultaneously providing the basis for analyzing the performance of the lines of business. Although the description casts the concept of a key data entity (or KDE) in terms of its business use, a typical explanation will characterize the KDE in its technical sense. For example, in a dimensional database such as those used by a data warehouse, the key data entities are reflected as dimensions. In a master data management environment, data objects that are designated as candidates for mastering are likely to be the key data entities. Managing uniquely accessible instances of key data entities is a core driver for MDM, especially because of their inadvertent replication across multiple business applications.

Governing the quality and acceptability of a key data entity will emerge as a critical issue within the organization, mostly because of the political aspects of data ownership. In fact, data ownership itself is always a challenge, but when data sets are associated with a specific application, there is a reasonable expectation that someone associated with the line of business using the application will (when push comes to shove) at least take on the responsibilities of ownership. But as key data entities are merged together into an enterprise resource, it is important to have policies dictating how ownership responsibilities are allocated and how accountability is assigned, and the management framework for ensuring that these policies are not just paper tigers.

4.9 **CRITICAL DATA ELEMENTS**

Critical data elements are those that are determined to be vital to the successful operation of the organization. For example, an organization may define its critical data elements as those that represent protected personal information, those that are used in financial reports (both internal and external), regulatory reports, the data elements that represent identifying information of master data objects (e.g., customer, vendor, or employee data), the elements that are critical for a decision-making process, or the elements that are used for measuring organizational performance.

Part of the governance process involves a collaborative effort to identify critical data elements, research their authoritative sources, and then agree on their definitions. As opposed to what our comment in Section 4.3.1 might imply, a mass assessment of all existing enterprise data elements is not the most efficient approach to identifying critical data elements.

Rather, the best process is to start at the end and focus on the information artifacts that end clients are using—consider all reports, analyses, or operations that are critical to the business, and identify every data element that impacts or contributes to each report element or analytical dimension. At the same time, begin to map out the sequence of processes from the original point of entry until the end of each critical operation. The next step is to assemble a target to source mapping: look at each of the identified data elements and then look for data elements on which the selected data element depends. For example, if a report tallies the total sales for the entire company, that total sales number is a critical data element. However, that data element's value depends on a number of divisional sales totals, which in turn are composed of business-line or product-line detailed sales. Each step points to more elements in the dependence chain, each of which is also declared to be a critical data element.

Each data element's criticality is proportional to its contribution to the ultimate end values that are used to run or monitor the business. The quality of each critical data element is related to the impact that would be incurred should the value be outside of acceptable ranges. In other words, the quality characteristics are based on business impact, which means that controls can be introduced to monitor data values against those quality criteria.

4.10 DEFINING INFORMATION POLICIES

Information policies embody the specification of management objectives associated with data governance, whether they are related to management of risk or general data oversight. Information policies relate specified business assertions to their related data sets and articulate how the business policy is integrated with the information asset. In essence, it is the information policy that bridges the gap between the business policy and the characterization of critical data element quality.

For example, consider the many regulations requiring customer knowledge, such as the anti-money laundering (AML) aspects required by the USA PATRIOT Act. The protocols of AML imply a few operational perspectives:

- Establishing policies and procedures to detect and report suspicious transactions
- Ensuring compliance with the Bank Secrecy Act
- Providing for independent testing for compliance to be conducted by outside parties

But in essence, AML compliance revolves around a relatively straightforward concept: know your customer. Because all monitoring centers on how individuals are conducting business, any organization that wants to comply with these objectives must have processes in place to identify and verify customer identity.

Addressing the regulatory policy of compliance with AML necessarily involves defining information policies for managing customer data, such as the suggestions presented in the sidebar. These assertions are ultimately boiled down into specific data directives, each of which is measurable and reportable, which is the cornerstone of the stewardship process.

AML INFORMATION POLICIES

- Identity of any individual involved in establishing an account must be verified.
- Records of the data used to verify a customer's identity must be measurably clean and consistent.
- Customers may not appear on government lists of known or suspected terrorists or belong to known or suspected terrorist organizations.
- A track record of all customer activity must be maintained.
- Managers must be notified of any behavior categorized as "suspicious."

4.11 **METRICS AND MEASUREMENT**

Any business policy will, by virtue of its implementation within an application system, require conformance to a set of information policies. In turn, each information policy should be described as a set of assertions involving one or more key data entities, examining the values of critical data elements, as can be seen in Figure 4.1. In other

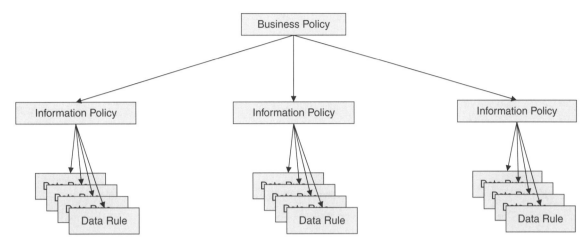

■ **FIGURE 4.1** A hierarchy of data rules is derived from each business policy.

words, the information policy might be further clarified into specific rules that would apply to both the master data set as well as the participating applications. In the example that required the tracking of customer activity, one might define a rule prescribing that each application that manages transactions must log critical data elements associated with the customer identity and transaction in a master transaction repository. Conformance to the rule can be assessed by verifying that all records of the master transaction repository are consistent with the application systems, where consistency is defined as a function of comparing the critical data values with the original transaction.

Metrics reflecting conformance with an information policy can be viewed as a rollup of the various data rules into which the policy was decomposed. As long as each rule is measurable, we can create a hierarchy of metrics that ultimately can be combined into key performance indicators for the purposes of data governance.

4.12 **MONITORING AND EVALUATION**

Essentially, measurements of conformance to business policies define the key performance indicators for the business itself. This collection of key performance indicators provides a high-level view of the organization's performance with respect to its conformance to defined information policies. In fact, we can have each indicator reflect the rolled-up measurements associated with the set of data rules for each information policy. Thresholds may be set that characterize levels of acceptability, and the metrics can be drilled through to isolate specific issues that are preventing conformance to the defined policy, enabling both transparency and auditability.

But for the monitoring to be effective, those measurements must be presented directly to the individual that is assigned responsibility for oversight of that information policy. It is then up to that individual to continuously monitor conformance to the policy and, if there are issues, to use the drill-through process to determine the points of failure and to initiate the processes for remediation.

4.13 **FRAMEWORK FOR RESPONSIBILITY AND ACCOUNTABILITY**

One of the biggest historical problems with data governance is the absence of follow-through; although some organizations may have well-defined governance policies, they may not have established the underlying organizational structure to make it actionable. This requires two things: the definition of the management structure to oversee the execution of the governance framework and a compensation model that rewards that execution.

A data governance framework must support the needs of all the participants across the enterprise, from the top down and from the bottom up. With executive sponsorship secured, a reasonable framework can benefit from enterprise-wide participation within a data governance oversight board, while all interested parties can participate in the role of data stewards. A technical coordination council can be convened to establish best practices and to coordinate technical approaches to ensure economies of scale. The specific roles include the following:

- Data governance director
- Data governance oversight board
- Data coordination council
- Data stewards

These roles are dovetailed with an organizational structure that oversees conformance to the business and information policies, as shown in Figure 4.2. Enterprise data management is integrated within the data coordination council, which reports directly to an enterprise data governance oversight board.

As mentioned at the beginning of the chapter, be aware that pragmatically the initial stages of governance are not going to benefit

Roles and Responsibilities

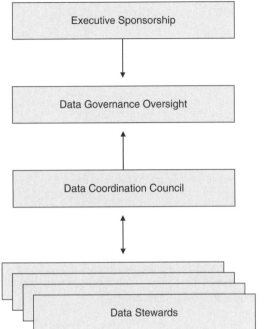

Executive Sponsorship

Provides senior management support at the C-level, warrants the enterprise's adoption of measurably high-quality data, and negotiates quality SLAs with external data suppliers.

Data Governance Oversight

Strategic committee composed of business clients to oversee the governance program, ensure that governance priorities are set and abided by, and delineate data accountability.

Data Coordination Council

Tactical team tasked with: ensuring that data activities have defined metrics and acceptance thresholds for quality, meeting business client expectations, managing governance across lines of business, setting priorities for business application data stewards, and communicating opportunities to Data Governance Oversight committee.

Data Stewards

At the deeper levels in the organization, the data governance structure defines data quality criteria for business applications, delineates stewardship roles, and reports activities and issues to Data Coordination Council.

■ **FIGURE 4.2** A framework for data governance management.

from a highly structured hierarchy; rather they are likely to roll the functions of an oversight board and a coordination council into a single working group. Over time, as the benefits of data governance are recognized, the organization can evolve the management infrastructure to segregate the oversight roles from the coordination and stewardship roles.

4.14 **DATA GOVERNANCE DIRECTOR**

The data governance director is responsible for the day-to-day management of enterprise data governance. The director provides guidance to all the participants and oversees adherence to the information policies as they reflect the business policies and necessary regulatory constraints. The data governance director plans and chairs the data governance oversight board. The director identifies the need for governance initiatives and provides periodic reports on data governance performance.

DGOB RESPONSIBILITIES

- Provide strategic direction for enterprise data governance
- Review corporate information policies and designate workgroups to transform business policies into information policies and then into data rules
- Approve data governance policies and procedures
- Manage the reward framework for compliance with governance policies
- Review proposals for data governance practices and processes
- Endorse data certification and audit processes

4.15 DATA GOVERNANCE OVERSIGHT BOARD

The data governance oversight board (DGOB) guides and oversees data governance activities. The DGOB is composed of representatives chosen from across the community. The main responsibilities of the DGOB are listed in the sidebar.

4.16 DATA COORDINATION COUNCIL

The actual governance activities are directed and managed by the data coordination council, which operates under the direction of the data governance oversight board. The data coordination council is a group composed of interested individual stakeholders from across the enterprise. It is responsible for adjusting the processes of the enterprise as appropriate to ensure that the data quality and governance expectations are continually met. As part of this responsibility, the data coordination council recommends the names for and appoints representatives to committees and advisory groups.

The data coordination council is responsible for overseeing the work of data stewards. The coordination council also does the following:

- Provides direction and guidance to all committees tasked with developing data governance practices
- Oversees the tasks of the committees and advisory groups related to data governance
- Recommends that the data governance oversight board endorse the output of the various governance activities for publication and distribution
- Recommends data governance processes to the data governance oversight board for final endorsement

- Nominates stewards and oversees the practices managed by the data stewards for data certification and managing audit information
- Advocates for enterprise data governance by leading, promoting, and facilitating the governance practices and processes developed
- Attends periodic meetings to provide progress reports, review statuses, and discuss and review the general direction of the enterprise data governance program

4.17 DATA STEWARDSHIP

The data steward's role essentially is to support the user community. This individual is responsible for collecting, collating, and evaluating issues and problems with data. Typically, data stewards are assigned either based on subject areas or within line-of-business responsibilities. However, in the case of MDM, because the use of key data entities may span multiple lines of business, the stewardship roles are more likely to be aligned along KDE boundaries. Prioritized issues must be communicated to the individuals who may be impacted. The steward must also communicate issues and other relevant information (e.g., root causes) to staff members who are in a position to influence remediation.

As the person accountable for the quality of the data, the data steward must also manage standard business definitions and metadata for critical data elements associated with each KDE. This person also oversees the enterprise data quality standards, including the data rules associated with the data sets. This may require using technology to assess and maintain a high level of conformance to defined information policies within each line of business, especially its accuracy, completeness, and consistency. Essentially, the data steward is the conduit for communicating issues associated with the data life cycle—the creation, modification, sharing, reuse, retention, and backup of data. If any issues emerge regarding the conformance of data to the defined policies over the lifetime of the data, it is the steward's responsibility to resolve them.

Data stewardship is not necessarily an information technology function, nor should it necessarily be considered to be a full-time position, although its proper execution deserves an appropriate reward. Data stewardship is a role that has a set of responsibilities along with accountability to the line-of-business management. In other words, even though the data steward's activities are overseen within the scope of the MDM program, the steward is accountable to his or her own line management to ensure that the quality of the data meets the needs of both the line of business and of the organization as a whole.

4.18 **SUMMARY**

For companies undertaking MDM, a hallmark of successful implementations will be the reliance and integration of data governance throughout the initiative. The three important aspects of data governance for MDM are managing key data entities and critical data elements, ensuring the observance of information policies and documenting and ensuring accountability for maintaining high-quality master data.

Keeping these ideas in mind during the development of the MDM program will ensure that the master data management program does not become relegated to the scrap heap of misfired enterprise information management initiatives. Rather, developing a strong enterprise data governance program will benefit the MDM program as well as strengthen the ability to manage all enterprise information activities.

Chapter 5

Data Quality and MDM

5.1 INTRODUCTION

One of the motivating factors for instituting an MDM program is the desire for consistency and accuracy of enterprise data. In fact, many MDM activities have evolved out of data cleansing processes needed for data warehousing or data migrations. The ability to use data parsing, standardization, and matching enabled the development of an "entity index" for people or products, which then was used for ongoing identity resolution and the elimination of duplicate entries. The realization that the entity index itself represented a valuable information resource was a precursor to the development of the master data environment altogether and the corresponding services supporting that master data environment.

When evaluating both the primary business objectives and the operational requirements for evolving toward an environment that relies on master data, there is going to be an underlying expectation that the instantiation of an MDM program necessarily implies improved data quality across the board. The reality is not so straightforward. By necessity, there will be some fundamental questions about the following:

- The definition of data quality
- The specification of the business data quality expectations
- Ways of monitoring those expectations to ensure that they are met in an acceptable manner

At a conceptual layer, these questions center on the trustworthiness of the data as it is extracted from the numerous sources and consolidated into the master repository. However, at the operational level, these questions begin to delve much deeper into the core definitions, perceptions, formats, and representations of the data elements that comprise the model for each master data object. The challenges of monitoring and ensuring data quality within the MDM environment become associated with identifying critical data elements, determining

87

which data elements constitute master data, locating and isolating master data objects that exist within the enterprise, and reviewing and resolving the variances between the different representations in order to consolidate instances into a single view. Even after the initial integration of data into a master data environment, there will still be a need to instantiate data inspection, monitoring, and controls to identify any potential data quality issues and prevent any material business impacts from occurring.

Data assessment, parsing, standardization, identity resolution, enterprise integration—all of these aspects of consolidation rely on data quality tools and techniques successfully employed over time for both operational and analytical (read: data warehousing) purposes. In this chapter, we will look at how the distribution of information leads to inconsistency, and then we explore the data quality techniques needed for MDM and how data quality tools meet those needs.

5.2 DISTRIBUTION, DIFFUSION, AND METADATA

Because of the ways that diffused application architectures have evolved across different project teams and lines of business, it is likely that although only a relatively small number of core master *objects* (or more likely, object types) are used, there are going to be many different ways that these objects are named, modeled, represented, and stored. For example, any application that must manage contact information for individual customers will rely on a data model that maintains the customer's name, but one application may maintain the individual's full name, whereas others might break up the name into its first, middle, and last parts. Conceptually, these persistent models are storing the same *content*, but the slightest variance in representation prevents most computer systems from recognizing the similarity between record instances.

Even when different models are generally similar in structure, there might still be naming differences that would confuse most applications. For example, the unique identifier assigned to a customer is defined as a 10-character numeric string, padded with zeros out to the left, and that format is used consistently across different applications. Yet even when the format and rules are identical, different names, such as CUST_NUM versus CUSTOMER_NUMBER versus CUST_ID, may still confuse the ability to use the identifier as a foreign key among the different data sets. Alternatively, the same data element concept may be represented with slight variations, manifested in data types and lengths. What may be represented as a numeric field in one table may be alphanumeric in another, or similarly named attributes may be of slightly different lengths.

Ultimately, to consolidate data with a high degree of confidence in its quality, the processes must have an aligned view of what data objects are to be consolidated and what those objects look like in their individual instantiations. Therefore, an important process supporting the data quality objectives of an MDM program involves collecting the information to populate a metadata inventory. Not only is this metadata inventory a resource to be used for identification of key data entities and critical data elements, it also is used to standardize the definitions of data elements and connect those definitions to authoritative sources, harmonizing the variances between data element representations as well as identifying master data objects and sources. Collecting and managing the various kinds of master metadata is discussed in Chapter 6.

5.3 DIMENSIONS OF DATA QUALITY

We must have some yardstick for measuring the quality of master data. Similar to the way that data quality expectations for operational or analytical data silos are specified, master data quality expectations are organized within defined data quality dimensions to simplify their specification and measurement/validation. This provides an underlying structure to support the expression of data quality expectations that can be reflected as rules employed within a system for validation and monitoring. By using data quality tools, data stewards can define minimum thresholds for meeting business expectations and use those thresholds to monitor data validity with respect to those expectations, which then feeds into the analysis and ultimate elimination of root causes of data issues whenever feasible.

Data quality dimensions are aligned with the business processes to be measured, such as measuring the quality of data associated with data element values or presentation of master data objects. The dimensions associated with data values and data presentation lend themselves well to system automation, making them suitable for employing data rules within the data quality tools used for data validation. These dimensions include (but are not limited to) the following:

- Uniqueness
- Accuracy
- Consistency
- Completeness
- Timeliness
- Currency

5.3.1 **Uniqueness**

Uniqueness refers to requirements that entities modeled within the master environment are captured, represented, and referenced uniquely within the relevant application architectures. Asserting uniqueness of the entities within a data set implies that no entity logically exists more than once within the MDM environment and that there is a key that can be used to uniquely access each entity (and only that specific entity) within the data set. For example, in a master product table, each product must appear once and be assigned a unique identifier that represents that product across the client applications.

The dimension of uniqueness is characterized by stating that no entity exists more than once within the data set. When there is an expectation of uniqueness, data instances should not be created if there is an existing record for that entity. This dimension can be monitored two ways. As a static assessment, it implies applying duplicate analysis to the data set to determine if duplicate records exist, and as an ongoing monitoring process, it implies providing an identity matching and resolution service inlined within the component services supporting record creation to locate exact or potential matching records.

5.3.2 **Accuracy**

Data accuracy refers to the degree with which data correctly represent the "real-life" objects they are intended to model. In many cases, accuracy is measured by how the values agree with an identified source of correct information (such as reference data). There are different sources of correct information: a database of record, a similar corroborative set of data values from another table, dynamically computed values, or perhaps the result of a manual process. Accuracy is actually quite challenging to monitor, not just because one requires a secondary source for corroboration, but because real-world information may change over time. If corroborative data are available as a reference data set, an automated process can be put in place to verify the accuracy, but if not, a manual process may be instituted to contact existing sources of truth to verify value accuracy. The amount of effort expended on manual verification is dependent on the degree of accuracy necessary to meet business expectations.

5.3.3 **Consistency**

Consistency refers to data values in one data set being consistent with values in another data set. A strict definition of consistency specifies that two data values drawn from separate data sets must not conflict with each other. Note that *consistency* does not necessarily imply *correctness*.

The notion of consistency with a set of predefined constraints can be even more complicated. More formal consistency constraints can be encapsulated as a set of rules that specify consistency relationships between values of attributes, either across a record or message, or along all values of a single attribute. However, there are many ways that process errors may be replicated across different platforms, sometimes leading to data values that may be consistent even though they may not be correct.

An example of a consistency rule verifies that, within a corporate hierarchy structure, the sum of the number of customers assigned to each customer representative should not exceed the number of customers for the entire corporation.

CONSISTENCY CONTEXTS

- Between one set of attribute values and another attribute set within the same record (record-level consistency)
- Between one set of attribute values and another attribute set in different records (cross-record consistency)
- Between one set of attribute values and the same attribute set within the same record at different points in time (temporal consistency)
- Across data values or data elements used in different lines of business or in different applications
- Consistency may also take into account the concept of "reasonableness," in which some range of acceptability is imposed on the values of a set of attributes.

5.3.4 **Completeness**

The concept of completeness implies the existence of non-null values assigned to specific data elements. Completeness can be characterized in one of three ways. The first is asserting mandatory value assignment—the data element must have a value. The second expresses value optionality, essentially only forcing the data element to have (or not have) a value under specific conditions. The third is in terms of data element values that are inapplicable, such as providing a "waist size" for a hat.

5.3.5 **Timeliness**

Timeliness refers to the time expectation for accessibility and availability of information. Timeliness can be measured as the time between when information is expected and when it is readily available for use. In the MDM environment, this concept is of particular interest, because synchronization of data updates to application data with the centralized resource supports the concept of the common, shared, unique representation. The success of business applications relying on master data depends on consistent and timely information. Therefore, service levels specifying how quickly the data must be propagated through the centralized repository should be defined so that compliance with those timeliness constraints can be measured.

5.3.6 **Currency**

Currency refers to the degree to which information is up to date with the world that it models and whether it is correct despite possible time-related changes. Currency may be measured as a function of the expected frequency rate at which the master data elements are expected to be updated, as well as verifying that the data are up to date, which potentially requires both automated and manual processes. Currency rules may be defined to assert the "lifetime" of a data value before it needs to be checked and possibly refreshed. For example, one might assert that the telephone number for each vendor must be current, indicating a requirement to maintain the most recent values associated with the individual's contact data. An investment may be made in manual verification of currency, as with validating accuracy. However, a more reasonable approach might be to adjust business processes to verify the information at transactions with counterparties in which the current values of data may be established.

5.3.7 **Format Compliance**

Every modeled object has a set of rules bounding its representation, and conformance refers to whether data element values are stored, exchanged, and presented in a format that is consistent with the object's value domain, as well as consistent with similar attribute values. Each column has metadata associated with it: its data type, precision, format patterns, use of a predefined enumeration of values, domain ranges, underlying storage formats, and so on. Parsing and standardization tools can be used to validate data values against defined formats and patterns to monitor adherence to format specifications.

5.3.8 **Referential Integrity**

Assigning unique identifiers to those data entities that ultimately are managed as master data objects (such as customers or products, etc.) within the master environment simplifies the data's management. However, the need to index every item using a unique identifier introduces new expectations any time that identifier is used as a foreign key across different data applications. There is a need to verify that every assigned identifier is actually assigned to an entity existing within the environment. Conversely, for any "localized" data entity that is assigned a master identifier, there must be an assurance that the master entity matches that identifier. More formally, this is referred to as referential integrity. Rules associated with referential integrity often are manifested as constraints against duplication (to ensure that each entity is represented once, and only once) and reference integrity rules, which assert that all values used for all keys actually refer back to an existing master record.

5.4 **EMPLOYING DATA QUALITY AND DATA INTEGRATION TOOLS**

Data quality and data integration tools have evolved from simple standardization and pattern matching into suites of tools for complex automation of data analysis, standardization, matching, and aggregation. For example, data profiling has matured from a simplistic distribution analysis into a suite of complex automated analysis techniques that can be used to identify, isolate, monitor, audit, and help address anomalies that degrade the value of an enterprise information asset. Early uses of data profiling for anomaly analysis have been superseded by more complex uses that are integrated into proactive information quality processes. When coupled with other data quality technologies, these processes provide a wide range of functional capabilities. In fact, there is a growing trend to employ data profiling for identification of master data objects in their various instantiations across the enterprise.

A core expectation of the MDM program is the ability to consolidate multiple data sets representing a master data object (such as "customer") and to resolve variant representations into a conceptual "best representation" whose presentation is promoted as representing a master version for all participating applications. This capability relies on consulting metadata and data standards that have been discovered through the data profiling and discovery process to parse, standardize, match, and resolve the surviving data values from identified replicated records. More relevant is that the tools and techniques used to identify duplicate data and to *identify* data anomalies are exactly the same ones used to facilitate an effective strategy for *resolving* those anomalies within an MDM framework. The fact that these capabilities are available from traditional data cleansing vendors is indicated by the numerous consolidations, acquisitions, and partnerships between data integration vendors and data quality tools vendors, but this underscores the conventional wisdom that data quality tools are required for a successful MDM implementation.

Most important is the ability to transparently aggregate data in preparation for presenting a uniquely identifiable representation via a central authority and to provide access for applications to interact with the central authority. In the absence of a standardized integration strategy (and its accompanying tools), the attempt to transition to an MDM environment would be stymied by the need to modernize all existing production applications. Data integration products have evolved to the point where they can adapt to practically any data representation framework and can provide the means for transforming existing data into a form that can be materialized, presented, and manipulated via a master data system.

5.5 ASSESSMENT: DATA PROFILING

Data profiling originated as a set of algorithms for statistical analysis and assessment of the quality of data values within a data set, as well as for exploring relationships that exist between value collections within and across data sets. For each column in a table, a data profiling tool provides a frequency distribution of the different values, offering insight into the type and use of each column. Cross-column analysis can expose embedded value dependencies, whereas intertable analysis explores overlapping value sets that may represent foreign key relationships between entities. It is in this way that profiling can be used for anomaly analysis and assessment. However, the challenges of master data integration have presented new possibilities for the use of data profiling, not just for analyzing the quality of source data but especially with respect to the discovery, assessment, and registration of enterprise metadata as a prelude to determining the best sources for master objects, as well as managing the transition to MDM and its necessary data migration.

5.5.1 Profiling for Metadata Resolution

If the objective of an MDM program is to consolidate and manage a uniquely referenceable centralized master resource, then before we can materialize a single master record for any entity, we must be able to do the following:

1. Discover which enterprise data resources may contain entity information
2. Understand which attributes carry identifying information
3. Extract identifying information from the data resource
4. Transform the identifying information into a standardized or canonical form
5. Establish similarity to other standardized records

This entails cataloging the data sets, their attributes, formats, data domains, definitions, contexts, and semantics, not just as an operational resource but rather in a way that can be used to automate master data consolidation and govern the ongoing application interactions with the master repository. In other words, to be able to manage the master data, one must first be able to manage the master metadata.

Addressing these aspects suggests the need to collect and analyze master metadata in order to assess, resolve, and unify similarity in both structure and semantics. Although many enterprise data sets may have documented metadata (e.g., RDBMS models, COBOL copybooks) that reveal structure, some of the data—such as fixed-format or character-separated files—may have little or no documented metadata at all. The MDM team must be able to resolve master metadata in terms of formats at the element level and structure at the instance level. Among a number of surveyed case studies, this requirement is best addressed by creatively applying data profiling techniques. To best collect comprehensive and consistent metadata from all enterprise sources, the natural technique is to employ both the statistical and analytical algorithms provided by data profiling tools to drive the empirical assessment of structure and format metadata while simultaneously exposing embedded data models and dependencies.

Profiling is used to capture the relevant characteristics of each data set in a standard way, including names and source data type (e.g., RDBMS table, VSAM file, CSV file), as well as the characteristics of each of its columns/attributes (e.g., length, data type, format pattern, among others). Creating a comprehensive inventory of data elements enables the review of meta-model characteristics such as frequently used names, field sizes, and data types. Managing this knowledge in a metadata repository allows again for using the statistical assessment capabilities of data profiling techniques to look for common attribute names (e.g., "CUSTOMER") and their assigned data types (e.g., VARCHAR(20)) to identify (and potentially standardize against) commonly used types, sizes, and formats. This secondary assessment highlights differences in the forms and structures used to represent similar concepts.

Commonalities among data tables may expose the existence of a master data object. For example, different structures will contain names, addresses, and telephone numbers. Iterative assessment using data profiling techniques will suggest to the analyst that these data elements are common characteristics of what ultimately resolves into a "party" or "customer" type. Approaches to these processes for metadata discovery are covered in greater detail in Chapter 7.

5.5.2 Profiling for Data Quality Assessment

The next use of data profiling as part of an MDM program is to assess the quality of the source data sets that will feed the master repository. The result of the initial assessment phase will be a selection of candidate data sources to feed the master repository, but it will be necessary to evaluate the quality of each data source to determine the degree to which that source conforms to the business expectations. This is where data profiling again comes into play. Column profiling provides statistical information regarding the distribution of data values and associated patterns that are assigned to each data attribute, including range analysis, sparseness, format and pattern evaluation, cardinality and uniqueness analysis, value absence, abstract type recognition, and attribute overloading analysis.

These techniques are used to assert data attribute value conformance to the quality expectations for the consolidated repository. Profiling also involves analyzing dependencies across columns (looking for candidate keys, looking for embedded table structures, discovering business rules, or looking for duplication of data across multiple rows). When applied across tables, profiling evaluates the consistency of relational structure, analyzing foreign keys and ensuring that implied referential integrity constraints actually hold. Data rules can be defined that reflect the expression of data quality expectations, and the data profiler can be used to validate data sets against those rules. Characterizing data quality levels based on data rule conformance provides an objective measure of data quality that can be used to score candidates for suitability for inclusion in the master repository.

5.5.3 Profiling as Part of Migration

The same rules that are discovered or defined during the data quality assessment phase can be used for ongoing conformance as part of the operational processes for streaming data from source data systems into the master repository. By using defined data rules to proactively validate data, an organization can distinguish those records that conform to defined data quality expectations and those that do not. In turn, these defined data rules can contribute to baseline measurements and ongoing auditing for data stewardship and governance. In fact, embedding data profiling rules within the data integration framework makes the validation process for MDM relatively transparent.

5.6 **DATA CLEANSING**

The original driver for data quality tools was correcting what was perceived to be "bad" data associated with database marketing, and so the early data quality tools focused on customer name and address cleansing. This typically consists of the following:

- Customer record parsing, which will take semistructured customer/entity data and break it up into component pieces such as title, first name, last name, and suffix. This also looks for connectives (DBA, AKA, &, "IN TRUST FOR") that indicate multiple parties in the data field.
- Address parsing, which is a similar activity for addresses.
- Address standardization, which makes sure that addresses conform to a published postal standard, such as the postal standard of the U.S. Postal Service. This includes changing street designations to the standard form (e.g., ST for Street, AVE for Avenue, W for West).
- Address cleansing, which fills in missing fields in addresses (such as ZIP codes, ZIP+4, or area codes) and corrects mistakes in addresses, such as fixing street names, or reassigning post office locality data or changing the City field in an address from a vanity address ("ROLLING HILLS HEIGHTS" to "SMALL VALLEY").

The cleansing process for a data value (usually a character string) typically follows this sequence:

- Subject the candidate string to parsing to identify key components, called "tokens," within the string.
- Determine whether the components reflect a recognized pattern (such as "First Name, Middle Initial, Last Name" for customer names).
- If so, map the recognized tokens to the corresponding components of the pattern.

- Apply any rules for standardizing the tokens (such as changing "Mike" to "Michael").

- Apply any rules for standardizing the collection of tokens together (such as mapping tokens extracted from a NAME data element into a FIRST_NAME, MIDDLE_NAME, LAST_NAME).

- If the components do not map to a recognized pattern, attempt to determine whether there are similarities to known patterns. This will help in figuring out whether there are specific errors in the data value that can be reviewed by one of the data stewards responsible for overseeing the quality of that specific master data object type.

Once a value has been transformed into a standard representation, existing master reference lists can be searched for the standardized entity name. If a match is found, the candidate record is compared with the existing master entry. Any discrepancies can also be called out into the stewardship process for resolution, with resulting updates communicated into either the master index or the record being evaluated.

Over time, cleansing has become more sophisticated; now we rely on the master repository for cleanliness, but the methods necessary to integrate stewardship roles in making corrections as well as learning from made decisions need to be introduced into the automation processes. For example, early cleansing processes were performed in batch, with out files provided to analysts for "postmortem" review and decision making. Modifications to actual records were performed manually, with all the associated challenges of synchronization and propagation of changes to dependent data sets downstream.

The automation process for MDM at the service layer must now be able to embed the functionality supporting the data stewardship part of the business process. Instead of batch processing for cleansing, services can now inline the identity resolution as part of data acquisition. If the identity can be resolved directly, no interaction with the business client is needed. However, if there are potential match discrepancies, or if no exact matches are found, the application itself can employ the underlying MDM service to prompt the business user for more information to help in the resolution process.

Enabling real-time decisions to be made helps in eliminating the introduction of duplicate or erroneous data at the earliest point of the work stream. At an even higher level of sophistication, there are techniques for learning from the decisions made by users to augment the rule sets for matching, thereby improving the precision of future matching and resolution. The use of parsing, standardization, and matching for master data consolidation is discussed in greater detail in Chapter 10.

5.7 **DATA CONTROLS**

Business processes are implemented within application services and components, which in turn are broken down into individual processing stages, with communication performed via data exchanges. Within the MDM environment, the business processing stages expect that the data being exchanged are of high quality, and the assumption of data appropriateness is carried over to application development as well.

However, no system is immune to the potential for introduction of flawed data into the system, especially when the acquired data are being repurposed across the enterprise. Errors characterized as violations of expectations for completeness, accuracy, timeliness, consistency, and other dimensions of data quality often impede the ability of an automated task to effectively complete its specific role in the business process. Data quality control initiatives are intended to assess the potential for the introduction of data flaws, determine the root causes, and eliminate the source of the introduction of flawed data if possible.

If it is not possible to eliminate the root cause, it may be necessary to use a data source that is known to have flaws. However, being aware of this possibility, notifying the downstream clients, and enabling the staff to mitigate any impacts associated with known flawed data helps to control any potential damage if that is the only source available for the needed data

But the reality is that even the most sophisticated data quality management activities do not prevent all data flaws. Consider the concept of data accuracy. Although we can implement automated processes for validating that values conform to format specifications, belong to defined data domains, or are consistent across columns within a single record, there is no way to automatically determine if a value is *accurate*. For example, salespeople are required to report their daily sales totals to the sales system, but if one salesperson inadvertently transposed two digits on one of the sales transaction amounts, the sales supervisor would not be able to determine the discrepancy without calling the sales team to verify their numbers (and even *they* might not remember the right numbers!).

The upshot is that despite your efforts to ensure quality of data, there are always going to be data issues that require attention and remediation. The goal is to determine the protocols that need to be in place to determine data errors as early as possible in the processing stream(s), whom to notify to address the issue, and whether the issue can be resolved appropriately within a "reasonable" amount of time. These protocols are composed of two aspects: controls, which are used to determine the issue, and service level agreements, which specify the reasonable expectations for response and remediation.

5.7.1 **Data and Process Controls**

In practice, every processing stage has embedded controls, either of the "data control" or "process control" variety. The objective of the control process is to ensure that any issue that might incur a significant business impact late in the processing stream is identified early in the processing stream. The effectiveness of a control process is demonstrated when the following occurs:

- Control events occur when data failure events take place.
- The proper mitigation or remediation actions are performed.
- The corrective actions to correct the problem and eliminate its root cause are performed within a reasonable time frame.
- A control event for the same issue is never triggered further downstream.

Contrary to the intuitive data quality ideas around defect prevention, the desire is that the control process discovers many issues, because the goal is assurance that if there are any issues that would cause problems downstream, they can be captured very early upstream.

5.7.2 **Data Quality Control versus Data Validation**

Data quality control differs from data validation in that validation is a process to review and measure conformance of data with a set of defined business rules, but control is an ongoing process to reduce the number of errors to a reasonable and manageable level and to institute a mitigation or remediation of the root cause within an agreed-to time frame. A data quality control mechanism is valuable for communicating data trustworthiness to enterprise stakeholders by demonstrating that any issue with a potential impact would have been caught early enough to have been addressed and corrected, thereby preventing the impact from occurring altogether.

5.8 MDM AND DATA QUALITY SERVICE LEVEL AGREEMENTS

A data quality control framework bolsters the ability to establish data quality service level agreements by identifying the issues and initiating processes to evaluate and remediate them. Pushing the controls as far back as possible in each process stream increases trust, especially when the control is instantiated at the point of data acquisition or creation. In retrospect, the master data repository can be used to validate data quality, and, as we will explore in Chapter 12, the component service layer will embed the validation and control across the data life cycle.

A key component of establishing the control framework is a data quality service level agreement (SLA); the sidebar lists what should be in a data quality SLA.

A DATA QUALITY SLA DESCRIBES

- Which data assets are covered by the SLA
- The business impacts associated with data flaws
- The data quality dimensions associated with each data element
- Characterizations of the data quality expectations for each data element for each identified dimension
- How conformance to data quality expectations is measured along with the acceptability threshold for each measurement
- The individual to be notified in case the acceptability threshold is not met
- The times for expected resolution or remediation of discovered issues and an escalation strategy when the resolution times are not met
- A process for logging issues, tracking progress in resolution, and measuring performance in meeting the SLA

5.8.1 Data Controls, Downstream Trust, and the Control Framework

Data controls evaluate the data being propagated from business customer-facing applications to the master data environment and ensure that the data sets conform to quality expectations defined by the business users. Data controls can be expressed at different levels of granularity. At the most granular level, data element level controls review the quality of the value in the context of its assignment to the element. The next level of granularity includes data record level controls, which examine the quality of the set of (element, value) pairs within the context of the record. An even higher level incorporates data set and data collection level controls, which focus on completeness of the data set, availability of data, and timeliness in its delivery.

In essence data quality management for MDM must provide a means for both error prevention and error detection and remediation. Continued monitoring of conformance to data expectations only provides some support to the ability to keep the data aspect of business processes under control. The introduction of a service level agreement, and certifying that the SLAs are being observed, provides a higher level of trust at the end of the business process that any issues with the potential for significant business impact that *might* have appeared will have been caught and addressed early in the process.

5.9 **INFLUENCE OF DATA PROFILING AND QUALITY ON MDM (AND VICE VERSA)**

In many master data management implementations, MDM team members and their internal customers have indicated that data quality improvement is both a driver and a by-product of their MDM or Customer Data Integration (CDI) initiatives, often citing data quality improvement as the program's major driver. Consider these examples:

- A large software firm's customer data integration program was driven by the need to improve customer data integrated from legacy systems or migrated from acquired company systems. As customer data instances were brought into the firm's Customer Relationship Management (CRM) system, the MDM team used data profiling and data quality tools to understand what data were available, to evaluate whether the data met business requirements, and to resolve duplicate identities. In turn, the master customer system was adopted as the baseline for matching newly created customer records to determine potential duplication as part of a quality identity management framework.

- An industry information product compiler discussed its need to rapidly and effectively deploy the quality integration of new data sources into its master repository because deploying a new data source could take weeks, if not months. By using data profiling tools, the customer could increase the speed of deploying a new data source. As a by-product, the customer stated that one of the ways it could add value to the data was by improving the quality of the source data. This improvement was facilitated when this company worked with its clients to point out source data inconsistencies and anomalies, and then provided services to assist in root-cause analysis and elimination.

5.10 **SUMMARY**

Because the MDM program is intended to create a synchronized, consistent repository of quality master information, data quality integration incorporates data profiling, parsing, standardization, and resolution aspects to both inventory and identify candidate master object sets as well as to assess that data's quality. However, this must be done in a way that establishes resolution and the management of the semantics, hierarchies, taxonomies, and relationships of those master objects, and this process will be explored in Chapters 6 and 10. On the other hand, we have seen (in Chapter 4) that the benefits of imposing an enterprise data governance framework include the oversight of critical data elements, clear unambiguous definitions, and collaboration among multiple organizational divisions.

For MDM, these two ideas converge in the use of data profiling and data quality tools for assessment, semantic analysis, integration, data inspection and control, and monitoring—essentially across the board. Using profiling to assess and inventory enterprise metadata provides an automated approach to the fundamental aspects of building the master data model. Data profiling and data quality together are used to parse and monitor content within each data instance. This means that their use is not just a function of matching names, addresses, or products, but rather automating the conceptual understanding of the information embedded within the representative record. This knowledge is abstracted as part of a "metadata control" approach, with a metadata registry serving as the focus of meaning for shared information. Fully integrating data quality control and management into the organization is one of the single most important success factors for MDM.

6

Metadata Management
for MDM

6.1 **INTRODUCTION**

At a purely technical level, there is a significant need for coordination to oversee and guide the information management aspects of an enterprise initiative such as MDM. The political and organizational aspects of this coordination are addressed as part of the governance program that must accompany an MDM program. However, all aspects of determining need, planning, migration strategy, and future state require a clarified view of the information about the data that is used within the organization—its metadata.

It is easy for us to fall into the trap of referring to metadata by its industry-accepted definition: data about the data. This relatively benign description does not provide the depth of understanding that adds value to the MDM deployment. Instead, the metadata associated with an enterprise master data set does more than just describe the size and types of each data element. It is the historically distributed application and data silos that are impacted by the variance in meaning and structure that necessitated MDM in the first place. Therefore, to develop a model, framework, and architecture that provide a unified view across these applications, there must be a control mechanism, or perhaps even a "clearing house," for unifying the view when possible and for determining when that unification is not possible.

In fact, the scale of metadata management needed for transitioning enterprise data sets into a master data environment differs from the relatively simple data dictionary-style repositories that support individual applications. Sizes and types are just the tip of the iceberg. Integration of records from different data sets can only be done when it is clear that data elements have the same meaning, that their valid data domains are consistent, that the records represent similar or the same real-world entities. Not only that, but there are more complex dependencies as

105

well: Do client applications use the same entity types? Do different applications use different logical names for similar objects? How is access for reading and writing data objects controlled? These and many other important variable aspects must be addressed.

There is value in looking at a conceptual view of master metadata that starts with basic building blocks and grows to maintain comprehensive views of the information that is used to help an organization achieve its business objectives. The metadata stack described in this chapter is driven by business objectives from the top down and from the bottom up, and it is intended to capture as much information as necessary to drive the following elements:

- The analysis of enterprise data for the purpose of structural and semantic discovery
- The correspondence of meanings to data element types
- The determination of master data element types
- The models for master data object types
- The interaction models for applications touching master data
- The information usage scenarios for master data
- The data quality directives
- Access control and management
- The determination of core master services
- The determination of application-level master services
- Business policy capture and correspondence to information policies

We can look at seven levels of metadata that are critical to master data management, starting from the bottom up:

Business definitions. Look at the business terms used across the organizations and the associated meanings

Reference metadata. Detail data domains (both conceptual domains and corresponding value domains) as well as reference data and mappings between codes and values

Data element metadata. Focus on data element definitions, structures, nomenclature, and determination of existence along a critical path of a processing stream

Information architecture. Coagulates the representations of data elements into cohesive entity structures, shows how those structures reflect real-world objects, and explores how those objects interact within business processes

Data governance management. Concentrates on the data rules governing data quality, data use, access control, and the protocols for rule observance (and processes for remediation of rule violations)

Service metadata. Look at the abstract functionality embedded and used by the applications and the degree to which those functions can be described as stand-alone services, along with the mapping from service to client applications and at the top of the stack

Business metadata. Capture the business policies that drive application design and implementation, the corresponding information policies that drive the implementation decisions inherent in the lower levels of the stack, and the management and execution schemes for the business rules that embody both business and information policies

Given this high-level description of a metadata stack, the challenge is to look at how these levels interact as part of an overall metadata management strategy. This view, shown as a whole in Figure 6.1, enables us to consider metadata as a "control panel," because the cumulative knowledge embedded within the metadata management framework will ultimately help to determine of the most appropriate methods for delivering a master data asset that is optimally suited to the organization. In this chapter, we will look at each layer of metadata from the bottom up and review its relevance to the master data management framework.

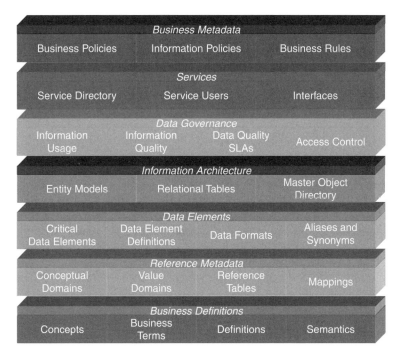

■ **FIGURE 6.1** The MDM metadata stack.

Valuable work has been invested in developing standards for managing metadata repositories and registries as part of an International Standards Organization activity. The resulting standard for Metadata Registries, ISO/IEC 11179 (see *www.metadata-stds.org*), is an excellent resource for learning more about metadata management, and some of the material in this chapter refers to the 11179 standard.

One word of caution, though: the rampant interconnectedness of the information that is to be captured within the metadata model implies that analysts must take an iterative approach to collecting the enterprise knowledge. Business process models will reveal new conceptual data elements; relationships between master data object types may not be completely aligned until business process flows are documented. The effective use of metadata relies on its existence as a living artifact, not just a repository for documentation.

Within this stack, there are many components that require management. Although numerous metadata tools may supplement the collection of a number of these components, the thing to keep in mind is not the underlying tool but the relevance of each component with respect to MDM, and the processes associated with the collection and use of master metadata. Standard desktop tools can be used as an initial pass for capturing master metadata. Once processes are in place for reaching consensus across the stakeholder community as to what will ultimately constitute the metadata asset, requirements can be identified for acquiring a metadata management tool.

6.2 BUSINESS DEFINITIONS

One of the key technical drivers for MDM is the reconciliation of meanings that have diverged in accordance with distributed application development. Therefore, it should come as no surprise that the foundation of master metadata is based on collecting (and, one hopes, standardizing) the definitions for the business terms commonly used across the organization. This layer initiates the high-level notions that are associated with business activities, and the process of collecting the information allows an open environment for listing the business concepts and terms that are commonly used. Then, as concepts are identified, there is an opportunity for the stakeholders to explore the differences and commonalities between the concepts, standardize definitions when possible, and distinguish between concepts when it is not possible to standardize their meanings.

6.2.1 **Concepts**

A concept represents a core unit of thought, such as a "person," "product," or "supplier." A concept is associated with core characteristics. For example, a "residential property" is associated with a geographic region, a mailing address, an owner, an appraised value, possibly a mortgage, and a real estate tax assessment, among others. In turn, the characteristics may themselves be concepts as well.

Each environment may have a specific set of concepts that are relevant to the business processes, and some concepts transcend specific divisions, organizations, or even industries. Within the organization, a good place to seek out concepts is with the business process model, as was described in Chapter 2. At the macro level, standards for information exchange among participants within the same industry provide an ample resource from which concepts can be identified as well.

As part of the process of enumerating business concepts, participants may find that some concepts are referred to with a variety of words or phrases. At the same time, one may discover that certain words are overloaded and refer to more than a single concept. Collecting the concepts and their names leads to the next component of the business definitions layer: business terms.

6.2.2 **Business Terms**

How is the term "customer" used? Many words and terms are used so frequently within a business environment that they eventually lose their precise meaning in deference to a fuzzy understanding of the core concept. Alternatively, many organizations have a regimented lingo that confuses almost everyone except for the hardcore organizational veterans. Both ends of this spectrum reflect different aspects of the same problem: organizational knowledge locked inside individual's minds, with no framework for extracting that knowledge and clarifying it in a way that can be transferred to others within the organization. It is this gap that the business terms component is intended to alleviate, which naturally follows from the identification of the business concepts described in Section 6.2.1.

Given a list of business concepts, the next step is to identify the different terms used in reference to each concept and create a mapping through which the subject matter experts can browse. The simplest approach is to develop a direct mapping between the concept and its various aliases. For example, for the concept of "customer," the terms "customer" and "account" may have the same intention. However, this process should not be limited to developing a direct mapping between terms and concepts, but it should also include any business terms used in any type of reference. This will include the different terms used for the concept "customer" as well as the terms used for the characteristics of a customer ("customer type," "relationship start date," "contact mechanism," etc.).

6.2.3 **Definitions**

The metadata asset also supports a process for determining what each business term means in each of its contexts. Again, referring back to the business processes, evaluate the use of the business term, connect it to a business concept, and seek a clear definition for each business term in relation to a business concept drawn from an authoritative source. The range of authoritative sources includes internal documentation and external directives. For example, the concept of a "customer" may exist in one form in relation to the sales staff based on internal memos and corporate dictates. However, when reporting the count of customers in regulatory reports to government bodies, the definition of the "customer" concept may be taken from the regulatory guidelines. Both are valid uses of a concept, but it may turn out that ultimately, based on the different definitions, the business term "customer" actually is defined in two *different* ways, meaning that the term is used in reference to two different concepts! This dichotomy must be documented, and the semantics component (see Section 6.2.4) is the best place to capture that.

The definitions component harmonizes term usage and enables users to distinguish concepts based on classification by authoritative source. This includes the listing of authoritative sources and prioritization key for those sources so that if there is a conflict between two definitions, one can use the prioritization key to break the tie. Recognize though, that if one were to assess the different uses of the same business terms and find multiple definitions, it may turn out that despite the use of the same term, we really have multiple concepts that must be distinguished through some type of qualification. This is also documented as part of the semantics component.

6.2.4 **Semantics**

The semantics components is intended to capture information about how business terms are mapped to concepts, whether business terms are mapped to multiple concepts, and whether concepts are mapped to multiple business terms, as well as to describe how the business concepts are related within the organization. To some extent, the semantics component captures the interconnectedness of the business concepts, business terms, and the definitions. Documenting business definitions using prioritized authoritative sources is a relatively formal practice that some people may find constraining, especially when attempting to shoehorn multiple concepts into one specific definition. The semantic component enables a more fluid practice, allowing the coexistence of concepts that are similarly named as long as their meanings are qualified.

This is the component in which practitioners collect similar concepts and terms together, qualify their meanings, and determine if there is any overlap among or between them. If there is, then the relationship is documented; if not, then the specific differences must be clearly specified and a means for distinguishing the meanings in application contexts determined.

6.3 **REFERENCE METADATA**

One might question the difference between "master data" and "reference data," as in some cases both appear to be the same thing. For our purposes, "reference data" refers to the collections of values that are used to populate the existing application data stores as well as the master data model. This section looks at two core constructs: data domains and mappings.

6.3.1 **Conceptual Domains**

An evaluation of the business concepts will reveal hierarchies associating specific logical notions or objects together. For example, there is a concept of a "U.S. state," which represents a geopolitical subregion of a country (another concept) named "United States of America," which in its own right is a concept. Whereas the "U.S. state" conceptual domain is composed of the concepts representing each of the states of the Unites States of America—Alabama, Alaska, and so forth through Wyoming—the conceptual domain does not direct the way the concepts are represented; this is done using value domains.

Despite the fact that they are "conceptual," there will typically be some basic representation for the objects that compose the domain set. Continuing the "U.S. state" example, there must be some representation of each of the states that conveys the standard agreed-to meaning. Therefore, one of any number of value domains may be selected as that basic representation, as we see in the next section.

6.3.2 **Value Domains**

A value domain is a collection of representations of the values in a conceptual domain. To continue our example, we can define a collection of character strings that refer to each of the states of the United States of America: "Alabama," "Alaska," and so on.

As Figure 6.2 shows, different value domains may be associated with a single conceptual domain. In this case, U.S. states are represented by their full names, by their U.S. Postal Service two-character codes, by Federal Information Processing System (FIPS) two-digit codes, or even by graphical images showing each state's boundaries. Each of these data sets is a value domain, each has a unique representation for a concept (each individual state) that is included in the higher-level concept (U.S. states), and, in fact, each value in one value domain maps to a corresponding value in the other value domains. This means that we

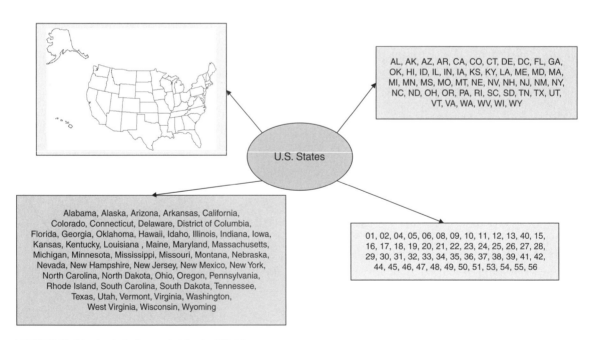

■ **FIGURE 6.2** Value domains for the conceptual domain of U.S. states.

may have data sets that are intended to represent the same concept yet use different value sets in representation; capturing this information within the metadata repository enables making the necessary links when determining ways to integrate and consolidate data sets.

On the other hand, we may have a value domain that is used to represent different conceptual domains. Figure 6.3 shows a value domain consisting of the numerals 0, 1, 2, 3, 4, 5, and 6 used to represent four different conceptual domains. So even though the same *values* are used, their use across different data does not necessarily imply that the data sets represent the same business concepts. Again, capturing this in the metadata repository is critical when considering approaches to data integration and consolidation.

6.3.3 **Reference Tables**

For any given conceptual domain, there must be a way to document the connection with a specific value domain and how the values within the value domain refer to the objects within the conceptual domain. Reference tables essentially capture this information by providing a direct one-to-one mapping between an enumeration of the basic representation of a value domain representing the conceptual domain and a value domain used in an application data context. These are often manifested in the organization as "code tables" or "lookup tables."

For each of the conceptual domains shown in Figure 6.3 that use the same value domain, there is a direct reference table showing the relationship between concept to value. Consider the example of "Weekdays" presented in Table 6.1.

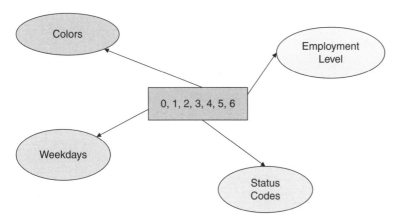

■ **FIGURE 6.3**   The same value domain may be used for different conceptual domains.

Table 6.1 Reference Table for "Weekdays"

Weekday	Value
Sunday	0
Monday	1
Tuesday	2
Wednesday	3
Thursday	4
Friday	5
Saturday	6

6.3.4 **Mappings**

Another artifact of the historical variance of data representations is that different information architects may have selected different value domains to represent objects within the same conceptual domain. Yet before integrating records drawn from different data sets, one must know when different value domains are used to represent the same conceptual domain. Contrast the reference table in Table 6.2 for weekdays with the one in Table 6.1. The same conceptual domain is associated with two different value domains, and to appropriately establish that two records contain the same weekday value, one must know the mapping demonstrating equivalence between the two value domains.

Table 6.2 An Alternate Reference Table for "Weekdays"

Weekday	Value
Sunday	SU
Monday	MO
Tuesday	TU
Wednesday	WE
Thursday	TH
Friday	FR
Saturday	SA

Table 6.3 Mapping between "Weekday" Value Domains

Weekday	WD Value 1	WD Value 2
Sunday	0	SU
Monday	1	MO
Tuesday	2	TU
Wednesday	3	WE
Thursday	4	TH
Friday	5	FR
Saturday	6	SA

Empirical data analysis (such as that performed using data analytics or data profiling tools) can reveal the mappings between value domains within the context of the conceptual domain. A mapping for our weekday example would show the relationship between the reference data sets (Table 6.3).

6.4 **DATA ELEMENTS**

At the next level of the metadata stack, we start to see the objects used to create the information models used in the different application data sets. According to the ISO/IEC 11179 standard, a data element is "a unit of data for which the definition, identification, representation and permissible values are specified by means of a set of attributes." More simply, a data element is the basic building block for data models, and each data element is specified in terms of a definition, a name, a representation, and a set of valid values.

All data assets are composed of data elements, intentionally or not. Data sets designed before the use of comprehensive data modeling tools still conform to the use of data elements, although the associated constraints may not have been formally defined. In these cases, data analytics tools can again be used to evaluate the de facto rules, which can then be reverse-engineered and validated with subject matter experts.

Ultimately, the master metadata repository should maintain information about every data element that might contribute to the master data asset. However, the scope of analyzing, validating, and formally capturing metadata about every single data element may prove to be overwhelming and could become a bottleneck to MDM success. Therefore, it may be worthwhile to initially concentrate on the *critical* data elements.

6.4.1 **Critical Data Elements**

Of the thousands of data elements that could exist within an organization, how would one distinguish "critical" data elements from your everyday, run-of-the-mill data elements? There is a need to define what a critical data element means within the organization, and some examples were provided earlier in this chapter. For an MDM program, the definition of a critical data element should frame how *all* instances of each conceptual data element are used within the context of *each* business application use. For example, if the master data is used within a purely analytical/reporting scenario, the definition might consider the dependent data elements used for quality analytics and reporting (e.g., "A critical data element is one that is used by one or more external reports.")

On the other hand, if the master data asset is driving operational applications, the definition might contain details regarding specific operational data use (e.g., "A critical data element is one that is used to support part of a published business policy or is used to support regulatory compliance."). Some other examples define critical data elements as follows:

- "… supporting part of a published business policy"
- "… contributing to the presentation of values published in one or more external reports"
- "… supporting the organization's regulatory compliance initiatives"
- "containing personal information protected under a defined privacy or confidentiality policy"
- "containing critical information about an employee"
- "containing critical information about a supplier"
- "containing detailed information about a product"
- "required for operational decision processing"
- "contributing to key performance indicators within an organizational performance scorecard"

Critical data elements are used for establishing information policy and, consequently, business policy compliance, and they must be subjected to governance and oversight, especially in an MDM environment.

6.4.2 **Data Element Definition**

As data elements will ultimately reflect the instantiation of the concepts and business terms described in Section 6.2, it is important to capture precise definitions of the data elements that will contribute to the master model. In fact, one might consider the requirements to precisely define data elements to be as great, if not greater than that for business terms.

Sections 4.1 and 4.2 of Part 4 of the ISO/IEC 11179 standard provide guidance for data definitions, and we can apply these to the definition of a data element. A definition should state what the data element is (not what it "does" or what is isn't), be stated with descriptive phrases, not rely on uncommon abbreviations, and be expressed without incorporating definitions of other data concepts or elements. In addition, a definition should state the essential meaning of the data element, be precise and unambiguous, be concise, and avoid circular reasoning. Avoid using a data element's functional use as its definition or including procedural information.

6.4.3 **Data Formats**

In modern data modeling environments, every data element is attributed by a data type (e.g., integer, varchar, timestamp) and a size or length, but there are still many data environments that are less structured. Older file-based systems were defined with specific data element sizes but without enforcing any rules regarding data type compliance. As part of the data format component of the metadata repository, each captured data element will also be attributed with the format of the valid value set.

This may be limited to data type, such as CHAR(2) for a "U.S. state" data element that uses a U.S. Postal Service state postal code for its value domain. Alternatively, the format may contain a more complex formatting information that reflects a greater degree of constraint, such as limiting North American Numbering Plan telephone numbers to data type of CHAR(12) and a format "999-999-9999," where the 9's represent digits only; any value that does not conform to the format must be invalid. Lastly, specifying an enumerated data value domain to a data element provides a greater degree of format constraint, because the data element's value *must* be selected from that set of values.

6.4.4 **Aliases/Synonyms**

Recognizing that different data elements ultimately contain data that represent the same underlying business concept allows the metadata analyst to establish a relationship between those data elements in that they are *aliases* or *synonyms*. Synonym data elements may or may not share the same value domains, data element formats, names, and other components, but through their connections within the metadata hierarchy one can determine that they represent the same notions and must be associated.

This observation underscores the value of the hierarchical layering of master metadata. This value is driven by the exposure of concept and type inheritance, because it provides the ability to determine that two

Table 6.4 Data Elements Metadata		
Data Element Name	**Data Element Type**	**Value Domain**
DayOfWeek Metadata DayOfWeek	Integer(1)	WD Value 1
Weekday Metadata Weekday	CHAR(2)	WD Value 2

data elements refer to the same concept, even if empirically they look completely different. Let us revisit our example of documenting mappings between value domains associated with the same conceptual domain from Section 6.3.4. Suppose the metadata analyst were presented with two data elements. The first is called "DayOfWeek" and details are presented in Table 6.4; the second is called "Weekday" and details also are presented in Table 6.4.

In isolation, other than slight similarity between the names, empirical analysis of the data elements' values would not suggest any similarity between them, yet the connectivity established in the metadata registry shows that both data elements employ data value domains that are mapped together. Documenting data element synonyms is valuable when determining data extract and transformation rules for master data integration.

6.5 **INFORMATION ARCHITECTURE**

For MDM, we would expect to see two views of information models: the current state view consisting of the existing models used to represent master objects and the conformed model to be used for the master repository. In fact, there may be an additional model defined as well as a canonical model used for exchange or migration between existing models and the master model.

Both the logical models and their physical counterparts are constructed from the data elements documented in the previous level of the metadata stack. And within the information architecture level, we see a logically "interleaved" assembly, driven on the conceptual front by descriptions of master data object types and their structure and driven on the more concrete front using defined data models.

6.5.1 **Master Data Object Class Types**

Analysts can speculate on which master data object class types exist within the organization. Typical lists start with customer, product,

employee, and supplier—the conceptual entities with which the organization does business. Yet there is a difference between the conceptual
entities that the applications are expected to use and the actual instances
in which these entities are documented and ultimately managed.

Analysis of the data sets from the bottom up and the business processes
from the top down will help subject matter experts identify recurring
concepts, manifested as information entities that share similar, if not
identical structures. These similar entities reflect themes that are commonly used across the application fabric, and patterns will emerge to
expose the conceptual master objects in the organization. Cataloging
the details of agreed-to master data object types that are used (or will
be used) helps in later processes for mapping existing instance models to the master model for each object type. In turn, a focused review
of the data objects that are used and shared across applications will
reveal a more comprehensive list of potential master data objects.

This component of the metadata model is used to maintain the set
of master object types and will incorporate a list of the master object
concepts with a logical enumeration of the high-level structure. More
important, this layer should also document the relationships that are
manifested through the business process and work flows.

6.5.2 **Master Entity Models**

Having articulated the types of each master object used in the organization, a resolved master model for each object type will be developed
as the core representation. Each logical model reflects the attribution
for the master object, referring to data elements defined at the data element layer. This will, by default, also provide the associated agreed-to
definitions for the data elements.

The existence of defined models drives three management activities related
to application migration and development. First, the model becomes the
default for persistence of master data. Although the actual architecture will
depend on many operational and functional requirements, the core model
managed within the metadata repository is the logical starting point for
any stored data systems. Second, within each business area, there must be
object models suitable for application program manipulation, and these
object models must correspond to the persistent view. Third, master data
will be shared among applications, some of which may be legacy applications that require wrappers and facades along with transformations
into and back out of the master model, suggesting the need for defined
exchange model for information sharing.

6.5.3 **Master Object Directory**

To facilitate the development of a migration strategy for legacy applications, as well as to document entity use for planning and impact analysis, the metadata repository should also maintain a directory that maps the applications that use specific master objects. The mapping should describe whether the application uses the version of the master data object as presented by the MDM environment or whether the application uses an internal data structure that represents (and perhaps copies data in from and out to) a corresponding master data object structure. In other words, this component tracks how master object types are mapped to the applications that use them.

6.5.4 **Relational Tables**

Lastly, the metadata repository will maintain the actual relational data models for both the master object types and the instance representations used by the applications.

6.6 **METADATA TO SUPPORT DATA GOVERNANCE**

In Chapter 4 we looked at the necessity for data governance as part of MDM. Data governance, which is a collection of processes for overseeing the alignment of data use with achieving business objectives, is supported through documenting the directives for oversight derived from the information policies associated with the business policies that are managed at the highest level of the metadata stack. At this level, we capture the information quality rules and how they are applied to the information objects, as well as the service level agreements (SLAs) that dictate the contract between data suppliers and data consumers in terms of data quality metrics, measurement, and information acceptability.

6.6.1 **Information Usage**

Just as we maintain a mapping from the logical use of master data objects to their use by applications, a more general mapping from the data entities and their associated data elements to their application use can be maintained within the metadata repository. This mapping is critical for assessing the need for data transformations, data migrations, and the development of functional infrastructure supporting the movement of instance data from the application silo to the master data asset.

6.6.2 **Information Quality**

The business policies and their corresponding information policies provide the context for assessing the available data sources and how those data sources are used to populate the master data asset. More important, that process also will result in sets of data rules and directives that indicate quantifiable measures of information quality. These rules are managed as content and can even be linked to tools that automate data inspection, monitoring, event notification, and continuous reporting of master data quality.

6.6.3 **Data Quality SLAs**

A key component of establishing data governance is through the use of SLAs. That data quality SLA should delineate the location in the processing stream that it covers, the data elements covered by the agreement, and additional aspects of overseeing the quality, as listed in the sidebar. All of these will be documented as metadata within the repository, which will simplify the data stewards' ability to manage observance of the agreements.

SLA ATTRIBUTES FOR OVERSEEING QUALITY

- Business impacts associated with potential flaws in the data elements
- Data quality dimensions associated with each data element
- Assertions regarding the expectations for quality for each data element for each identified dimension
- Methods for measuring conformance to those expectations (automated or manual)
- The acceptability threshold for each measurement
- The individual to be notified in case the acceptability threshold is not met
- An explanation of how often monitoring is taking place
- A clarification of how results and issues will be reported
- A description of to whom and how often issues are reported
- The times for expected resolution or remediation of the issue
- A description of the escalation strategy that will be enforced when the resolution times are not met
- A process for logging issues, tracking progress in resolution, and measuring performance in meeting the SLA

6.6.4 **Access Control**

Consolidating data instances into a master data view presents some potential issues regarding security and privacy, necessitating policies for access rights and observing access control according to those policies. Consider that capturing identifying information in a master registry does not only enable the *consolidation* of data—it also enables the *segregation* of data when needed. For business processes that must enforce policies restricting access to protected information, policy compliance can be automated in an auditable manner.

There must be defined roles associated with master data access, whether by automated process or by individuals. In turn, each of these roles will be granted certain rights of access, which can restrict access at a level as granular as the data element level within record sets limited by specified filters. Individuals and stakeholders within the organization are then assigned roles and corresponding access rights; these assignments are archived within the metadata repository as well.

6.7 **SERVICES METADATA**

Master data management is largely seen as providing value to client applications by virtue of providing access to a high quality data asset of uniquely identifiable master objects synchronized across the enterprise. However, it turns out that master service consolidation is a strong motivating factor for MDM, even (at times) trumping the value of the consolidated data asset. The process of analyzing the use of master data objects exposes the ways in which different applications create, access, modify, and retire similar objects, and this analysis helps in determining which data sets represent recognized master object types. The by-product of this analysis is not just knowledge of the master objects but also knowledge about the functionality applied to those objects.

The upshot is that as consolidated multiple master object views are aggregated into a single master model, the functionality associated with the life cycle of master objects can also be consolidated as well—there is no need to have three or four processes for creating a new customer or product when one will suffice. This becomes particularly valuable when add-on software applications are integrated into the environment—applications whose licensing, maintenance, and operations costs can be reduced when the data sets they were intended to support become reduced into a single master view.

6.7.1 **Service Directory**

There will be two collections of services. The first is an enumeration of the essential services employed by client business applications at a conceptual level, such as "create a customer" or "update a telephone number." Master services can be segmented as well into core object services that address typical data life cycle events, such as "create or modify an object," or business services applied as part of the business process workflow, such as "generate invoice" or "initiate product shipment."

The second collection is a current view of the (possibly multiple) ways that each conceptual master service is actually deployed within the current environment. This is intended to assist in the development of an implementation road map by identifying the functional components to be ultimately replaced that will require an engineered wrapper during the migration process.

6.7.2 **Service Users**

In addition to documenting the list of services and the way each is currently deployed, the services metadata layer will also list the clients of the services. This is a list of both automated clients and individuals that invoke the functionality that will ultimately be implemented within the set of enumerated services. This inverse mapping from service to client also is used in impact analysis and migration planning, both for the determination of risk during the transition from the legacy framework to the MDM environment and for ongoing management, maintenance, and improvement of master data services.

6.7.3 **Interfaces**

There are metadata representing the different types of services and the users of those services. What is left will comprise the third component of master data services metadata, which captures the interfaces used by the clients (both automated and human) to invoke those services. Consolidating functionality into services must ensure that the newly created services support the application's current functional requirements, and that includes details about the different ways the services must be invoked and, consequently, any necessary parameterization or customization for the service layer. Alternatively, as functions are evaluated and their invocation methods reviewed, it may become apparent that even though the functionality appears to be the same across a set of applications, the ways that the functionality is invoked may signal discrete differences in the effects intended to occur. Capturing this information interface layer will help analysts to make this assessment.

6.8 BUSINESS METADATA

As we have seen, a master data environment can be valuable because it gives analysts the ability to consolidate more than just data, or even services; doing so will provide expected benefits in terms of improving data quality and reducing the complexity of developing and maintaining system functionality. Additional, and potentially greater, value can be achieved through the implementation of business policies imposed on the ways that processes interact with master objects.

It is one thing to consider the integration of all customer data records, and another to impose policy constraints such as those regarding the protection of private personal information or the segregation of access between different groups. In fact, many policies used to run the business correspond to information policies applied to master data, creating the opportunity for organizations to manage and control the observance of business policies as part of the MDM program.

Driving policy observance via metadata requires that the business policies themselves be documented and that their relationship to information policies be made explicit. In turn, the subject matter experts determine how the information policies reflect specific business rules to be applied to the data. The successive refinement of business policies down to information business rules opens opportunities for automating the way that business rule observance is monitored as well as rolling up to gauge business policy compliance. Business rules engines can be used to implement the monitoring of compliance and how that compliance rolls back up along the hierarchy, as is shown in Figure 6.4.

As an example, consider a business policy that restricts the organization from sharing customer information with trusted partners if the customer is under the age of 13 unless the organization has the customer's parental consent. This business policy, expressed in natural language, restricts a business process ("information sharing") based on attribution of specific data instances (namely, birth date and parental

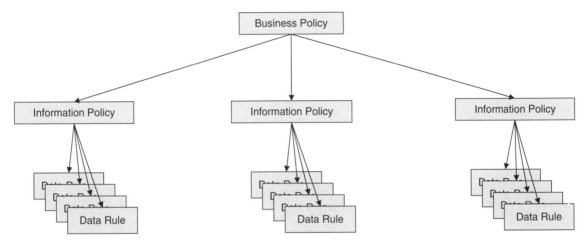

■ **FIGURE 6.4** Observance of business rules can be rolled up to report policy compliance.

consent). Therefore, this business policy suggests a number of information policies:

■ The organization must capture customer birth date.
■ The organization must conditionally capture parental consent.
■ Only records for customers over the age of 13 and those that are under the age of 13 with parental consent may be shared.

In turn, there are business rules to be imposed regarding the structure of the master model, the completeness of the master records, and the implementation of the constraint during the process for data extraction in preparation for sharing. Each of these aspects represents pieces of knowledge to be documented and controlled via the master metadata repository.

6.8.1 **Business Policies**

At a simplistic level, a business policy is a statement that guides or constrains a business process as a way of controlling the outcome as well as side effects of the business process. Business policies, which may be either documented or undocumented, reflect general practices to be observed by those within an organization along with those that do business with the organization.

Business policies are expressed in natural language, but requiring subject matter experts to capture these policies within the metadata repository is a way to encourage more precision in expressing policies. The objective is to specify business policies in a manner that can be linked to the ways that the applications enforce them. Presumably, it may be possible to meet this objective by using information already managed within the metadata repository: concepts, business terms, business definitions, and semantics that are associated with commonly used business language. Business policies are more likely to be well structured if they have been specified using terms with agreed-to definitions.

6.8.2 **Information Policies**

The difference between a business policy and an information policy is that a business policy guides the business process whereas an information policy guides information architecture and application design. An information policy specifies one (of possibly many) information management requirements to support the observance of business policies. In the data-sharing example in Section 6.8, one business policy translated into three information policies. In turn, an information policy may guide the specification of one or more business rules.

6.8.3 **Business Rules**

A business rule specifies one particular constraint or directive associated with a data element, a collection of data elements, one record, a set of records, and so forth. A rule may specify a constraint and be used to filter or distinguish compliant data instances from noncompliant ones, and it could also trigger one or more actions to be taken should some condition evaluate to true. One or more business rules can be derived from an information policy, and documenting these rules within the metadata repository enables the application of the rules to be automated via an associated rules engine. The metadata repository provides a centralized location for the subject matter to be reviewed by experts before it is deployed into the rules engine.

6.9 **SUMMARY**

The metadata requirements for master data management exceed the typical demands of application development, because the ability to consolidate and integrate data from many sources is bound to be hampered by variant business terms, definitions, and semantics. But once a decision is made to use metadata as a lever for enabling the migration to the master data environment, it is wise to consider the more sophisticated means for enterprise information management that can be activated via the metadata management program. The general processes for metadata management have been articulated here; evaluating the specific needs within an organization should lead to the definition of concrete information and functional requirements. In turn, the MDM team should use these requirements to identify candidate metadata management tools that support the types of activities described in this chapter.

Finally, the technology should not drive the process, but it should be the other way around. Solid metadata management supports more than just MDM—good enterprise information management relies on best practices in *activating* the value that metadata provides.

Identifying Master Metadata and Master Data

7.1 INTRODUCTION

After a determination is made regarding the development and deployment of an MDM program, a number of architectural decisions need to be addressed, including the determination of an architectural approach, the analysis of tools and technology to support the operational aspects of MDM, the evaluation of existing technical capabilities underlying those operational aspects, and the identification of component services to meet enterprise requirements. However, to some extent the questions raised by this decision-making process are premature. Before determining *how* to manage the enterprise master data asset, more fundamental questions need to be asked and comprehensively explored regarding the assets themselves, such as the following:

- Which data objects are highlighted within the business processes as master data objects?
- Which data elements are associated with each of the master data objects?
- Which data sets would contribute to the organization's master data?
- How do we locate and isolate master data objects that exist within the enterprise?
- How can we employ approaches for metadata and data standards for collecting and managing master metadata?
- How do we assess the variances between the different representations in order to determine standardized models for data extraction and data consolidation?
- How do we apply techniques to consolidate instances in a standardized representation into a single view?

Because of the ways that diffused application architectures have evolved within different divisions within the organization, it is likely that despite the conceptually small number of core master objects used, there are going to be many ways that these objects are modeled, represented, and stored.

For example, there may be different applications that require details of sets of products, such as product category. Any application that maintains product details data will rely on a defined data model that maintains the category. Yet one application will track category through classification codes, others may maintain both codes and category descriptions, and others may embed the category data within other attributes. Those that maintain the product category codes and descriptions will do it differently. Scan through the product data sets within your own organization, and you are likely to find "CATEGORY" and "CTGRY_CODE" attributes with a wide range of field lengths.

The same thing can be said for customer data. Applications managing contact information for individual customers depend on data sets that maintain the customer's name. As noted in Chapter 5, whereas one application contains data elements to store an individual's full name, others may break up the name into its first, middle, and last parts. And even for those that have data elements for the given and family names of a customer, various names and field lengths are employed, as Figure 7.1 illustrates.

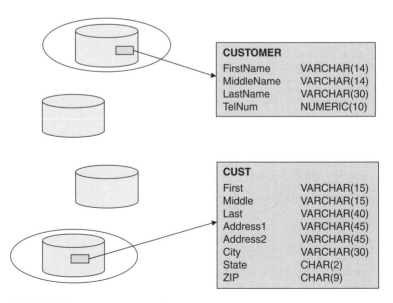

■ **FIGURE 7.1** Variance in data types for similar data elements.

These variations may pose a barrier to consolidation (and subsequent ongoing data synchronization), but they also are a rich source of knowledge about the ways that the core objects are attributed. The definition of a data object's data type is sometimes consistent with the application use, but just as often as not, the lengths and types are based on speculation of how the data elements will be used over time. In the latter case, there are opportunities for reviewing data element usage with respect to architecture, as part of a process for identifying the objects that represent master data.

The challenges are not limited to determining what master objects are used but rather to incorporating the need to find *where* master objects are used and to chart a strategy for standardizing, harmonizing, and consolidating their components in a way that enables the presentation of a master data asset. When the intention is to create an organizational asset that is not just another data silo, it is imperative that your organization provide the means for both the consolidation and integration of master data as well as facilitate the most effective and appropriate sharing of that master data.

7.2 CHARACTERISTICS OF MASTER DATA

The master data identification process consists of two main activities. One is a top-down process for reviewing the enterprise data model(s) and any documented business process models to identify which data objects are critical within the many business application work streams. The other is a bottom-up process that evaluates the enterprise data assets to find applications that use data structures that reflect what can be identified as master data objects and resolve them into a proposed master data environment. Both approaches examine business process dependence on information and the ways that the data objects are categorized and organized for the different business purposes. Ultimately, the path taken to identify master data will probably combine aspects of both approaches, coupled with some feet-on-on-the-ground knowledge along with some common sense.

7.2.1 Categorization and Hierarchies

Let's review our definition of master data from Chapter 1:

> *Master data objects are those core business objects used in the different applications across the organization, along with their associated metadata, attributes, definitions, roles, connections, and taxonomies. Master data objects are those key "things" that matter the most— the things that are logged in our transaction systems, measured and reported in reporting systems, and analyzed in analytical systems.*

Aside from the preceding description, though, master data objects share certain characteristics:

- The real-world objects modeled within the environment as master data objects will be referenced in multiple business areas and business processes. For example, the concept of a "vendor" is relevant to procurement, purchasing, accounting, and finance.

- Master data objects are referenced in both transaction and analytical system records. Both the sales and the customer service systems may log and process the transactions initiated by a customer. Those same activities may be analyzed for the purposes of segmentation, classification, and marketing.

- Master data objects may be classified within a semantic hierarchy, with different levels of classification, attribution, and specialization applied depending on the application. For example, we may have a master data category of "party," which in turn is comprised of "individuals" or "organizations." Those parties may also be classified based on their roles, such as "prospect," "customer," "supplier," "vendor," or "employee."

- Master data objects may have specialized application functions to create new instances as well as to manage the updating and removal of instance records. Each application that involves "supplier" interaction may have a function enabling the creation of a new supplier record.

- They are likely to have models reflected across multiple applications, possibly embedded in legacy data structure models or even largely unmodeled within flat file structures.

- They are likely to be managed separately in many systems associated with many different applications, with an assumption within each that their version is the only correct version.

For any conceptual master data type there will be some classifications or segmentations that naturally align along hierarchies, such as corporate ownership for organizations, family households for individuals, or product classification. However, the ways that even some of these hierarchical classification schemes (also referred to as "taxonomies") are applied to the data instances themselves might cross multiple segments. For example, a "party" may represent either an individual or an organization; however, a party categorized as an individual may be further classified as both a "customer" and an "employee."

As a valuable by-product of evaluating and establishing the hierarchies and taxonomies, we gain a degree of consistency that relates operations to reporting. The same master data categories and their related taxonomies would then be used for transactions, reporting, and analysis. For example, the headers in a monthly sales report may be derived from the master data categories and their qualifiers (e.g., sales by customer by region by time period). Enabling transactional systems to refer to the same data objects as the subsequent reporting systems ensures that the analysis reports are consistent with the transaction systems.

7.2.2 **Top-Down Approach: Business Process Models**

The top-down approach seeks to determine which business concepts are shared in practice across the different business processes. Because the operations of a business are guided by defined performance management goals, an efficient organization will define its business policies to be aligned with the organization's strategic imperatives and then implement business processes that support those policies. A business process, in this environment, is a coordinated set of activities intended to achieve a desired goal or produce a desired output product. Business process models are designed to capture both the high level and detail of the business process, coupled with the underlying business rules originating from the business objectives and subsequent auxiliary material that accompanies the corresponding definitions.

The traditional approach to designing business applications involves documenting the end clients' needs and then refining the ways that available technical solutions can be used to meet those needs. In essence, business objectives lead to formalizing the business policies. Those business policies then drive the definition of functional and informational requirements. The applications are then designed to implement these requirements as business logic operating on the underlying data objects.

Although as a matter of fact many application architectures emerge organically, the developed business applications are always intended to implement the stated business policies. Therefore, application designers should always strive to synchronize the way they implement policies with the ways that other applications in the enterprise implement business policies. To do this, the organization must maintain the relationships between business strategy and the components of the application's model:

- The business policies derived from the business objectives
- Business process models that reflect the work streams
- The orchestrations and the functional specifications that define high-level process-oriented services

- The enterprise data objects on which the processes operate
- The common semantics (for terms and facts) associated with the data objects and their corresponding business rules

Given an understanding of the way that a business application can be designed and implemented, we can apply the top-down approach to identifying the sources for master data by reviewing the business process models and identifying which data objects are critical within the processing streams of more than one application. What we will find is that individual business activities depend on the sharing or exchange of data objects. Those objects that would be shared are the ones that analysts can anticipate to be managed as master data.

Each shared data object has underlying metadata, a role within the business process, as well as its representation within the environment, suggesting a characterization as key data entities (as was discussed in Chapter 4). These key data entities reflect the business terms employed within the process, and those business terms are eventually rolled up into facts about the business process and its operations. Those key data entities that appear with relevant frequency as touch points within the business process models become the logical candidates for data mastering.

7.2.3 **Bottom-Up Approach: Data Asset Evaluation**

The bottom-up approach seeks to identify the master data objects that are already in use across the organization. This approach evaluates the enterprise data assets to locate applications using what are, in effect, replicas of master data objects and then enable their resolution into a proposed master data environment This is more of a widespread assessment of the data sets performed using data discovery tools and documenting the discoveries within a metadata management framework, as suggested in Chapter 6. This process incorporates these stages, which are examined in greater detail in this chapter:

- Identifying structural and semantic metadata and managing that metadata in a centralized resource
- Collecting and analyzing master metadata from empirical analysis
- Evaluating differences between virtually replicated data structures and resolving similarity in structure into a set of recognized data elements
- Unifying semantics when possible and differentiating meanings when it is not possible
- Identifying and qualifying master data
- Standardizing the representative models for extraction, persistence, and sharing of data entities managed as master data objects

7.3 **IDENTIFYING AND CENTRALIZING SEMANTIC METADATA**

One of the objectives of a master data management program is to facilitate the effective management of the set of key data entity instances that are distributed across the application environment as a single centralized master resource. But before we can materialize a single master record for any entity, we must be able to do the following:

1. Discover which data resources contain entity information.
2. Determine which data resources act as the authoritative source for each attribute.
3. Understand which of the entity's attributes carry identifying information.
4. Extract identifying information from the data resource.
5. Transform the identifying information into a standardized or canonical form.
6. Establish similarity to other records that have been transformed into a standardized form.

Fully blown, this process entails cataloging the data sets, their attributes, formats, data domains, definitions, contexts, and semantics, not just as an operational resource, but rather in a way that can be used to catalog existing data elements and automate master data consolidation, along with governing the ongoing application interactions with the MDM service layers.

In other words, to manage the master data, one must first be able to manage the master *metadata*. But as there is a need to resolve multiple variant models into a single view, the interaction with the master metadata must facilitate resolution of the following elements:

- *Format* at the element level
- *Structure* at the instance level
- *Semantics* across all levels

7.3.1 **Example**

In Figure 7.2, we look at the example of the two different representations for "customer" first displayed in Figure 7.1. Note that we are only looking at resolving the *representations* for data entities, not their actual values—that is discussed in Chapter 10 on data consolidation.

The first representation has four attributes (FirstName, MiddleName, LastName, and TelNum), whereas the second representation has eight

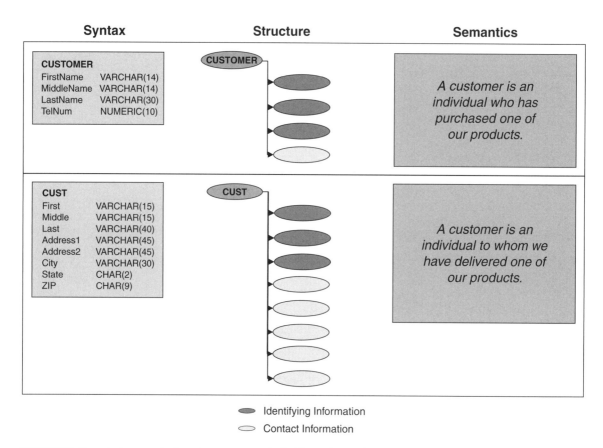

■ **FIGURE 7.2** Preparation for a master data integration process must resolve the differences between the syntax, structure, and semantics of different source data sets.

(First, Middle, Last, Address1, Address2, City, State, and Zip). The data elements are reviewed at the three levels (syntactic, structural, and semantic). At the syntactic level, we can compare the data types and sizes directly and see that there are apparently minor differences—first and middle names are of length 14 in the top example but are of length 15 in the bottom; there is a similar difference for the corresponding last name fields.

At the structural level, though, we see some more pointed differences. Reviewing the data elements shows that each of these entities contains data related to two different aspects of the "person" master data type. One aspect is the identifying information, which incorporates the data values used to make a distinction between specific instances, such as name or assigned identifiers (social security numbers, customer account numbers, etc.). The other aspect is related entity data that is not necessarily required for disambiguation. In this example, there are data elements associated with contact information that could potentially have been isolated as its own conceptual master data object type.

Lastly, reviewing the semantics of the business terms associated with the data entities reveals another subtle difference between the two data models. In one application, the concept of customer refers to those who have "purchased one of our products," whereas the other defines a customer as a person to whom we have "delivered one of our products." The latter definition is a bit broader than the first in some ways (e.g., items such as marketing material sent free of charge to prospects may be categorized as products) and is limiting in others (e.g., service customers are not included).

7.3.2 **Analysis for Integration**

The sidebar highlights the three stages in master data resolution that need to dovetail as a prelude to any kind of enterprise-wide integration, suggesting three corresponding challenges for MDM.

THREE STAGES OF MASTER DATA RESOLUTION

1. Collecting and analyzing master metadata so that there is a comprehensive catalog of existing data elements
2. Resolving similarity in structure to identify differences requiring structural reorganization for application interaction
3. Understanding and unifying master data semantics to ensure that objects with different underlying data types are not inadvertently consolidated in error

---

7.3.3 **Collecting and Analyzing Master Metadata**

One approach involves analyzing and documenting the metadata associated with all data objects across the enterprise, in order to use that information to guide analysts seeking master data. The challenge with metadata is that to a large extent it remains sparsely documented. However, many of the data sets may actually have some of the necessary metadata documented. For example, relational database systems allow for querying table structure and data element types, and COBOL copybooks reveal some structure and potentially even some alias information about data elements that are components of a larger logical structure.

On the other hand, some of the data may have little or no documented metadata, such as fixed-format or character-separated files. If the objective is to collect comprehensive and consistent metadata, as well as ensure that the data appropriately correlates to its documented metadata, the analysts must be able to discover the data set's metadata, and for this, data profiling is the tool of choice. Data profiling tools apply both statistical and analytical algorithms to characterize data sets, and the result of this analysis can drive the empirical assessment of structure and format metadata while simultaneously exposing embedded data models and dependencies.

Discoveries made through the profiling process should be collected into a metadata repository, and this consolidated metadata repository will eventually enumerate the relevant characteristics associated with each data set in a standardized way, including the data set name, its type (such as different storage formats, including relational tables, indexed flat VSAM file, or comma-separated files), and the characteristics of each of its columns/attributes (e.g., length, data type, format pattern, among others).

At the end of this process, we will not just have a comprehensive catalog of all data sets, but we will also be able to review the frequency of metamodel characteristics, such as frequently used names, field sizes, and data types. Capturing these values with a standard representation allows the metadata characteristics themselves to be subjected to the kinds of statistical analysis that data profiling provides. For example, we can assess the dependencies between common attribute names (e.g., "CUSTOMER") and their assigned data types (e.g., VARCHAR(20)) to identify (and potentially standardize against) commonly used types, sizes, and formats.

7.3.4 **Resolving Similarity in Structure**

Despite the expectations that there are many variant forms and structures for your organization's master data, the different underlying models of each master data object are bound to share many commonalities. For example, the structure for practically any "residential" customer table will contain a name, an address, and a telephone number. Interestingly, almost any vendor or supplier data set will probably also contain a name, an address, and a telephone number. This similarity suggests the existence of a de facto underlying concept of a "party," used as the basis for both customer and vendor. In turn, the analyst might review any model that contains those same identifying attributes as a structure type that can be derived from or is related to a party type.

Collecting the metadata for many different applications that rely on the same party concept allows the analyst to evaluate and document the different data elements that attribute a party in its different derivations. That palette of attributes helps the analyst to assess how each model instance maps to a growing catalog of data models used by each master data entity type.

There are two aspects to analyzing structure similarity for the purpose of identifying master data instances. The first is seeking out overlapping structures, in which the core attributes determined to carry identifying information for one data object are seen to overlap with a similar set of attributes in another data object. The second is identifying where one could infer "organic derivation" or inheritance of core attributes in some sets of data objects that are the same core data attributes that are completely embedded within other data objects, as in the case of the "first name," "middle name," and "last name" attributes that are embedded within both structures displayed in Figure 7.2. Both cases indicate a structural relationship. When related attributes carry identifying information, the analyst should review those objects to determine if they indeed represent master objects.

7.4 **UNIFYING DATA OBJECT SEMANTICS**

The third challenge focuses on the qualitative differences between pure syntactic or structural metadata (as we can discover through the profiling process) and the underlying semantic metadata. This involves more than just analyzing structure similarity. It involves understanding what the data mean, how that meaning is conveyed, how that meaning "connects" data sets across the enterprise, how the data are used, and approaches to capturing semantics as an attribute of your metadata framework.

As a data set's metadata are collected, the semantic analyst must approach the business client to understand that data object's business meaning. One step in this process involves reviewing the degree of semantic consistency in how data element naming relates to overlapping data types, sizes, and structures, such as when "first" and "first name" both refer to an individual's given name. The next step is to document the business meanings assumed for each of the data objects, which involves asking questions such as these:

- What are the definitions for the individual data elements?
- What are the definitions for the data entities composed of those data elements?
- Are there authoritative sources for the definitions?
- Do similar objects have different business meanings?

The answers to these question not only help in determining which data sets truly refer to the same underlying real-world objects, they also contribute to an organizational resource that can be used to standardize a representation for each data object as its definition is approved through the data governance process. Managing semantic metadata as a central asset enables the metadata repository to grow in value as it consolidates semantics from different enterprise data collections.

7.5 IDENTIFYING AND QUALIFYING MASTER DATA

Many master data object types are largely similar and reflect generic structural patterns (such as party, location, time, etc.). We can attempt to leverage standard or universal models and see if it is necessary to augment these models based on what is discovered empirically. This essentially marries the top-down and the bottom-up approaches and enables the analyst to rely on "off-the-shelf" master data models that have been proven in other environments. Those universal models can be adapted as necessary to meet the business needs as driven by the business application requirements.

Once the semantic metadata has been collected and centralized, the analyst's task of identifying master data should be simplified. As more metadata representations of similar objects and entities populate the repository, the frequency with which specific models or representations appear will provide a basis for assessing whether the attributes of a represented object qualify the data elements represented by the model as master data. By adding characterization information for each data set's metadata profile, more knowledge is added to the process of determining the source data sets that are appropriate for populating a master data repository, which will help in the analyst's task.

7.5.1 Qualifying Master Data Types

The many data types that abound, especially within the scope of the built-in types, complicate the population of the metadata repository. Consider that numbers can be used for quantity as easily as they can be used for codes, but a data profile does not necessarily indicate *which* way the values are being used within any specific column. One approach to this complexity is to simplify the characterization of the value set associated with each column in each table.

At the conceptual level, designating a value set using a simplified classification scheme reduces the level of complexity associated with data variance and allows for loosening the constraints when comparing multiple metadata instances. For example, we can limit ourselves to the six data value classes shown in the sidebar.

SELECTED DATA VALUE CLASSES

1. *Boolean or flag.* There are only two valid values, one representing "true" and one representing "false."
2. *Time/date stamp.* A value that represents a point in time.
3. *Magnitude.* A numeric value on a continuous range, such as a quantity or an amount.
4. *Code enumeration.* A small set of values, either used directly (e.g., using the colors "red" and "blue") or mapped as a numeric enumeration (e.g., 1 = "red," 2 = "blue").
5. *Handle.* A character string with limited duplication across the set, which may be used as part of an object name or description (e.g., name or address_line_1 fields contain handle information).
6. *Cross-reference.* An identifier (possibly machine-generated) that either is uniquely assigned to the record or provides a reference to that identifier in another data set.

7.5.2 **The Fractal Nature of Metadata Profiling**

At this point, each data attribute can be summarized in terms of a small number of descriptive characteristics: its data type, length, data value domain, and so on. In turn, each data set can be described as a collection of its component attributes. Looking for similar data sets with similar structures, formats, and semantics enables the analyst to assess each data set's "identifying attribution," try to find the collections of data sets that share similar characteristics, and determine if they represent the same objects.

Using data profiling to assess data element structure allows the analyst to collect structural metadata into a metadata repository. The analysis to evaluate the data attributes to find the ones that share similar characteristics is supplemented by data profiling and parsing/standardization tools, which also help the analyst to track those attributes with similar names. The analyst uses profiling to examine the data value sets and assign them into value classes and then uses the same tools again to detect similarities between representative data metamodels.

In essence, the techniques and tools we can use to determine the sources of master data objects are essentially the same types of tools that we will use later to consolidate the data into a master repository. Using data profiling, parsing, standardization, and matching, we can facilitate the process of identifying which data sets (tables, files, spreadsheets, etc.) represent which master data objects.

7.5.3 **Standardizing the Representation**

The analyst is now presented with a collection of master object representations. But as a prelude to continuing to develop the consolidation process, decisions must be made as part of the organization's governance process. To consolidate the variety of diverse master object representations into an environment in which a common master representation can be materialized, the relevant stakeholders need to agree on common representations for data exchange and for persistence, as well as the underlying semantics for those representations. This common model can be used for both data exchange and master data persistence itself; these issues are explored further in Chapter 8.

As discussed in Chapter 4, MDM is a solution that integrates tools with policies and procedures for data governance, so there should be a process for defining and agreeing to data standards. It is critical that a standard representation be defined and agreed to so that the participants expecting to benefit from master data can effectively share the data, and the techniques discussed in Chapter 10 will support the organization's ability to share and exchange data.

7.6 **SUMMARY**

This chapter has considered the challenge of master data discovery. That process depends on the effective collection of metadata from the many application data sets that are subject to inclusion in the master data repository. This depends on a process for analyzing enterprise metadata—assessing the similarity of syntax, structure, and semantics as a prelude to identifying enterprise sources of master data.

Because the objective in identifying and consolidating master data representations requires empirical analysis and similarity assessment as part of the resolution process, it is reasonable to expect that tools will help in the process. Luckily, the same kinds of tools and techniques that will subsequently be used to facilitate data integration can also be employed to isolate and catalog organizational master data.

Chapter 8

Data Modeling for MDM

8.1 INTRODUCTION

In Chapter 2, we looked at collecting business data requirements, and in Chapters 6 and 7, we looked at the documentation and annotation of metadata for proposed master data objects and existing replicas of master data objects. But a core issue for MDM is the ability to capture, consolidate, and then deliver the master representation for each uniquely identifiable entity. At this point, assume that the MDM team has successfully traversed the critical initial stages of the master data management program—most important, clarifying the business need, assessing the information architectures, and profiling available data sets to identify candidate sources for materializing the master data asset.

Having used our tools and techniques to determine our master data types and determine where master data are located across organization applications, we are now at a point when we must consider bringing the data together into a managed environment. Yet here we have a challenge: the data sources that contribute to the creation of the master representation may have variant representations, but at some point there must be distinct models for the managing and subsequent sharing of master data.

In this chapter we look at the issues associated with developing models for master data—from extraction, consolidation, persistence, and delivery. We explore the challenges associated with the variant existing data models and then look at some of the requirements for developing the models used for extraction, consolidation, persistence, and sharing. It is important to realize that becoming a skilled practitioner of data modeling requires a significant amount of training and experience, and this chapter is mostly intended to highlight the more significant issues to be considered when developing models for MDM.

8.2 **ASPECTS OF THE MASTER REPOSITORY**

For the most part in the previous chapters, we have shied away from making any assumptions about the logical or physical formats of a persistent "master repository," because there are different architectural styles that will rely on different sets of master data elements. The details of these different architectural styles are treated in greater detail in Chapter 9, but the common denominator among the different styles is the need to model the *identifying attributes* of each master entity. As we will see in Chapter 10, the ability to index the master registry and consolidate records drawn from multiple data sources hinges on matching records against those same identifying attributes.

8.2.1 **Characteristics of Identifying Attributes**

Within every master data model, some set of data attribute values can be combined to provide a candidate key that is used to distinguish each record from every other, and because each unique object can be presumably identified using this combination of data values, the underlying data attributes are referred to as the "identifying attributes," and the specific values are "identifying information." Identifying attributes are those data elements holding the values used to differentiate one entity instance from every other entity instance.

For example, consider a master object for a "consulting agreement." For the most part, legal documents like consulting agreements are largely boilerplate templates, attributed by the specifics of a business arrangement, such as the names of the counterparties, the statement of work, and financial details. One might consider that one agreement could be distinguished from another based on the names of the counterparties, yet every agreement is in relation to a specific set of counterparties for specific tasks and may not cover other sets of tasks or statements of work. Therefore, that pair of attributes (the name of the organization specifying the engagement and the one being contracted to perform the tasks) is not sufficient to identify the agreement itself. Instead, one must look to the set of attributes that essentially creates a unique key. In this case, we might add on the date of the agreement and a task order identifier to differentiate one agreement from all others.

8.2.2 **Minimal Master Registry**

No matter which architectural approach is used, the common denominator is the existence of a set of data attributes to formulate a keyed master index that can be used to resolve unique identities. This index is the resource consulted when new records are presented into the master environment to determine if there is an existing master data instance. As the following chapters will show, the master index may hold a number of common data attributes. However, the minimal set of attributes is the set of identifying attributes.

8.2.3 Determining the Attributes Called "Identifying Attributes"

Identifying attributes are interesting in that their usefulness depends on their content. The implication is that a set of data attributes is determined to be made up of identifying attributes because the assigned values in each record essentially *describe* the individual object represented by the record, whether that is a person, a company, a product, or some other entity. Therefore, the combination of values within each set of identifying attributes projected across the entire set must be unique, suggesting that any unique key is a candidate. The challenge with determining what the identifying attributes are lies in recognizing that defined key attributes (such as generated identifiers or generated primary or surrogate keys) do not naturally describe the represented object. A generated key tells you nothing about the record itself. In fact, generated keys are only useful inside the individual system and cannot be used across systems unless you develop a cross-referencing system to transform and map identifiers from one system to those in another.

The objective of the process for determining identifying attributes is to find the smallest set of data attributes within a data set whose values are unique across the data set *and* the potential combination of values in a new record that is not likely to duplicate those found in one of the existing records. In other words, the data values are unique for the initial data set and are expected to remain unique for any newly introduced records. To do this, one heuristic is to use what amounts to a reverse decision tree:

1. Limit the data elements to those that are truly descriptive of the represented entity.
2. Let the identifying information element set I begin with the empty set.
3. Seek out the data element d whose values are the most distinct.
4. Add d to the identifying information element set I.
5. If, for each record, the composed values in the data elements from I are not unique, return to step 3.
6. Information element set I is complete.

This process should yield a set of data elements that can be used to uniquely identify every individual entity. Remember that the uniqueness must be retained even after the data set has been migrated into the master environment as well as in production as the master data set grows.

In practice, this process will be performed using a combination of tools and careful consideration. Realize that data profiling tools will easily support the analysis. Frequency analysis, null value analysis, and uniqueness assessment are all functions that are performed by a data profiler and whose results are used to determine good value sets for identifying attributes.

8.3 INFORMATION SHARING AND EXCHANGE

If, as we have discussed before, the basic concept of MDM is to provide transparent access to a unified representation of each uniquely identifiable data instance within a defined entity class, it means that no matter what the ultimate representation will be, there must be models to accommodate absorbing data from multiple data sets, combining those data sets, identifying and eliminating duplicates, addressing potential mismatches, consolidating records, creating a master index or registry, and then publishing the master data back out to client applications. Basically, the essence of MDM revolves around data sharing and interchange.

8.3.1 Master Data Sharing Network

There are a number of interchanges of data within an MDM environment, as Figure 8.1 shows.

As part of the initial data integration and consolidation process, data will be extracted from the source data sets and moved to a consolidation platform. After the master consolidation process is complete, the core master records will be moved to a master repository. (Note that implementations may merge the consolidation platform with the persistent repository.) Third, master records are made available to the application system (via query/publication services) and must be properly packaged. Last, the applications will need to unbundle the data from the exchange model in preparation for reintegration.

8.3.2 Driving Assumptions

Again we face a challenge: despite the fact that we have been able to identify sources of master data, the underlying formats, structures, and content are bound to be different. To accommodate the conceptual

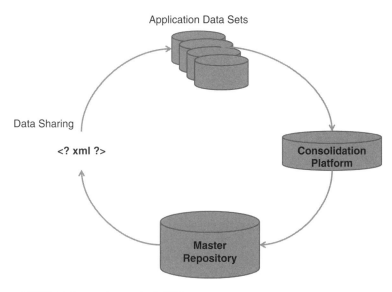

Application Data Sets

Data Sharing

<? xml ?>

Consolidation
Platform

Master
Repository

■ **FIGURE 8.1** Data interchange within the MDM environment.

master repository, though, all of the data in these different formats
and structures need to be consolidated *at some point* into a centralized
resource that can both accommodate those differences and, in turn,
feed the results of the consolidation back into those different original
representations when necessary. This implies the following:

1. There must be a representative model into which data from
   source systems is extracted as a prelude to consolidation.
2. There must be a consolidated master representation model to act
   as the core repository.
3. Processes for capturing data, resolving the variant references
   into a single set, selecting the "best" record, and transforming the
   data into the repository model must be defined.
4. Processes must be created to enable the publication and sharing
   of master data back to the participating applications

Most of these issues are dependent on two things: creating suitable
and extensible models for master data and providing the management
layer that can finesse the issue of legacy model differences.

To meet the objectives of the MDM initiative, the data from participating business applications will eventually be extracted, transformed,
and consolidated within a master data object model. Once the master

data repository is populated, depending on the architectural style selected for the MDM implementation, there will be varying amounts of coordinated interaction between the applications and the master repository, either directly, or indirectly through the integration process flow.

Figure 8.2 presents a deeper look into the general themes of master data integration: connectors attach to production data sources and data sets are extracted and are then transformed into a canonical form for consolidation and integrated with what will have evolved into the master data asset. The integrated records populate the master repository, which then serves as a resource to the participating applications through a service layer. This service layer becomes the broker through which interactions occur between the applications and the master data asset. This means that we must look at both the conceptual issues of

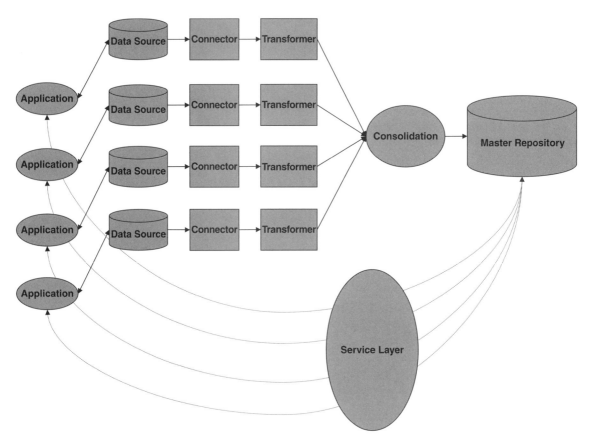

■ **FIGURE 8.2** The master data integration process flow.

modeling an extraction and exchange model along with a manageable centralized repository that can be used for consolidation, identity management, publication, and access management.

8.3.3 **Two Models: Persistence and Exchange**

The conclusion is that we actually need at least *two* models: one for data exchange and sharing and one for persistence. We'll use the term "repository model" for the persistent view and "exchange model" for the exchange view.

8.4 **STANDARDIZED EXCHANGE AND CONSOLIDATION MODELS**

Master data are distributed across data sets supporting numerous enterprise applications, each with its own data/object models and data life cycle processes. As Figure 8.3 shows, different data sets may capture similar information about master data objects, but there are likely to be differences in the content across both the syntactic and the semantic dimensions.

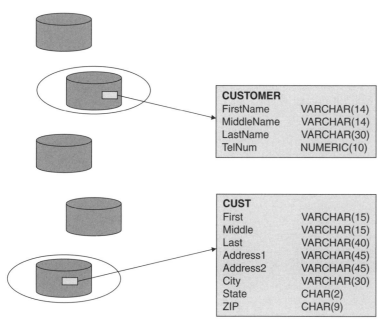

■ **FIGURE 8.3** Different metadata representing similar objects.

Syntactic differences refer to the structure of the objects, such as differences in column sizes or the specific data attributes collected within each table. In our example, consider the difference in the column lengths for the field representing a customer's last name—in one table it is 30 characters long, whereas in the other it is 40 characters long. Semantic differences refer to the underlying meaning—for example, in one data set a "customer" is a person to whom an item has shipped, whereas in another data set a "customer" is someone who has purchased an item.

The master exchange model must be able to accommodate data from all the source data sets. Subtle differences may be irrelevant out of context, but in the consolidation process, merging data sets together implies that the specific data instances in each set represent the same business concepts. Therefore, great precision in both *definition* and *structure* are necessary to ensure that the resulting master data set accurately reflects reality. The details of the source metadata are easily captured and managed in an enterprise metadata registry. This provides the basic information for the data model used for data exchange.

8.4.1 **Exchange Model**

The exchange model should be a standard representation for capturing the attributes relevant to the common business data elements to support the MDM program. This standard representation will be able to accommodate all of the data attribute types and sizes to enable information to be captured about each master object type. This scenario expects that the exchange model's set of data attributes will not prohibit the collection of any important (i.e., shared) attributes from each of the application models, and the format and structures for each attribute must support all the formats and structures used for that attribute across the many variant models.

The process for creating a canonical representation for the exchange model involves the steps shown in the following sidebar.

The resulting model for exchange can be manifested in different ways. A simple representation consists of a fixed-field table, where each field length for each attribute is as wide as the largest data element that holds values for that attribute. Other file formats might include data elements separated by special characters. More sophisticated approaches would rely on standard design schema such as XML to model data instances. Either way, the exchange representation is basically a linearized (that is, one whose relational structure is flattened

---

CREATING AN EXCHANGE MODEL CANONICAL REPRESENTATION

1. *Start with a business model.* Define an implementation-independent business model that represents the conceptual details of the shared object as a model for mapping client systems' data representations to candidate shared attributes.

2. *Enumeration of master data attributes.* This requires reviewing the different representations associated with the business requirements that suggest the components of the conceptual master data object and then listing each of the data attributes with its corresponding metadata: table, data element name(s), sizes, and so on. For example, one customer data set may maintain names and addresses, whereas another may maintain names, addresses, and telephone numbers.

3. *Resolution of master attribute structure.* Some conceptual data attributes may be represented using multiple columns, whereas some data fields may hold more than one attribute. Some attributes are managed within wide tables, whereas others are associated using relational structures. This step requires clarifying the names and definitions of the core data attributes, determining a table structure that is best suited to exchange, and documenting how the source data sets are mapped to each core attribute.

4. *Resolution of master attribute type.* At this point the structure has been defined, but the type and size of each master representation of each element still needs to be defined to hold any of the values managed within any of the source data attributes.

---

to fit within a transferable message) format of the most "liberal" size representation for each data element. This does not mean forcing all applications to be modified to meet this model, but rather adopting an exchange model that does not eliminate any valuable data from contributing to the matching and linkage necessary for integration.

8.4.2 Using Metadata to Manage Type Conversion

Metadata constraints must be employed when transforming data values into and out of the standardized format to prevent inappropriate type conversions. For example, in one system, numeric identifiers may be represented as decimal numbers, whereas in another the same identifiers may be represented as alphanumeric character strings. For the purposes of data extraction and sharing, the modeler will select one standard representation for the exchange model to characterize that identifier, and services must be provided to ensure that data values are converted into and out of that standardized format when (respectively) extracted from or published back to the client systems.

8.4.3 **Caveat: Type Downcasting**

There is one issue that requires some careful thought when looking at data models for exchange. Extracting data in one format from the contributing data sources and transforming that data into a common standardized form benefits the consolidation process, and as long as the resulting integrated data are not cycled back into application data sets, the fact that the exchange model is set to accommodate the liberal set of data values is not an issue.

The problem occurs when copying data from the exchange model back into the application data sets when the application data elements are not of a size large enough to accommodate the maximum sized values. In the example shown in Figure 8.3, the exchange model would have to allow for a length of 40 for the "Last Name" data attribute. However, the data element for LastName in the table called "CUSTOMER" only handles values of length 30. Copying a value for last name from the exchange model back into the CUSTOMER table might imply truncating part of the data value.

The risk is that the result of truncation is that the stored value is no longer the same as the perceived master data value. This could cause searches to fail, create false positive matches in the application data set, or even cause false positive matches in the master data set during the next iteration of the consolidation phase. If these risks exist, it is worth evaluating the effort to align the application data set types with the ones in the exchange model. One approach might be considered drastic but ultimately worth the effort: recasting the types in the application data stores that are of insufficient type or size into ones that are not inconsistent with the standardized model. Although this approach may appear to be invasive, it may be better to bite the bullet and upgrade insufficient models into sufficient ones instead of allowing the standardized representative model to devolve into a least-common-denominator model that caters to the weakest links in the enterprise information chain.

8.5 **CONSOLIDATION MODEL**

There may also be a master data model used for consolidating data instances that will have a logical structure that both reflects the views provided by the source data sets and provides a reasonable (perhaps even partially denormalized) relational structure that can be used as an efficient key-oriented index. This model is optimized for the consolidation process (as we will describe in Chapter 10) and may be an adaptation of the ultimate model used for persisting master data objects.

The process for designing this model is an iterative one—more careful data element definitions may impact the table structure or even suggest a different set of master data attributes. Experimentation with source data values, target data representations, and the determination of identifying values will lead to adjustments in the set of data elements to drive consolidation. Guidance from the MDM solution provider may drive the consolidation model, either because of the analysis necessary for the initial migration and subsequent inline integration or because of the underlying matching and identity resolution services that support the master consolidation process. Fortunately, many MDM solutions provide base models for common master data objects (such as customer, or product) that can be used as a starting point for the modeling process.

8.6 PERSISTENT MASTER ENTITY MODELS

Let's turn to the persistent master model. As previously discussed, a master data management initiative is intended to create a registry that uniquely enumerates all instances from a class of information objects that are relevant to a community of participants. In turn the registry becomes the focal point of application functionality for the different stages of the information object's life cycle: creation, review, modification, and retirement.

8.6.1 Supporting the Data Life Cycle

Supporting life cycle activities requires more comprehensive oversight as the expectations of the trustworthiness of the data grow and the number of participants increases. This becomes implicit in the system development life cycle for MDM, in which the quality of the managed content has to be ensured from the beginning of the project and as the sidebar that follows suggests.

Taking these points into consideration will help ensure that the models designed for master data management will be flexible enough to allow for growth while ensuring that the quality of the information is not compromised. To some extent, the modeling process is iterative, because there are interdependencies between the decisions regarding

ENSURING QUALITY MANAGED CONTENT

1. The business objectives will drive the determination of what master objects will be managed, which attributes will be included, and what level of consolidation will be expected for the master registry or repository.

2. The policies and protocols governing the extraction, consolidation, and historical management of entity information need to be addressed before any extraction, transformation, or linkage management applications are designed in order to make sure that the proper controls are integrated into the MDM solution. Realize that as a by-product of the data integration process, some policies may emerge from the ETL and data quality processes, may be applied to the master data asset, but may also be pushed further back in the processing streams to help in flagging issues early in the information streams.

3. The models to be used for consolidation must be robust enough to capture the data extracted from the participant applications as well as complete enough for the resolution of identities and consolidation into a master index.

4. The models must also support the functional components to support creating, breaking, and remediating errors in entity linkage.

architecture, decisions regarding the services to be provided, decisions regarding data standards, and decisions regarding the models. To this end, there are some concepts that are valuable to keep in mind during this iterative process.

8.6.2 **Universal Modeling Approach**

One way to do this is to develop the model in a way that provides flexibility when considering that real-world entities may play multiple roles in multiple environments yet carry identifying information relevant to the long-term business expectations associated with a master representation. One approach is to use universal model representations for common data objects that can be adapted to contain as many (or as few) attributes as required. In turn, subclassed entities can be derived from these core representations to take advantage of entity inheritance.

For example, look at an organization that, among its master data object types, has a "customer" master object and an "employee" master object. The customer object contains information about identifying

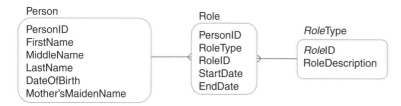

■ **FIGURE 8.4** Example of employing a universal model object.

the specific customer: first name, last name, middle initial, customer identifier, and a link to a set of contact mechanisms. The employee object contains information about identifying the specific employee: first name, last name, middle initial, employee number, and a link to a set of contact information. For the most part, in this case "customers" and "employees" are both individuals, with mostly the same degree of attribution.

If the conceptual representations for customer and employee are basically the same (with some minor adjustments), it is reasonable to consider a common representation for "individual" and then take one of two approaches. The first is to develop subclasses for both "customer" and "employee" that are derived from the base "individual" entity, except both are enhanced with their own unique attributes. The second approach is to use the core underlying model for each individual and augment that model with their specific roles. This allows for inheritance of shared characteristics within the model.

In Figure 8.4, we see the use of a core model object for a *person*, which is then associated with one or more *roles*. For our example, we would have a *customer* role type and an *employee* role type. The beauty of this approach is that it enables identity resolution centered on the individual in a way that is isolated from the context in which the entity appears. An employee may also be a customer and may appear in both data sets, providing two sources of identifying values for the individual. The universal modeling approach provides the flexibility to hierarchically segregate different levels of description relevant to the end-client application as opposed to the attributes for MDM.

8.6.3 **Data Life Cycle**

The persistent model must consistently support, within the master environment, the business operations that the client applications are expected to perform. If the master model is solely used as a lookup table for identity resolution and materialization of a master record on demand, then the requirements will be different than if the master data system is used as the sole resource for both operational and analytical applications.

Data life cycle events will be documented as a result of the process modeling. The typical CRUD (create, read, update, and delete) actions will be determined as a by-product of use cases, and the persistent model must reflect the core services supporting the defined requirements.

8.7 **MASTER RELATIONAL MODEL**

The universal modeling approach also paves the way for capturing the relationships that exist across the different master entity hierarchies, both through the inheritance chain and the entity landscape.

8.7.1 **Process Drives Relationships**

There are three kinds of relationships we want to capture:

Reflexive relationships. The existence of data instances in the same or different data sets referring to the same real-world object. Our example of an individual who plays both an employee role and a customer role demonstrates this type of relationship.

Process relationships. The connectivity associated with the business processes as reflected in the process model, use cases, and the business rules. Assertions regarding the way the business operates reveal the types of relationships at a high level (such as "customer buys products"), and this will be captured in the enterprise master model, especially in the context of transactional operations.

Analytical relationships. The connectivity that is established as a result of analyzing the data. An example might look at the set of customers and the set of suppliers and see that one of the customers works for one of the suppliers.

In essence, the "relationships" described here actually document business policies and could be characterized as business metadata to be captured in the metadata management system (as described in Chapter 6).

8.7.2 **Documenting and Verifying Relationships**

A process for verifying the modeled relationships is valuable, because it provides some level of confidence that both the explicit relationships and any discovered relationships are captured within the master models.

From a high-level perspective, this can be done by reviewing the business process model and the metadata repository for data accesses, because the structure of any objects that are touched by more than one activity should be captured within the master models.

8.7.3 **Expanding the Model**

Lastly, there are two scenarios in which the master models are subject to review and change. The first is when a client application must be modified to reflect changes in the dependent business processes, and this would require modifications to its underlying model. The second, which may be more likely, occurs when a new application or data set is to be incorporated into the master data environment.

The first scenario involves augmenting the existing business process models with the tasks and data access patterns associated with the inclusion of the new application capabilities. The second scenario may also demand revision of the business process model, except when one is simply integrating a data set that is unattached to a specific application. In both cases, there are situations in which the models will be expanded. One example is if there is a benefit to the set of participating client applications for including additional data attributes. Another example is if the inclusion of a new data set creates a situation in which the values in the existing set of identifying attributes no longer provide unique identification, which would drive the creation of a new set of identifying attributes. A third example involves data attributes whose types and sizes cannot be accommodated within the existing models, necessitating a modification.

8.8 **SUMMARY**

The creation of data models to accommodate the master data integration and management processes requires a combination of the skills a data modeler has acquired and the understanding of the business process requirements expected during a transition to a master data environment. The major issues to contend with for data modeling involve the following:

- Considering the flow and exchange of master data objects through the enterprise
- The iterative review of the business process model and discovered metadata to determine the identifying data attributes for the master data

- The creation of a linearized data model for data extraction and exchange
- The creation of a data model for consolidation
- The creation of a core master data model for persistent storage of master data

It is wise to consider using a universal modeling approach, and an excellent resource for universal data models is Len Silverston's books (*The Data Model Resource Book*, volumes 1 and 2). The books provide a library of common data models that are excellent as starting points for developing your own internal master data object models.

MDM Paradigms and Architectures

9.1 **INTRODUCTION**

The value of master data lies in the ability for multiple business applications to access a trusted data asset that can serve up the unique representation of any critical entity relevant within the organization. However, while we have focused on the concepts of a virtual means for managing that unique representation (the "what" of MDM), we have been relatively careful so far in asserting an architectural framework for implementing both the logical and the physical structure for managing master data (the "how" of MDM). This caution is driven by the challenges of not just designing and building the master data environment and its service layers, but also of corralling support from all potential stakeholders, determining the road map for implementation, and, most critically, applying migration to use the master data environment.

In fact, many organizations have already seen large-scale technical projects (e.g., Customer Relationship Management, data warehouses) that drain budgets, take longer than expected to bring into production, and do not live up to their expectations, often because the resulting technical solution does not appropriately address the business problems. To avoid this trap, it is useful to understand the ways that application architectures adapt to master data, to assess the specific application's requirements, and to characterize the usage paradigms. In turn, this will drive the determination of the operational service-level requirements for data availability and synchronization that will dictate the specifics of the underlying architecture.

In this chapter, we look at typical master data management usage scenarios as well as the conceptual architectural paradigms. We then look at the variable aspects of the architectural paradigms in the context of the usage scenarios and enumerate the criteria that can be used to determine the architectural framework that best suits the business needs.

9.2 **MDM USAGE SCENARIOS**

The transition to using a master data environment will not hinge on an "all or nothing" approach; rather it will focus on particular usage situations or scenarios, and the services and architectures suitable to one scenario may not necessarily be the best suited to another scenario. Adapting MDM techniques to qualify data used for analytical purposes within a data warehouse or other business intelligence framework may inspire different needs than an MDM system designed to completely replace all transaction operations within the enterprise.

In Chapter 1, we started to look at some of the business benefits of MDM, such as comprehensive customer knowledge, consistent and accurate reporting, improved risk management, improved decision making, regulatory compliance, quicker results, and improved productivity, among others. A review of this list points out that the use of master data spans both the analytical and the operational contexts, and this is accurately reflected in the categorization of usage scenarios to which MDM is applied.

It is important to recognize that master data objects flow into the master environment through different work streams. However, business applications treat their use of what will become master data in ways that are particular to the business processes they support, and migrating to MDM should not impact the way those applications work. Therefore, although we anticipate that our operational processes will directly manipulate master data as those applications are linked into the master framework, there will always be a need for direct processes for creating, acquiring, importing, and maintaining master data. Reviewing the ways that data is brought into the master environment and then how it is used downstream provides input into the selection of underlying architectures and service models.

9.2.1 **Reference Information Management**

In this usage scenario, the focus is on the importation of data into the master data environment and the ways that the data is enhanced and modified to support the dependent downstream applications. The expectation is that as data is incorporated into the master environment, it is then available for "publication" to client applications, which in turn may provide feeds back into the master repository.

For example, consider a catalog merchant that resells product lines from numerous product suppliers. The merchant's catalog is actually composed of entries imported from the catalogs presented by each of the suppliers. The objective in this reference information usage scenario is to create the master catalog to be presented to the ultimate customers by combining the product information from the supplier catalogs. The challenges associated with this example are largely driven by unique identification: the same products may be provided by more than one supplier, whereas different suppliers may use the same product identifiers for different products within their own catalogs. The desired outcome is the creation of a master catalog that allows the merchant to successfully complete its order-to-cash business process.

In this scenario, data enter the master repository from multiple streams, both automated and manual, and the concentration is on ensuring the quality of the data on entry. Activities that may be performed within this scenario include the following:

Creation. Creating master records directly. This is an entry point for data analysts to input new data into the master repository, such as modifying enterprise metadata (definitions, reference tables, value formats) or introducing new master records into an existing master table (e.g., customer or product records).

Import. Preparing and migrating data sets. This allows the data analysts to convert existing records from suitable data sources into a table format that is acceptable for entry into the master environment. This incorporates the conversion process that assesses the mapping between the original source and the target model and determines what data values need to be input and integrated with the master environment. The consolidation process is discussed in detail in Chapter 10.

Categorization. Arranging the ways that master objects are organized. Objects are grouped based on their attributes, and this process allows the data analyst to specify the groupings along with their related metadata and taxonomies, as well as defining the rules by which records are grouped into their categories. For example, products are categorized in different ways, depending on their type, use, engineering standards, target audience, size, and so on.

Classification. Directly specifying the class to which a master record will be assigned. The data steward can employ the rules for categorization to each record and verify the assignment into the proper classes.

Quality validation. Ensuring that the data meet defined validity constraints. Based on data quality and validity rules managed within the metadata repository, both newly created master records and modifications to existing records are monitored to filter invalid states before committing the value to the master repository.

Modification. Directly adjusting master records. Changes to master data (e.g., customer address change, update to product characteristics) may be made. In addition, after being alerted to a flaw in the data, the data steward may modify the record to "correct" it or otherwise bring it into alignment with defined business data quality expectations.

Retirement/removal. Records that are no longer active may be assigned an inactive or retired status, or the record may be removed from the data set. This may also be done as part of a stewardship process to adjust a situation in which two records referring to the same object were not resolved into a single record and must be manually consolidated, with one record surviving and the other removed.

Synchronization. Managing currency between the master repository and replicas. In environments where applications still access their own data sets that are periodically copied back and synchronized with the master, the data steward may manually synchronize data values directly within the master environment.

9.2.2 **Operational Usage**

In contrast to the reference information scenario, some organizations endeavor to ultimately supplement all application data systems with the use of the master environment. This means that operational systems must execute their transactions against the master data environment instead of their own data systems, and as these transactional business applications migrate to relying on the master environment as the authoritative data resource, they will consume and produce master data as a by-product of their processing streams.

For example, an organization may want to consolidate its views of all customer transactions across multiple product lines to enable real-time up-sell and cross-sell recommendations. This desire translates into a need for two aspects of master data management: managing the results of customer analytics as master profile data and real-time monitoring of all customer transactions (including purchases, returns, and all inbound call center activities). Each customer transaction may trigger some event that requires action within a specified time period, and all results must be logged to the master repository in case adjustments to customer profile models must be made.

Some of the activities in this usage scenario are similar to those in Section 9.2.1, but here it is more likely to be an automated application facilitating the interaction between the business process and the master repository. Some activities include the following:

Creation. The direct creation of master records. This is an entry point for both data stewards and business applications to stream new data into the master repository as a result of executing defined business workflows.

Access. The process of searching the master repository. This activity is likely to be initiated frequently, especially by automated systems validating a customer's credentials using identity resolution techniques, classifying and searching for similar matches for product records, or generally materializing a master view of any identified entity for programmatic manipulation.

Quality validation. The process of ensuring data quality business rules. Defined quality characteristics based on business expectations can be engineered into corresponding business data rules to be applied at various stages of the information processing streams. Quality validation may be as simple as verifying conformance of a data element's value within a defined data domain to more complex consistency rules involving attributes of different master objects.

Access control. Monitoring individual and application access. As we describe in Chapter 6 on metadata, access to specific master objects can be limited via assignment of roles, even at a level as granular as particular attributes.

Publication and sharing. Making the master view available to client applications. In this scenario, there may be an expectation that as a transaction is committed, its results are made available to all other client applications. In reality, there may be design constraints that may drive the definition of service level agreements regarding the timeliness associated with publication of modifications to the master data asset.

Modification. Making changes to master data. In the transactional scenario, it is clear that master records will be modified. Coordinating multiple accesses (reads *and* writes) by different client applications is a must and should be managed within the master data service layer.

Synchronization. Managing coherence internally to the master repository. In this situation, many applications are touching the master repository in both querying and transactional modes, introducing the potential for consistency issues between reads and writes whose serialization has traditionally been managed within the database systems themselves. The approach to synchronizing any kinds of accesses to master data becomes a key activity to ensure a consistent view, and we address this issue in greater detail in Chapter 11.

Transactional data stewardship. Direct interaction of data stewards with data issues as they occur within the operational environment.

Addressing data issues in real time supports operational demands by removing barriers to execution, and combining hands-on stewardship with the underlying master environment will lead to a better understanding of the ways that business rules can be incorporated to automatically mitigate issues when possible and highlight data issues when a data steward is necessary.

9.2.3 **Analytical Usage**

Analytical applications can interact with master data two ways: as the dimensional data supporting data warehousing and business intelligence and for embedded analytics for inline decision support. One of the consistent challenges of data warehousing is a combination of the need to do the following:

- Cleanse data supplied to the warehouse to establish trustworthiness for downstream reporting and analysis
- Manage the issues resulting from the desire to maintain consistency with upstream systems

Analytical applications are more likely to use rather than create master data, but these applications also must be able to contribute information to the master repository that can be derived as a result of analytical models. For example, customer data may be managed within a master model, but a customer profiling application may analyze customer transaction data to classify customers into threat profile categories. These profile categories, in turn, can be captured as master data objects for use by other analytical applications (fraud protection, bank secrecy act compliance, etc.) in an embedded or inlined manner. In other words, integrating the results of analytics within the master data environment supplements analytical applications with real-time characteristics.

Aside from the activities mentioned in previous sections, some typical activities within the analytical usage scenario include the following:

Access. The process of searching and extracting data from the master repository. This activity is invoked as part of the process for populating the analytical subsystems (e.g., the fact tables in a data warehouse).

Creation. The creation of master records. This may represent the processes invoked as a result of analytics so that the profiles and enhancements can be integrated as master data. Recognize that in the analytical scenario, the creation of master data is a less frequent activity.

Notification. Forwarding information to business end clients. Embedded analytical engines employ master data, and when significant events are generated, the corresponding master data are composed with the results of the analytics (customer profiles, product classifications, etc.) to inform the end client about actions to be taken.

Classification. Applying analytics to determine the class to which a master record will be assigned. Rules for classification and categorization are applied to each record, and data stewards can verify that the records were assigned to the proper classes.

Validation. Ensuring that the data meet defined validity constraints. Based on data quality and validity rules managed within the metadata repository, both newly created master records and modifications to existing records are monitored to filter invalid states before committing the value to the master repository.

Modification. The direct adjustment of master records. Similarly to the reference data scenario, changes to master data (e.g., customer address change, update to product characteristics) may be made. Data stewards may modify the record to bring it into alignment with defined business data quality expectations.

9.3 **MDM ARCHITECTURAL PARADIGMS**

All MDM architectures are intended to support transparent, shared access to a unique representation of master data, even if the situations for use differ. Therefore, all architecture paradigms share the fundamental characteristics of master data access, namely fostered via a service layer that resolves identities based on matching the core identifying data attributes used to distinguish one instance from all others.

However, there will be varying requirements for systems supporting different usage situations. For example, with an MDM system supporting the reference data scenario, the applications that are the sources of master data might operate at their own pace, creating records that will (at some point) be recognized as master data. If the reference MDM environment is intended to provide a common "system of record" that is not intricately integrated into real-time operation, the actual data comprising the "master record" may still be managed by the application systems, using the MDM environment solely as an index for searching and identification.

In this case, the identifying attributes can be rationalized on a periodic basis, but there is no need for real-time synchronization.

An architecture to support this approach may require a master model that manages enough identifying information to provide the search/index/identification capabilities, as long as the remainder of the master data attributes can be composed via pointers from that master index.

In the fully operational usage scenario, all interactions and transactions are applied to the master version, and the consistency requirements must be enforced at a strict level. As opposed to the reference scenario, this situation is much less tolerant of replicating master data and suggests a single master repository accessed only through a service layer that manages serialization and synchronization.

The analytical scenario presents less stringent requirements for control over access. Much of the data that populates the "master record" are derived from source application data systems, but only data necessary for analysis might be required in the master repository. Because master records are created less frequently, there are fewer stringent synchronization and consistency constraints. In this environment, there may be some combination of a master index that is augmented with the extra attributes supporting real-time analytics or embedded monitoring and reporting. These concepts resolve into three basic architectural approaches for managing master data (see sidebar).

ARCHITECTURAL APPROACHES TO MANAGE MASTER DATA

- A virtual master data index, frequently implemented using a *registry*
- A fully consolidated master data set for synchronized access, implemented as a *transaction hub*
- Some combination of these approaches in a *hybrid* model

9.3.1 **Virtual/Registry**

In a registry-style architecture (as shown in Figure 9.1), a thin master data index is used that captures the minimal set of identifying attribute values. Any presented record's identifying values are indexed by identity search and match routines (which are discussed in greater detail in Chapter 10). The master index provided in a registry model contains pointers from each uniquely identified entity to the source systems maintaining the balance of the master data attributes (see Figure 9.1). Accessing the "master record" essentially involves the following tasks:

- Searching through the master registry index to find candidate matches
- Evaluating similarity of candidates to the sought-after record to determine a close match
- Once a match has been found, accessing the registry entries for that entity to retrieve the pointers into the application data systems containing records for the found entity
- Accessing the application data systems to retrieve the collection of records associated with the entity
- Applying a set of survivorship rules to materialize a consolidated master record

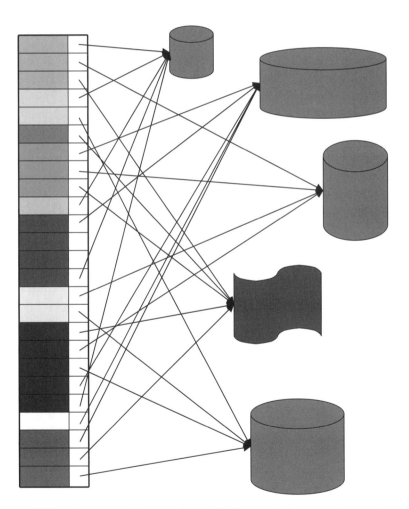

■ **FIGURE 9.1** A registry-style architecture provides a thin index that maps to data instances across the enterprise.

The basic characteristics of the registry style of MDM are as follows:

- A thin table is indexed by identifying attributes associated with each unique entity.
- Each represented entity is located in the registry's index by matching values of identifying attributes.
- The registry's index maps from each unique entity reference to one or more source data locations.

The following are some assumptions regarding the registry style:

- Data items forwarded into the master repository are linked to application data in a silo repository as a result of existing processing streams.
- All input records are cleansed and enhanced before persistence.
- The registry includes only attributes that contain the identifying information required to disambiguate entities.
- There is a unique instance within the registry for each master entity, and only identifying information is maintained within the master record.
- The persistent copies for all attribute values are maintained in (one or more) application data systems.
- Survivorship rules on consolidation are applied at time of data access, not time of data registration.

9.3.2 **Transaction Hub**

Simply put, a transaction hub (see Figure 9.2) is a single repository used to manage all aspects of master data. No data items are published out to application systems, and because there is only one copy, all applications are modified to interact directly with the hub. Applications invoke access services to interact with the data system managed within the hub, and all data life cycle events are facilitated via services, including creation, modification, access, and retirement.

Characteristics of the transaction hub include the following:

- All attributes are managed within the master repository.
- All access to master data is managed through the services layer.
- All aspects of the data instance life cycle are managed through transaction interfaces deployed within the services layer.
- The transaction hub functions as the only version of the data within the organization.

The following are some assumptions that can be made regarding the development of a repository-based hub:

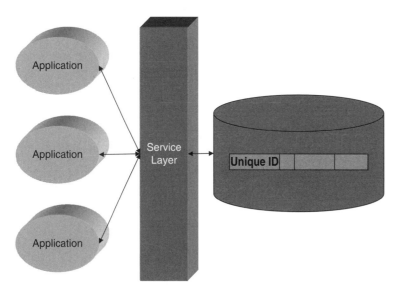

■ **FIGURE 9.2** All accesses to a transaction hub are facilitated via a service layer.

- All input records from original sources are consolidated during an initial phase into a single "golden" repository.
- There is a unique record for each master entity.
- Data quality techniques (parsing, standardization, normalization, cleansing) are applied to all input records.
- Identifying information includes attributes required to disambiguate entities.
- Data quality rules and enhancements are applied to each attribute of any newly created master record.

9.3.3 **Hybrid/Centralized Master**

A happy medium in contrast to both the "thin" model of the registry and the "thick" transaction hub provides a single model to manage the identifying attributes (to serve as the master data index) as well as common data attributes consolidated from the application data sets. In this approach, shown in Figure 9.3, a set of core attributes associated with each master data model is defined and managed within a single master system. The centralized master repository is the source for managing these core master data objects, which are subsequently published out to the application systems. In essence, the centralized master establishes the standard representation for each entity. Within each

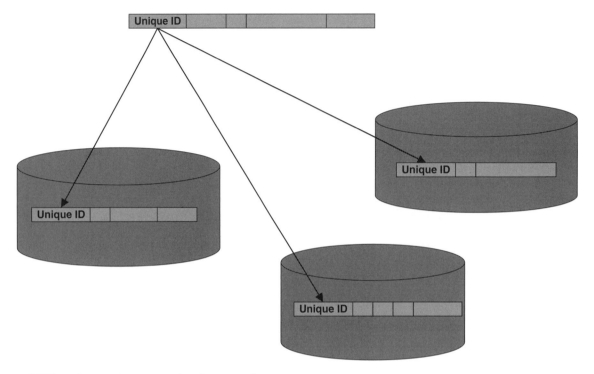

■ **FIGURE 9.3** Common attributes are managed together in a mapped master.

dependent system, application-specific attributes are managed locally but are linked back to the master instance via a shared global primary key.

The integrated view of common attributes in the master repository provides the "source of truth," with data elements absorbed into the master from the distributed business applications' local copies. In this style, new data instances may be created in each application, but those newly created records must be synchronized with the central system. Yet if the business applications continue to operate on their own local copies of data also managed in the master, there is no assurance that the values stored in the master repository are as current as those values in application data sets. Therefore, the hybrid or centralized approach is reasonable for environments that require harmonized views of unique master objects but do not require a high degree of synchronization across the application architecture.

Some basic characteristics of the hybrid or centralized master architecture include the following:

- Common attributes are managed within a central repository.
- Applications maintain their own full local copies of the master data.
- Instances in the centralized master are the standardized or harmonized representations, and their values are published out to the copies or replicas managed by each of the client applications.
- A unique identifier is used to map from the instance in the master repository to the replicas or instances stored locally by each application.
- Application-specific attributes are managed by the application's data system.
- Consolidation of shared attribute values is performed on a periodic basis.
- Rules may be applied when applications modify their local copies of shared master attributes to notify the master or other participating applications of the change.

9.4 **IMPLEMENTATION SPECTRUM**

There may be differences between the ways that each of these architectures supports business process requirements, and that may suggest that the different architecture styles are particularly distinct in terms of design and implementation. In fact, a closer examination of the three approaches reveals that the styles represent points along a spectrum of design that ranges from thin index to fat repository. All of the approaches must maintain a registry of unique entities that is indexed and searchable by the set of identifying attributes, and each maintains a master version of master attribute values for each unique entity.

As Figure 9.4 shows, the styles are aligned along a spectrum that is largely dependent on three dimensions:

1. The number of attributes maintained within the master data system
2. The degree of consolidation applied as data are brought into the master repository
3. How tightly coupled applications are to the data persisted in the master data environment

At one end of the spectrum, the registry, which maintains only identifying attributes, is suited to those application environments that are loosely coupled and where the drivers for MDM are based more on harmonization of the unique representation of master objects on demand. The transaction hub, at the other end of the spectrum, is well suited to environments requiring tight coupling of application

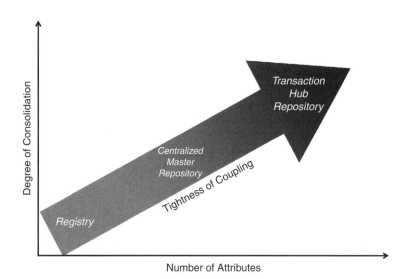

■ **FIGURE 9.4** MDM architectural styles along a spectrum.

interaction and a high degree of data currency and synchronization. The central repository or hybrid approach can lie anywhere between these two ends, and the architecture can be adjusted in relation to the business requirements as necessary; it can be adjusted to the limitations of each application as well. Of course, these are not the only variables on which the styles are dependent; the complexity of the service layer, access mechanics, and performance also add to the reckoning, as well as other aspects that have been covered in this book.

9.5 APPLICATIONS IMPACTS AND ARCHITECTURE SELECTION

To some extent, this realization simplifies some of the considerations regarding selection of an underlying architecture. Instead of assessing the organization's business needs against three apparently "static" designs, one may look at the relative needs associated with these variables and use that assessment as selection criteria for the underlying MDM architecture. As an example, a template like the one shown in Figure 9.5 can be used to score the requirements associated with the selection criteria. The scores can be weighted based on identified key aspects, and the resulting assessment can be gauged to determine a reasonable point along the implementation spectrum that will support the MDM requirements.

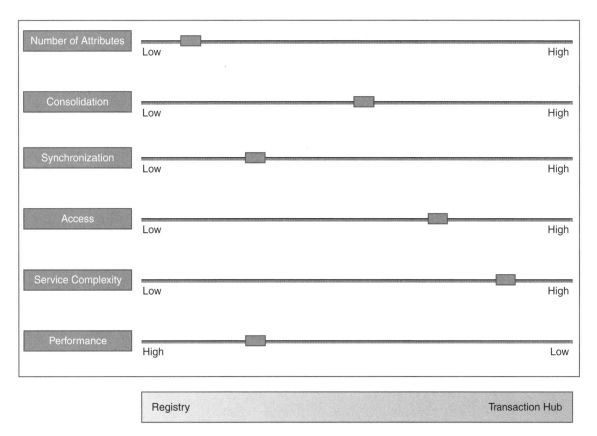

■ **FIGURE 9.5** Using the requirements variables as selection criteria.

This template can be adjusted depending on which characteristics emerge as most critical. Variables can be added or removed, and corresponding weights can be assigned based on each variable's relative importance.

9.5.1 **Number of Master Attributes**

The first question to ask focuses on the number of data attributes expected to be managed as master data. Depending on the expected business process uses, the master index may be used solely for unique identification, in which case the number of master attributes may be limited to the identifying attributes. Alternatively, if the master repository is used as a shared reference table, there may be an expectation that as soon as the appropriate entry in the registry is found, all other attributes are immediately available, suggesting that there be an expanded number of attributes. Another consideration is that there may be a limited set of shared attributes, even though each system may have a lot of attributes that it alone uses. In this case, you may decide to limit the number of attributes to only the shared ones.

9.5.2 **Consolidation**

The requirement for data consolidation depends on two aspects: the number of data sources that feed the master repository and the expectation for a "single view" of each master entity. From the data input perspective, with a greater number of sources to be fed into the master environment there is greater complexity in resolving the versions into the surviving data instance. From the data access perspective, one must consider whether or not there is a requirement for immediate access to all master records such as an analytics application. Immediate access to all records would require a higher degree of record consolidation, which would take place before registration in the master environment, but the alternative would allow the survivorship and consolidation to be applied on a record-by-record basis upon request. Consolidation is discussed at great length in Chapter 10.

9.5.3 **Synchronization**

As we will explore in greater detail in Chapter 11, the necessary degrees of timeliness and coherence (among other aspects of what we will refer to as "synchronization") of each application's view of master data are also critical factors in driving the decisions regarding underlying architectures. Tightly coupled environments, such as those that are intended to support transactional as well as analytical applications, may be expected to ensure that the master data, as seen from every angle, looks exactly the same. Environments intended to provide the "version of the truth" for reference data may not require that all applications be specifically aligned in their view simultaneously, as long as the values are predictably consistent within reason. In the former situation, controlling synchronization within a transaction hub may be the right answer. In the latter, a repository that is closer to the registry than the full-blown hub may suffice.

9.5.4 **Access**

This aspect is intended to convey more of the control of access rather than its universality. As mentioned in Chapter 6, master data management can be used to both consolidate and segregate information.

The creation of the master view must not bypass observing the policies associated with accessing authorization, authenticating clients, managing and controlling security, and protecting private personal information. The system designers may prefer to engineer observance of policies restricting and authorizing access to protected information into the service layer. Controlling protected access through a single point may be more suited to a hub style. On the other hand, there are environments whose use of master data sets might not necessarily be subject to any of these policies. Therefore, not every business environment necessarily has as strict a requirement for managing access rights and observing access control. The absence of requirements for controlling access enables a more flexible and open design, such as the registry approach. In general, the hub-style architecture is better suited for environments with more constrained access control requirements.

9.5.5 **Service Complexity**

A reasonable assessment of the business functionality invoked by applications should result in a list of defined business services. A review of what is necessary to implement these services in the context of MDM suggests the ways that the underlying master objects are accessed and manipulated using core component services. However, the degree of complexity associated with developing business services changes depending on whether the MDM system is deployed as a thin repository or as a heavyweight hub. For example, complex services may be better suited to a hub, because the business logic can be organized within the services and imposed on the single view instead of attempting to oversee the application of business rules across the source data systems as implemented in a registry.

9.5.6 **Performance**

Applications that access and modify their own underlying data sets are able to process independently. As designers engineer the consolidation and integration of replicated data into a master view, though, they introduce a new data dependence across the enterprise application framework. An MDM program with a single consolidated data set suddenly becomes a bottleneck, as accesses from multiple applications must be serialized to ensure consistency. This bottleneck can impact performance if the access patterns force the MDM services to continually (and iteratively) lock the master view, access or modify, then release the lock. A naively implemented transaction hub may be subject to performance issues.

Of course, an application environment that does not execute many transactions touching the same master objects may not be affected by the need for transaction serialization. Even less constrained systems that use master data for reference (and not transactional) purposes may be best suited to the registry or central repository approaches.

9.6 **SUMMARY**

There has been a deliberate delay in discussing implementation architectures for master data management because deciding on a proper approach depends on an assessment of the business requirements and the way these requirements are translated into characteristic variables that impact the use, sustainability, and performance of the system. Understanding how master data are expected to be used by either human or automated business clients in the environment is the first step in determining an architecture, especially when those uses are evaluated in relation to structure.

While there are some archetypical design styles ranging from a loosely coupled, thin registry, to a tightly coupled, thick hub, these deployments reflect a spectrum of designs and deployments providing some degree of flexibility over time. Fortunately, a reasonable approach to MDM design will allow for adjustments to be made to the system as more business applications are integrated with the master data environment.

10

Data Consolidation and Integration

10.1 INTRODUCTION

Once the master data model issues have been resolved, the project reaches the point where data from the identified source data sets can be consolidated into the master environment. To develop the master repository, there are a number of considerations that must be thought out. First of all, one must always keep in mind that there are two aspects to consolidation and integration: the initial migration of data from source data and the ongoing integration of data instances created, modified, or removed from the master environment. The first aspect will be familiar to anyone involved in building a data warehouse or in any kind of data cleansing activity; the second aspect essentially moves inlined integration (which embeds consolidation tasks within operational services that are available any time new information is brought into the system) and consolidation into production systems as a way of preserving the consistency of the master data set.

So what is data integration? The most common understanding is that data integration comprises the processes for collecting data from different sources and making that data accessible to specific applications. Because data integration has largely been used for building data warehouses, it is often seen as part of collecting data for analysis, but as we see more operational data sharing activities, we can see that data integration has become a core service necessary for both analytics and operations. In this chapter, we explore the techniques employed in extracting, collecting, and merging data from various sources. The intention is to identify the component services required for creating the virtual data set that has a single instance and representation for every unique master data object and then use the data integration and consolidation services to facilitate information sharing *through* the master data asset.

USING DATA INTEGRATION TOOLS TO SHARE INFORMATION

1. *Data extraction and consolidation.* Core master data attributes are brought from the source systems into the master repository.
2. *Data federation.* Complete master records are materialized on demand from the participating data sources.
3. *Data propagation.* Master data are synchronized and shared with (or "exported to") participating applications.

10.2 INFORMATION SHARING

The approaches to information sharing via an MDM system differ based on application business requirements, especially in the areas of enterprise data consistency, data currency and synchronization, and data availability and latency. Because a successful MDM initiative is driven by information sharing, as data is consolidated into the repository, the participating applications will derive the benefit of using master data. Information is shared using data integration tools in three ways, as shown in the sidebar.

10.2.1 Extraction and Consolidation

One significant responsibility of data integration services is the ability to essentially extract the critical information from different sources and ensure that a consolidated view is engineered into the target architecture. Data extraction presupposes that the technology is able to access data in a variety of source applications as well as being able to select and extract data instance sets into a format that is suitable for exchange. Essentially, the capability involves gaining access to the right data sources at the right times to facilitate ongoing information exchange; consequently, data integration products are designed to seamlessly incorporate the following elements:

Data transformation. Between the time that the data instances are extracted from the data source and delivered to the target location, data rules may be triggered to transform the data into a format that is acceptable to the target architecture. These rules may be engineered directly within the data integration tool or may be alternate technologies embedded within the tool.

Data monitoring. A different aspect of applying business rules is the ability to introduce filters to monitor the conformance of the data to business expectations (such as data quality) as it moves from one location to another. The monitoring capability provides a way to incorporate the

types of data rules both discovered and defined during the data profiling phase to proactively validate data and distinguish records that
conform to defined data quality expectations and those that do not,
providing measurements for the ongoing auditing necessary for data
stewardship and governance.

Data consolidation. As data instances from different sources are brought
together, the integration tools use the parsing, standardization, harmonization, and matching capabilities of the data quality technologies to
consolidate data into unique records in the master data model.

Each of these capabilities contributes to the creation and consistency
of the master repository. In those MDM programs that are put in place
either as a single source of truth for new applications or as a master
index for preventing data instance duplication, the extraction, transformation, and consolidation can be applied at both an acute level
(i.e., at the point that each data source is introduced into the environment) and on an operational level (i.e., on a continuous basis, applied
to a feed from the data source).

10.2.2 **Standardization and Publication Services**

One might consider data integration from a services-oriented perspective. In this approach, we don't think about extraction and transformation but rather view each source data system "publishing" its data to
other service consumers. That service would take the data from internal,
private persistence, transform it to the standardized exchange format,
and then make it available for consumers. In this approach, transformations are handled within the source system's service layer, and no
other application would need to be aware of how data instances had
to be manipulated or transformed into the standardized form.

The benefit is that if all systems publish data into a standard schema,
using standard semantics, this approach eliminates the need for a
subsequent harmonization stage for master data objects. That way,
the work is done at the end points and the workload is shared at the
points where it can most easily be enforced close to the point of capture instead of waiting for the MDM layer that is consuming that data
to carry that performance load.

10.2.3 **Data Federation**

Although the holy grail of MDM is a single master data source completely synchronized with all enterprise applications, MDM can be
created by combining core identifying data attributes along with

associated relevant data attributes into a master repository, as well as an indexing capability that acts as a registry for any additional data that is distributed across the enterprise. In some cases, though, only demographic identifying data is stored within the master repository, with the true master record essentially materialized as a compendium of attributes drawn from various sources indexed through that master registry. In essence, accessing the master repository requires the ability to decompose the access request into its component queries and assemble the results into the master view.

This type of federated information model is often serviced via Enterprise Application Integration (EAI) or Enterprise Information Integration (EII) styles of data integration tools. This capability is important in MDM systems built on a registry framework or using any framework that does not maintain all attributes in the repository for materializing views on demand. This style of master data record materialization relies on the existence of a unique identifier with a master registry that carries both core identifying information and an index to locations across the enterprise holding the best values for designated master attributes.

10.2.4 **Data Propagation**

The third component of data integration—data propagation—is applied to support the redistribution and sharing of master data back to the participating applications. Propagation may be explicit, with replicated, read-only copies made available to specific applications, may be deployed through replication with full read/write access that is subsequently consolidated, or may be incorporated more strategically using a service-oriented approach. MDM applications that employ the replication approach will push data from the master repository to one or more replication locations or servers, either synchronously or asynchronously, using guaranteed delivery data exchange. Again, EAI products are suitable to this aspect of data integration.

The alternate approach involves the creation of a service layer on top of the master repository to supplement each application's master data requirements. At one extreme, the master data is used as a way to ensure against the creation of duplicate data. At the other extreme, the applications that participate in the MDM program yield their reliance on their own version of the data and instead completely rely on the data that have been absorbed into the master repository. This range of capabilities requires that the access (both request and delivery) be provided via services, and that in turn depends on the propagation of data out of the repository and delivery to the applications.

10.3 **IDENTIFYING INFORMATION**

As we discussed in Chapter 8, every record that will be incorporated into a master repository or registry must be uniquely identifiable. Within every master data model, some set of data attribute values can be combined to provide a candidate key that is used to distinguish each record from every other. We have referred to these underlying data attributes as the "identifying attributes," and the specific values are "identifying information." Chapter 8 provided a method for determining identifying attributes, and at the point of developing the integration framework, we employ those identifying attributes and their values to develop the master registry.

10.3.1 **Indexing Identifying Values**

No matter which architectural approach is taken for assembling the underlying MDM system, there must be an identification service that is queried whenever an application wants to access any master records. This service must ensure satisfaction of the uniqueness constraint that for every entity within the system there is one and only one entry, no entity is duplicated within the system, and that if the entity has not been registered within the system, the service will not locate an entry. The identification service is supported through the use of a registry of entities that is indexed using the values contained within the identifying attributes.

In simplest terms, the index maps the combination of the identifying attribute values to the master record. Therefore, whenever an application wants to access an existing master record, the identification service should take the identifying attribute values as input, locate the registration entry within the index, and locate the master record. If there is no record for the entity, there will be no entry within the index for that set of identifying values. A straightforward approach for creating this indexed registry is a simple one-to-one mapping created from the composed identifying values and a pointer to the location of the master record. This table can be indexed by sorting the composed identifying values, thereby optimizing the ability to look up any specific record.

It is also important to note that to some extent, the concept of uniqueness itself is not necessarily cast in stone. The number of attributes that essentially qualify unique identification may be greater or fewer depending on the business requirements. For example, to a catalog company, two records may represent the same person if they share a name and address, but a surgeon may require a lot more data to ensure that the person on the operating table is the one needing surgery.

In other words, the same set of records may be judged to be unique or not depending on the business client's perspective.

10.3.2 **The Challenge of Variation**

The indexed master registry of identifying values works well under one condition: that there is never a situation where there are variations in the identifying attributes for a specific entity. For example, as is displayed in Figure 10.1, many values may be assigned to an identifying attribute that might represent the same entity.

Alternatively, as is seen in Figure 10.2, it is possible that a combination of identifying values (name + "is an author") may seem to refer to the same underlying entity but in reality map to two separate individuals. Performing a search for books written by "David Loshin" will return a list of books with "David Loshin" as the author, yet there are actually two authors who have the same (relatively unusual) name!

Howard David Loshin
Howard Loshin
David Loshin
David Howard Loshin
H David Loshin
David H Loshin
David Loshing
David Losrin
David Lotion
David Loskin
David Lashin
David Lasrin
David Laskin
Mr. David Loshin
Loshin, Howard
Loshin David
D Loshin
Jill and David Loshin
Mr. Loshin
HD Loshin
The Loshin Family

■ **FIGURE 10.1** Multiple variant identifying values represent the same entity.

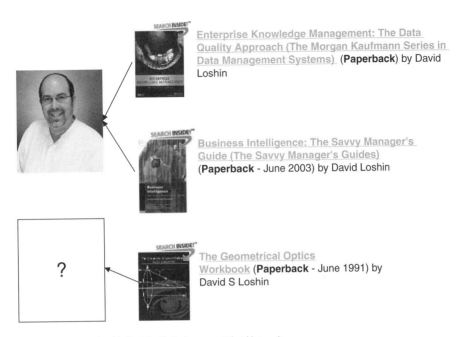

■ FIGURE 10.2 Of these three books authored by "David Loshin," only two are attributable to me!

The upshot is that there will be exceptions to the notion that every unique entity is likely to be referenced using variations of the identifying values. Consequently, the master identification service needs to incorporate a technique called *identity resolution* that finds close matches when an exact match cannot be found. Identity resolution relies on techniques that have been incorporated into data quality tools, and these sections review how these techniques are applied to enhance the master identification service.

10.4 CONSOLIDATION TECHNIQUES FOR IDENTITY RESOLUTION

Although the techniques used for data cleansing, scrubbing, and duplicate elimination have been around for a long time, their typical application was for static data cleanups, as part of preparation for migration of data into a data warehouse or migrations for application modernization. However, tools to help automate the determination of a "best record" clearly meet the needs of a master data consolidation activity as well, which is the reason that data quality tools have emerged as a critical component of MDM.

10.4.1 **Identity Resolution**

As introduced in Section 10.3, identity resolution refers to the ability to determine that two or more data representations can be resolved into one representation of a unique object. This resolution is not limited to people's names or addresses, because even though the bulk of data (and consequently, the challenge) is made up of person or business names or addresses, there is significant need for the resolution of records associated with other kinds of data, such as product names, product codes, object descriptions, reference data, and so forth.

For a given data population, identity resolution can be viewed as a two-stage process. The first stage is one of discovery and will combine data profiling activities with a manual review of data. Typically, simple probabilistic models can be evolved that then feed into the second stage, which is one of similarity scoring and matching for the purpose of record linkage. The model is then applied to a much larger population of records, often taken from different sources, to link and presumably to automatically establish (within predefined bounds) that some set of records refers to the same entity.

Usually, there are some bounds to what can be deemed an automatic match, and these bounds do not just depend on the quantification of similarity but must be defined based on the application. For example, there is a big difference between trying to determine if the same person is being mailed two catalogs instead of one and determining if the individual boarding the plane is on the terrorist list.

Identity resolution is similar, and it employs the tools and processes used for the determination of duplicates for the purpose of duplicate elimination or for value-added processes like householding. The following data quality tool functions are of greatest value to the master data integration process:

- *Parsing and standardization.* Data values are subjected to pattern analysis, and value segments are recognized and then put into a standard representation.
- *Data transformation.* Rules are applied to modify recognized errors into acceptable formats.
- *Record matching.* This process is used to evaluate "similarity" of groups of data instances to determine whether or not they refer to the same master data object.

In a number of cases, the use of data quality technology is critical to the successful implementation of a master data management program.

As the key component to determining variance in representations associated with the same real-world object, data quality techniques are used both in launching the MDM activity and in governing its continued trustworthiness.

10.4.2 **Parsing and Standardization**

The first step in identity resolution is to separate the relevant components of the identifying attribute values and organize them in a manner that is manipulated in a predictable way. However, identifying values such as names, descriptions, or locations often reflects a semistructured view, with the critical tokens being peppered throughout a character string. As was shown in Figure 10.1, "David Loshin," "Loshin, David," "H David Loshin," and "Howard Loshin" are examples of ways that a name can be represented; the important tokens, though, are **first_name**, **middle_name**, and **last_name**, each of which may (or may not) be provided within a specific name string. The important tokens are segregated using data parsing tools.

Data parsing tools enable the data analyst to define patterns that can be fed into rules engines that are used to distinguish between valid and invalid data values and to identify important tokens within a data field. When a specific pattern is matched, actions may be triggered. When a valid pattern is parsed, the separate components may be extracted into a standard representation. When an invalid pattern is recognized, the application may attempt to transform the invalid value into one that meets expectations.

Many data issues are attributable to situations where slight variance in representation of data values introduces confusion or ambiguity. For example, consider the different ways telephone numbers are formatted. Even though some have digits, some have alphabetic characters, and all use different special characters for separation, we all recognize each one as being a telephone number. However, to determine if these numbers are accurate (perhaps by comparing them to a master customer directory) or to investigate whether duplicate numbers exist when there should be only one for each supplier, the values must be parsed into their component segments (area code, exchange, and line) and then transformed into a standard format.

The human ability to recognize familiar patterns contributes to our ability to characterize variant data values belonging to the same abstract class of values; people recognize different types of telephone numbers because they conform to frequently used patterns. When an analyst can describe the format patterns that all can be used to represent a data object (e.g., Person Name, Product Description, etc.), a data quality tool can be used to parse data values that conform to any of those patterns and even transform them into a single, standardized form that will simplify the assessment, similarity analysis, and cleansing processes. Pattern-based parsing can automate the recognition and subsequent standardization of meaningful value components.

As data sources are introduced into the MDM environment, the analysts must assemble a mechanism for recognizing the supplied data formats and representations and then transform them into a canonical format in preparation for consolidation. Developed patterns are integrated with the data parsing components, with specific data transformations introduced to effect the standardization.

10.4.3 **Data Transformation**

Data standardization results from mapping the source data into a target structural representation. Customer name data provides a good example—names may be represented in thousands of semistructured forms, and a good standardizer will be able to parse the different components of a customer name (e.g., first name, middle name, last name, initials, titles, generational designations) and then rearrange those components into a canonical representation that other data services will be able to manipulate.

Data transformation is often rule based—transformations are guided by mappings of data values from their derived position and values in the source into their intended position and values in the target. Standardization is a special case of transformation, employing rules that capture context, linguistics, and idioms that have been recognized as common over time through repeated analysis by the rules analyst or tool vendor.

Interestingly, data integration tools usually provide data transformation ability and could perhaps even be used to support data quality activities. The distinction between data transformation engines and data parsing and standardization tools often lies in the knowledge base that is present in the data quality tools that drive the data quality processes.

10.4.4 **Normalization**

In some instances, there are different underlying data value domains for the same data element concept. For example, one data set describing properties may represent the number of bathrooms in terms of unites and fractions (e.g., 1½ baths), whereas another data set describing properties may represent the number of bathrooms using decimals (0.5 = ½ bath, 0.75 = a bathroom with a shower stall, and 1.0 is a bathroom with a tub and shower). A frequent occurrence is the use of code tables to represent encoded values, or different precision used for quantified values (gallons versus liters). In these cases, before the data can be used, the values must be normalized into a reference framework defined for each master data attribute. The normalization rules are applied as part of the data transformation task.

In essence, these underlying data domains constitute reference data sets, which themselves are a part of a master data environment. The difference between reference data and master data is subtle. For many purposes, reference data may be completely encompassed within the metadata stack, as discussed in Chapter 6.

10.4.5 **Matching/Linkage**

Record linkage and matching is employed in identity recognition and resolution, and it incorporates approaches used to evaluate "similarity" of records for customer data integration or master data management the same way it is used in duplicate analysis and elimination, merge/purge, householding, data enhancement, and cleansing. One of the most common data quality problems involves two sides of the same coin:

1. When there are multiple data instances that actually refer to the same real-world entity
2. Where there is the perception that a record does not exist for a real-world entity when in fact it really does

These are both instances of false negatives, where two sets of identifying data values should have matched, but did not. In the first situation, similar, yet slightly variant representations in data values may have been inadvertently introduced into the system. In the second situation, a slight variation in representation prevents the identification of an exact match of the existing record in the data set.

This is a fundamental issue for master data management, as the expectation is that the master repository will hold a unique representation for every entity. This implies that the identity resolution service can analyze and resolve object entities as a component service of all participating applications. These issues are addressed through a process called similarity analysis, in which the degree of similarity between any two records is scored, most often based on weighted approximate matching between the set of identifying attribute values between the two records. If the score is above a specific threshold, the two records are deemed to be a match and are presented to the end client as most likely to represent the same entity. It is through similarity analysis that slight variations are recognized, data values are connected, and that linkage is subsequently established.

Attempting to compare each record against all the others to provide a similarity score is not only ambitious but also time consuming and computationally intensive. Most data quality tool suites use advanced algorithms for blocking records that are more likely to contain matches into smaller sets, whereupon different approaches are taken to measure similarity. Identifying similar records within the same data set probably means that the records are duplicated and may be subjected to cleansing or elimination. Identifying similar records in different sets may indicate a link across the data sets, which facilitates cleansing, knowledge discovery, and reverse engineering—all of which contribute to master data aggregation. It is the addition of blocking, similarity scoring, and approximate matching that transforms the simplistic master index into an identity resolution service, and it is the approximate matching that truly makes the difference.

10.4.6 **Approaches to Approximate Matching**

There are two basic approaches to matching. Deterministic matching, like parsing and standardization, relies on defined patterns and rules for assigning weights and scores for determining similarity. Alternatively, probabilistic matching relies on statistical techniques for assessing the probability that any pair of records represents the same entity. Deterministic algorithms are predictable in that the patterns matched and the rules applied will always yield the same matching determination. Performance, however, is tied to the variety, number, and order of the matching rules. Deterministic matching works out of the box with relatively good performance, but it is only as good as the situations anticipated by the rules developers.

Probabilistic matching relies on the ability to take data samples for "training" purposes by looking at the expected results for a subset of the records and tuning the matcher to self-adjust based on statistical analysis. These matchers are not reliant on rules, so the results may be nondeterministic. However, because the probabilities can be refined based on experience, probabilistic matchers are able to improve their matching precision as more record sets are analyzed.

Which approach is better? In the abstract, this question may be premature when asked outside of a specific business context. There are pros and cons to both methods in terms of accuracy, precision, tunability, oversight, consistency, and performance, and before selecting either one, one must assess what the business needs are, how matching fits into the consolidation strategy, how it is used in the unique identification service, and what the service-level expectations are.

However, combining deterministic and probabilistic matching may ultimately be the best approach. By enabling some degree of deterministic rule-based control, a large part of organization-specific matching requirements can be met, and in the instances where no corporate lore exists, the probabilistic approach can supplement the balance of the needs. Of course, that can be described the opposite way as well: the probabilistic approach can hit a large part of the statistically relevant match opportunities, and the deterministic rules can be applied where there is not enough support from the probabilistic approach.

Another potential trick to improve the precision of matching is to use the discovered relationships between data instances to help in determining the likelihood that two instances refer to the same real-world entity. For example, for some reasons people may use several different names for themselves in different environments, and names are grossly inadequate in many cases. However, the knowledge derived from identity resolution coupled with known relationships will help narrow down matching.

10.4.7 The Birthday Paradox versus the Curse of Dimensionality

The ability to assign similarity scores takes the number of data attributes and their value variance into consideration. However, no matter how carefully you have selected your identifying attributes, there are two concepts that will interfere with consistently predictable identity resolution: the birthday paradox and the curse of dimensionality.

The birthday paradox is associated with the probability that a set of randomly selected individuals within a small population will share the same birthday. It turns out that when the population size is 23, there is a greater than 50% chance that two people share a birth date (month and date), and that for 57 or more people, the probability is greater than 99% that two people share a birth date. In other words, within a relatively small population, there is a great chance that two different people share the same piece of identifying information, and this suggests that even with a carefully selected set of identifying attributes, there is still a chance that enough overlap between two distinct entities will be incorrectly determined to represent the same entity, leading to false positives.

On the other hand, we can view the set of selected identifying attributes as referring to a multidimensional space and that each set of values represents a point in that space. Similarity scoring is equivalent to seeking out points in the multidimensional space that are near enough to each other to potentially represent the same true location. However, the curse of dimensionality refers to the increase in the "volume" of the search space as one adds additional dimensions. Two random points on a one-inch line are more likely to be close together than two random points in a 1-inch square, which in turn are more likely to be closer together than two random points in a 1-inch cube, and so on as more dimensions are added. The implication is that as one adds more data elements to the set of identifying attributes, the chance that two similar records will not be recognized as such increases, leading to false negatives.

So in turn we have an even greater paradox: one concept suggests adding more attributes, whereas the other suggests restricting the set of identifying attributes. The upshot is that in the presence of variant data values, there is always going to be some uncertainty regarding the identity resolution service, and it requires governance and oversight to maintain a level of predictability.

10.5 CLASSIFICATION

Most sets of data objects can be organized into smaller subsets as they reflect some commonalities, and master data objects are no exception. Master data objects can often be classified within logical hierarchies or taxonomies; sometimes these are based on predefined classes, whereas interestingly, other data sets are self-organized. For example, products may be segmented into one set of categories when manufactured, another set when transferred from the factory to the warehouse, and yet another set when presented for sale. This means that different applications will have different views of master data and suggests that entity classification enhances the ability to integrate applications with a master data repository.

Forcing a classification scheme requires a significant amount of prior knowledge of the objects, how their attribution defines the segmentation, and even the categories for classification. Many business clients can clearly articulate the taxonomies and classification criteria for the data their applications use, whereas in other environments the data can be subjected to an assessment and analysis in order to construct the hierarchies and categories.

10.5.1 **Need for Classification**

Why do master data systems use classification? The reasons have less to do with the management of the systems and more to do with the application requirements and how the data items are used. Overall, classification improves the consolidation process by providing a blocking mechanism that naturally reduces the search space when trying to locate matches for a specific query. In a way that is similar to unique identification, classification is a service that is driven by the content embedded within structured data. For example, customers may be categorized based on their geographical location, their purchasing patterns, or personal demographics such as age and gender. These classification frameworks can be applied to customer-facing applications to enable a customer service representative to provide the appropriate level of service to that customer.

Alternatively, searching and locating matching entries within a master product database may be limited when solely relying on the specific words that name or describe each object. Because different terms are used to describe similar products, the data entities may require detailed type classification based on semantics. For example, "leatherette," "faux leather," "vinyl," "pleather," "synthetic leather," and "patent leather" are all terms used to describe synthetic material that resembles leather. However, the use of any of these terms within a product description would indicate conceptual similarity among those products, but that would not necessarily be detected based on the text alone.

10.5.2 **Value of Content and Emerging Techniques**

Linking entities together based on the text tokens, such as first name or product code, restricts a master environment from most effectively organizing objects according to defined taxonomies. The classification process is intended to finesse the restriction by incorporating intelligence driven by the content and context. For example, a robust classifier can be trained to determine that the terms listed in Section 9.5.1 refer to synthetic leather, which in turn can be used to link entities together in which the descriptions have wide variance (e.g., a "vinyl pocketbook" and a "pleather purse" refer to the same type of product).

Text analysis of the semistructured or unstructured data can assign conceptual tags to text strings that delineate the text tokens that indicate their general semantics, and these semantic tags can be mapped to existing or emerging hierarchies. The result is that over time, an intelligent classification system can establish a "concept-based" connectivity between business terms, which then supports the precision of the categorization. Approaches such as text mining, text analysis, semantic analysis, meta-tagging, and probabilistic analysis all contribute to classification.

10.6 **CONSOLIDATION**

Consolidation is the result of the tasks applied to data integration. Identifying values are parsed, standardized, and normalized across the same data domains; subjected to classification and blocking schemes; and then submitted to the unique identification service to analyze duplicates, look for hierarchical groupings, locate an existing record, or determine that one does not exist. The existence of multiple instances of the same entity raises some critical questions shown in the sidebar.

The answers to the questions frame the implementation and tuning of matching strategies and the resulting consolidation algorithms. The decision to merge records into a single repository depends on a number of different inputs, and these are explored in greater detail in Chapter 9.

CRITICAL QUESTIONS ABOUT MULTIPLE INSTANCES OF ENTITIES

- What are the thresholds that indicate when matches exist?
- When are multiple instances merged into a single representation in a master repository as opposed to registration within a master registry?
- If the decision is to merge into a single record, are there any restrictions or constraints on how that merging may be done?
- At what points in the processing stream is consolidation performed?
- If merges can be done in the hub, can consuming systems consume and apply that merge event?
- Which business rules determine which values are forwarded into the master copy—in other words, what are the survivorship rules?
- If the merge occurs and is later found to be incorrect, can you undo the action?
- How do you apply transactions against the merged entity to the subsequently unmerged entities after the merge is undone?

10.6.1 **Similarity Thresholds**

When performing approximate matching, what criteria are used for distinguishing a match from a nonmatch? With exact matching, it is clear whether or not two records refer to the same object. With approximate matching, however, there is often not a definitive answer, but rather some point along a continuum indicating the degree to which two records match. Therefore, it is up to the information architect and the business clients to define the point at which two values are considered to be a match, and this is specified using a threshold score.

When identifying values are submitted to the integration service, a search is made through the master index for potential matches, and then a pair-wise comparison is performed to determine the similarity score. If that similarity score is above the threshold, it is considered a match. We can be more precise and actually define three score ranges: a high threshold above which indicates a match; a low threshold under which is considered not a match; and any scores between those thresholds, which require manual review to determine whether the identifying values should be matched or not.

This process of incorporating people into the matching process can have its benefits, especially in a learning environment. The user may begin the matching process by specifying specific thresholds, but as the process integrates user decisions about what kinds of questionable similarity values indicate matches and which do not, a learning heuristic may both automatically adjust the thresholds as well as the similarity scoring to yield a finer accuracy of similarity measurement.

10.6.2 **Survivorship**

Consolidation, to some extent, implies merging of information, and essentially there are two approaches: on the one hand, there is value in ensuring the existence of a "golden copy" of data, which suggests merging multiple instances as a cleansing process performed before persistence (if using a hub). On the other hand, different applications have different requirements for how data is used, and merging records early in the work streams may introduce inconsistencies for downstream processing, which suggests delaying the merging of information until the actual point of use. These questions help to drive the determination of the underlying architecture.

Either way, operational merging raises the concept of *survivorship*. Survivorship is the process applied when two (or more) records representing the same entity contain conflicting information to determine which record's value survives in the resulting merged record. This process must incorporate data or business rules into the consolidation process, and these rules reflect the characterization of the quality of the data sources as determined during the source data analysis described in Chapter 2, the kinds of transactions being performed, and the business client data quality expectations as discussed in Chapter 5.

Ultimately, every master data attribute depends on the data values within the corresponding source data sets identified as candidates and validated through the data requirements analysis process. The master data attribute's value is populated as directed by a source-to-target mapping based on the quality and suitability of every candidate source. Business rules delineate valid source systems, their corresponding priority, qualifying conditions, transformations, and the circumstances under which these rules are applied. These rules are applied at different locations within the processing streams depending on the business application requirements and how those requirements have directed the underlying system and service architectures.

Another key concept to remember with respect to survivorship is the retention policy for source data associated with the master view. Directed data cleansing and data value survivorship applied when each data instance is brought into the environment provides a benefit when those processes ensure the correctness of the single view at the point of entry. Yet because not all data instances imported into the system are used, cleansing them may turn out to be additional work that might not have been immediately necessary. Cleansing the data on demand would limit the work to what is needed by the business process, but it introduces complexity in managing multiple instances and history regarding when the appropriate survivorship rules should have been applied.

A hybrid idea is to apply the survivorship rules to determine its standard form, yet always maintain a record of the original (unmodified) input data. The reason is that a variation in a name or address provides extra knowledge about the master object, such as an individual's nickname or a variation in product description that may occur in other situations. Reducing each occurrence of a variation into a single form removes knowledge associated with potential aliased identifying data, which ultimately reduces your global knowledge of the underlying object. But if you can determine that the input data is just variations of one (or more) records that are already known, storing newly acquired versions linked to the cleansed form will provide greater knowledge moving forward, as well as enabling traceability.

10.6.3 **Integration Errors**

We have already introduced the concepts of the two types of errors that may be encountered during data integration. The first type of error is called a false positive, and it occurs when two data instances representing two distinct real-life entities are incorrectly assumed to refer to the same entity and are inadvertently merged into a single master representation. False positives violate the uniqueness constraint that a master representation exists for every unique entity. The second type of error is called a false negative, and it occurs when two data instances representing the same real-world entity are not determined to match, with the possibility of creating a duplicate master representation. False negatives violate the uniqueness constraint that there is one and only one master representation for every unique entity.

Despite the program's best laid plans, it is likely that a number of both types of errors will occur during the initial migration of data into the master repository, as additional data sets are merged in and as data come into the master environment from applications in production. Preparing for this eventuality is an important task:

- Determine the risks and impacts associated with both types of errors and raise the level of awareness appropriately. For example, false negatives in a marketing campaign may lead to a prospective customer being contacted more than once, whereas a false negative for a terrorist screening may have a more devastating impact. False positives in product information management may lead to confused inventory management in some cases, whereas in other cases they may lead to missed opportunities for responding to customer requests for proposals.

- Devise an impact assessment and resolution scheme. Provide a process for separating the unique identities from the merged instance upon identification of a false positive, in which two entities are incorrectly merged, and determine the distinguishing factors that can be reincorporated into the identifying attribute set, if necessary. Likewise, provide a means for resolving duplicated data instances and determining what prevented those two instances from being identified as the same entity.

These tasks both suggest maintaining historical information about the way that the identity resolution process was applied, what actions were taken, and ways to unravel these actions when either false positives or false negatives are identified.

10.6.4 **Batch versus Inline**

There are two operational paradigms for data consolidation: batch and inline. The batch approach collects static views of a number of data sets and imports them into a single location (such as a staging area or loaded into a target database), and then the combined set of data instances is subjected to the consolidation tasks of parsing, standardization, blocking, and matching, as described in Section 10.4. The inline approach embeds the consolidation tasks within operational services that are available at any time new information is brought into the system. Inlined consolidation compares every new data instance with the existing master registry to determine if an equivalent instance already exists within the environment. In this approach, newly acquired data instances are parsed and standardized in preparation for immediate comparison against the versions managed within the master registry, and any necessary modifications, corrections, or updates are applied as the new instance either is matched against existing data or is identified as an entity that has not yet been seen.

The approaches taken depend on the selected base architecture and the application requirements for synchronization and for consistency. Batch consolidation is often applied as part of the migration process to accumulate the data from across systems that are being folded into a master environment. The batch processing allows for the standardization of the collected records to seek out unique entities and resolve any duplicates into a single identity. Inlined consolidation is the approach used in operations mode to ensure that as data come into the environment, they are directly synchronized with the master.

10.6.5 **History and Lineage**

Knowing that both false positives and false negatives will occur directs the inclusion of a means to roll back modifications to master objects on determination that an error has occurred. The most obvious way to enable this capability is to maintain a full history associated with every master data value. In other words, every time a modification is made to a value in a master record, the system must log the change that was made, the source of the modification (e.g., the data source and set of rules triggered to modify the value), and the date and time that the modification was made. Using this information, when the existence of an error is detected, a lineage service can traverse the historical record for any master data object to determine at which point a change was made that introduced the error.

Addressing the error is more complicated, because not only does the error need to be resolved through a data value rollback to the point in time that the error was introduced, but any additional modifications dependent on that flawed master record must also be identified and rolled back. The most comprehensive lineage framework will allow for backtracking as well as forward tracking from the rollback point to seek out and resolve any possible errors that the identified flaw may have triggered. However, the forward tracking may be overkill if the business requirements do not insist on complete consistency—in this type of situation, the only relevant errors are the ones that prevent business tasks from successfully completing; proactively addressing potential issues may not be necessary until the impacted records are actually used.

10.7 ADDITIONAL CONSIDERATIONS

The process of data integration solves a technical challenge to consolidate data into the master repository, but there are other considerations that may impact the process from a nontechnical aspect, especially when it comes to information rights: ownership, usage, access, and so on. Within these areas, questions regarding *how* the master data asset is (or may be) used to intersect with those questioning *whether* the data can be used within specific contexts. Here we explore some straightforward examples where policies overrule use.

10.7.1 Data Ownership and Rights of Consolidation

The appeal of mastering disparate data sets that represent the same conceptual data objects often leads to an enthusiasm for consolidation in which individuals may neglect to validate that data ownership issues will not impede the program. In fact, many organizations use data sourced from external parties to conduct their business operations, and that external data may appear to suitably match the same business data objects that are to be consolidated into the master repository. This may sound like an excellent opportunity to incorporate an additional data set into the master repository, but in fact there are likely to be issues regarding ownership of the data and contractual obligations relating to the ways that the data are used, including the following:

Licensing arrangements. Data providers probably license the use of the data that are being provided, as opposed to "selling" the data for general use. This means that the data provider contract will be precise in detailing the ways that the data are licensed, such as for review by named individuals, for browsing and review purposes directly through provided software, or for comparisons but not copied or stored. License restrictions will prevent consolidating the external data into the master.

Usage restrictions. More precisely, some external data may be provided or shared for a particular business reason and may not be used for any other purpose. This differs subtly from the licensing restrictions in that many individuals may be allowed to see, use, or even copy the data, but only for the prescribed purpose. Therefore, using the data for any other purpose that would be enabled by MDM would violate the usage agreement.

Segregation of information. In this situation, information provided to one business application must deliberately be quarantined from other business applications because of a "business-sensitive" nature, which also introduces complexity in terms of data consolidation.

Obligations on termination. Typically, when the provider arrangement ends, the data customer is required to destroy all copies of provided data; if the provider data have been integrated into a master repository, to what degree does that comingling "infect" the master? This restriction would almost make it impossible to include external data in a master repository without introducing significant safeguards to identify data sources and to provide selective rollback.

10.7.2 **Access Rights and Usage Limitations**

Alternatively, there may be data sets that are consolidated into a master view, with the constraint that the visibility of certain data attributes and their values is limited based on designated access rights. For example, in a health care environment, a patient's health record may contain information accumulated from many sources, yet there are different roles that may have access to different parts of the health record, ranging from the identifying information (which may be necessary to validate patient identity) to the entire health history, access to which being limited to the patients themselves and primary caregivers. Disclosure of protected information to the wrong individual may have compliance and legal ramifications, necessitating strict compliance to managing security and access to authorized individuals based on their roles.

In addition, individuals within different roles may have different levels of access to the master data. Different roles may have different access capabilities (determination of record existence, read, read/write, read/write/delete, etc.), and at the same time specific attributes may be protected in accordance to role-based permissions. Role-based access control coupled with user authentication can be deployed as a collection of access controls ensuring conformance to specified access and usage limitation policies. Conformance to these policies is managed in accordance with the data governance framework, enabling access management services to become incorporated as part of the master data service layer.

10.7.3 **Segregation Instead of Consolidation**

The question of information segregation arises in environments that manage similar data sets for lines of business that are restricted from interaction. In these kinds of environments, one potential intention for master data management is not bringing all the line-of-business data sets into one massive repository but rather to be used as a management initiative to ensure that restricted line of business data sets are *not* mixed together. The master registry can be used to ensure against inadvertent consolidation by managing the data lineage (as described in Section 10.6.5) and determining at any point if data sources have been compromised.

10.8 **SUMMARY**

The central driver of master data management is the ability to locate the variant representations of any unique entity and unify the organization's view to that entity. The process by which this is accomplished must be able to access the candidate data sets, extract the appropriate identifying information, and then correctly assess similarity to a degree that allows for linkage between records and consolidation of the data into an application service framework that permits access to the unified view. The technical components of this process—parsing, standardization, matching and identity resolution, and consolidation—must be integrated within two aspects of the master environment: the underlying technical infrastructure and models that support the implementation, and the governance framework that oversees the management of information access and usage policies.

Master Data Synchronization

11.1 INTRODUCTION

What is the qualitative difference between the traditional manner that data quality tools are used for data cleansing and the way they are used for master data management? To a large degree, the approaches are the same when it comes to the mechanics of parsing, standardization, corrections, and consolidation and merging. But whereas static data cleansing focuses on one data set at a time in isolation, the same techniques used for master data do so in an active environment with dependent applications demanding access to that core data asset, even as it is being assessed and reviewed for improvement.

In other words, the answer is related to the way that business application owners have specified their needs for consistency and synchronization of the critical data assets for both consolidation and use. Traditional approaches to data cleansing focus on a static view of data sets—extracting data from sources; normalizing their structure; submitting to the cleansing process; and creating a newly formed, cleansed data silo. To the contrary, though, the master data asset is not a separate data silo but an intrinsic component of the operational, analytical, or combined application architecture. In essence, one of the core concepts of MDM is the dynamic availability of a representative master data set that by definition provides a consistent view across the enterprise. Correspondingly, the concept of an isolated consolidation of extracted data sets into a static repository of cleansed records is inconsistent with the business needs for the dynamically managed master view.

Our expectations for the master data asset availability are defined in terms of synchronization—between the client applications and the master data set, as well as between the components of the master data set itself. Synchronization can be characterized at a more refined level by looking at specific aspects of the shared consistent view of uniquely referenced objects:

- Timeliness
- Currency
- Latency
- Consistency
- Coherence
- Deterministic data access

Within the context of the shared master data asset, each of these notions has a subtly different meaning, and a combination of the business requirements for these execution aspects contributes the ultimate drivers for the selection of the underlying MDM architecture. In this chapter, we examine the meanings and implications of these system concepts, a model in which some of the issues have been addressed, and how we can adapt that model to the MDM program.

11.2 ASPECTS OF AVAILABILITY AND THEIR IMPLICATIONS

What do timeliness, currency, latency, consistency, coherence, and determinism mean in the context of synchronized master data? In Chapter 5 we explored the dimensions of data quality, yet the rules and thresholds for those dimensions are defined from the point of view of each of the business applications using the data sets. But as characteristics of a synchronized master view, these terms take on more operational meanings. Within each application, accesses to each underlying managed data set are coordinated through the internal system services that appropriately order and serialize data reads and writes. In this manner, consistency is maintained algorithmically, and the end users are shielded from having to be aware of the mechanics employed.

However, the nature of the different ways that master data are managed raises the question of consistency above the system level into the application service layer. This must be evaluated in the context of the degree of synchronization needed by the set of client applications using the master data asset. Therefore, the decisions regarding the selection of an underlying MDM architecture, the types of services provided, the application migration strategy, and the tools needed for integration and consolidation all depend on assessing the business process requirements (independently of the way the technology has been deployed!) for data consistency.

Each of the key characteristics impacts the maintenance of a consistent view of master data across the client application infrastructure, and each of the variant MDM architecture styles will satisfy demands across these different dimensions in different ways. Our goal is to first understand the measures of the dimensions of synchronization and how they address the consistency of master data. Given that understanding, the MDM architects would assess the applications that rely on the master data asset as well as the future requirements for applications that are planned to be developed and determine what their requirements are for master data synchronization. At this point, each of the architectural styles can be evaluated to determine how well each scores with respect to these dimensions. The result of these assessments provides input to inform the architect as to the best architecture to meet the organizational needs.

11.3 TRANSACTIONS, DATA DEPENDENCIES, AND THE NEED FOR SYNCHRONY

The need for synchronization is best illustrated using an example. Consider a company, WidgeCo, that for the benefit of its customers maintains a master product information management system that composes product data from multiple sources into a single view. Three suppliers sell a 3-inch widget, with unique product code WID-3IN, and for each of the suppliers (A, B, and C), there is an entry in the master data environment tracking the number of widgets the supplier has in stock and the current price at which the supplier is selling the widget.

Here are some of the use cases associated with that master product catalog:

- When one of WidgeCo's customers is interested in buying 3-inch widgets, a request is made from the master catalog to provide the best price and the quantity of widgets available at that price.
- When a customer makes a purchase, WidgeCo processes the transaction by forwarding the transaction to the supplier with the best price and arranging for drop shipping directly to the customer's location.
- Suppliers proactively provide data to WidgeCo, updating its product data.

In each of these use cases, the degree of synchronization and consistency of product data may impact whether the results of the transactions are what the customers think will happen. The issues emerge when the transactions triggered by these use cases are interleaved.

To follow the example, consider this sequence of events:

1. A customer requests prices for widgets.
2. WidgeCo returns result saying that supplier A has WID-3IN for $19 each.
3. Supplier B forwards an update of product data including a reduction in cost for WID-3IN to $18 each.
4. The customer orders 100 units of WID-3IN.

At this point, some of a number of actions might happen:

A. The customer's order is forwarded to supplier A, because at the time of the query, supplier A had the lowest price, or
B. The customer's order is forwarded to supplier B, who had the lowest price when the order was placed, and
C. The customer is charged for widgets at the rate of $19 each, which was the lowest price at the time of the query, or
D. The customer is charged for widgets at the rate of $18 each, which was the lowest price at the time of the order.

The potential for confusion revolves around how the master system's underlying master product information was implemented. In a database management system (DBMS) application, all the transactions would have been ordered in some way to prevent the potential for confusion. But the final outcomes of the process may be different, depending on how the applications participating in the MDM system access the master data stores, how the master data stores are configured, and how the master data service layer interleaves components of these transactions.

In fact, these issues might have serious business impact if WidgeCo has specified policies regarding service-level compliance, either with the customers or with the suppliers. For example, one policy might specify that the customer always receives the lowest price, whereas another might specify that the supplier whose price was quoted always receives the order. In this example, both of those policies cannot be observed at the same time.

11.3.1 **Data Dependency**

What we see in this example is that the execution sequence of transactions defines the outcome, and this is driven by the fact that each individual transaction is dependent on the result of a previous transaction. The price charged to the customer when the order is made *should be* related to the price reported to the customer after the initial price request, if that is what the company has stated as its definitive policy.

Because any master object can be either read or written, we want to ensure that the data dependencies are observed within any transaction. The combinations of read/write dependencies by different applications can be characterized as follows:

Read after read. In this situation, one transaction reads a data element, followed by another transaction reading the same data element. Here, there are not likely to be any issues; because there is no modification to the master object between the two reads, their order can even be interchanged.

Read after write. Here, one transaction writes the master object, then another transaction reads the same master object. In this case, the read action is dependent on the completion of the write, and here we cannot interchange the order of execution.

Write after read. In this case, one transaction writes the master object, then another transaction reads the same master object. Similarly to the "read after write," the value read is dependent on the successful completion of the preceding write, and here we cannot interchange the order of execution.

Write after write. In this case, one transaction writes the master object, then another transaction writes the same master object. The resulting persisted value is the last one that executed, and to some extent it does not matter which write "wins," as long as every participating application sees the same winner.

This last point is the critical one: maintaining consistency and synchronicity is related to ensuring that all participating applications see a consistent ordering of data dependent actions.

11.3.2 **Business Process Considerations**

Different aspects of coordinating the management of product WID-3IN's virtual master record show how reliant our applications are on particular systemic support for data synchronization. For example, the result of the customer's query could have been different if supplier B's product update had arrived earlier in the sequence, as would be the ultimate cost per widget, which highlights how the *timeliness* of master data transactions impacts the business process. In fact, the intermediate update to the product's master record in the middle of the customer interaction demonstrates the importance of having the most *current* data available.

The amount of time that it takes for the specific actions to be communicated may also impact the final outcome, because if supplier B's update takes a long time to be made generally available (in other words, has a long *latency*), the customer will be charged the higher amount. At the same time, the view to the customer displayed one lowest price, whereas the updated master data set contained a different lowest price—a lack of *consistency and coherence* that could impact the end result. Lastly, had the customer requested the price twice, it is possible that the result would have been different each time, exhibiting *nondeterministic* behavior with respect to data access. In general, within the DBMS, all of the peculiarities of concurrent interactions between these different aspects are handled as a by-product of transaction serialization.

11.3.3 **Serializing Transactions**

The fact is that almost any high-level transaction in any operational system is composed of multiple subtransactions, each of which is executed within a defined sequence. At the same time, other applications may be simultaneously executing transactions touching the same data sets. So how are these transactions (and their corresponding subtransactions) executed in a way that ensures that they don't step all over each other? Although the complexity of transaction serialization, multiphased commits, and locking are beyond the scope of this book, a simple overview can be somewhat illuminating.

The basic principle is that the underlying transaction management system must ensure a number of assertions that will guarantee a consistent view:

1. Each application's transactions will be executed in an order consistent with the order in which they were requested.
2. All transactions from all applications will be seen to have been executed in the same order.

The impact of the first assertion is the guarantee of a total ordering of the transactions performed by each distinct application. The second assertion enforces a consistent ordering of interleaved transactions from the different applications to enforce the view of data dependencies as described in Section 11.3.1. Simply put, database management systems employ processes to enforce these assertions by intermittently "locking" the underlying data asset being modified during any specific set of subtransactions until the system is able to guarantee the consistency of the entire transaction. Locking a data object means that no other transaction can modify that object, and any reads are likely to see the value before the start of the transaction sequence. When that guarantee is assured, the database system commits all the modifications and then releases the locks on each individual data object.

Because these locking and multiphase commit protocols are engineered into the database management system, their effect is completely transparent to any application developer or any application user. But because there are many different approaches to implementing master data management, the importance of incorporating these same protocols at the service layer is related to the degree to which the business requirements specify the need for the master data to be synchronized.

11.4 SYNCHRONIZATION

What are the characteristics of synchrony and consistency? Using the characteristic dimensions enumerated earlier in this chapter, we can explore the degree to which we can describe synchrony, as well as provide a means for comparing business application requirements and implementation support. This process helps refine the selection criteria for an underlying MDM architecture. The dimensions of synchronization are shown in the sidebar.

SYNCHRONIZATION DIMENSIONS

- *Timeliness.* Refers to the ability to ensure the availability of master data to the client applications and stakeholders within a reasonable window from the time that the data were initially created or introduced into the enterprise. Timeliness is essentially a gauge of the maximum time it takes for master data to propagate across the system, as well as the time window in which the underlying replicas of master data have potentially inconsistent values.

- *Currency.* Corresponds to the degree of "freshness" of master data, which measures the update times and frequency associated with any "expiration" time of data values.

- *Latency.* Refers to the time between an application's request for information and the time of its delivery.

- *Consistency.* A measure of the degree to which each application's view of master data is not different than any other application's view.

- *Coherence.* The ability to maintain predictable synchronization between local copies of master data and any master repository, or between any two local copies.

- *Determinism/idempotence.* Means that when the same query is performed more than once, it returns the same result.

11.4.1 **Application Infrastructure Synchronization Requirements**

Clearly, many MDM environments are not specifically designated as tightly coupled transaction processing systems, which means that the requirements are going to be determined in the context of the degree to which there is simultaneous master data access, as well as how that is impacted by our dimensions of synchronization. Therefore, the process for determining the requirements for synchronization begins with asking a number of questions:

1. Is the master data asset supporting more of a transactional or an analytical environment? A transactional system will require a greater degree of synchronization than one that is largely used solely for analytics.

2. How many applications will have simultaneous access to master data? An environment with many applications touching the master data repository will probably have more data dependencies requiring consistency.

3. What is the frequency of modifications to master data? Higher frequency may require greater assurance of coherence.

4. What is the frequency of data imports and loads? This introduces requirements for data currency and timeliness of delivery.

5. How tightly coupled are the business processes supported by different master data sets? Siloed master object repositories may be of use for specific business objectives, but fully integrated business processes that operate on collections of master objects will demand greater degrees of synchrony.

6. How quickly do newly introduced data need to be integrated into the master environment? Rapid integration will suggest a high degree of timeliness and currency.

7. What is the volume of new master records each day?

8. How many applications are introducing new master records? (This question and the previous one focus on the potential for large numbers of simultaneous transactions and how that would impact the need for coordination.)

9. What are the geographical distribution points for master data? In a replicated environment, this would impose coherence and consistency constraints that may be bound by network data transfer bandwidth.

This is just a beginning; the answers to these questions will trigger additional exploration into the nature of coordinating access to master data. The degree of synchronization relates to the ways that applications are using master data. When there is a high overlap in use of the same assets, there will be a greater need for synchrony, and a low degree of overlap reduces the need for synchrony.

It is valuable to note that one of the biggest issues of synchrony in an MDM environment leveraging a services-oriented architecture (SOA) is the degree to which end point systems can consume updates. In this asynchronous paradigm, if some end point systems cannot consume updates, for example, or there's a huge backlog of updates, you may have both performance and consistency issues.

11.5   CONCEPTUAL DATA SHARING MODELS

As is discussed in Chapter 9, the spectrum of MDM architectures ranges from the thin model embodied by the registry approach to the more comprehensive repository that captures the complete collection of master data attributes, with an increasing number of attributes being shared in different ways as the design moves along that spectrum. The registry and repository architectural styles describe data sharing models, and in fact we can consider a third data sharing model that supports the repository view.

11.5.1 Registry Data Sharing

In the registry architectural style, the only shared components are the identifying attributes, whereas the existing data sets contain the data that compose the conceptual master asset. Although individual applications still control these component data sources, master data services can only impose synchronization control on the shared registry, in which case the identifying attributes become the focus of the synchronization requirements. The characterization of the levels of each synchronization dimension for the registry model is shown in Figure 11.1. Because data are available as master data as soon as they have been persisted to an application's data store, timeliness and currency of master data are both high. However, the existence of variant copies of records representing the same master entity means that consistency will be low, and, by definition, the absence of strict coordination between these copies means that coherence will be low. Lastly, because the consolidated view is materialized on demand (through federation), intervening changes between any two access requests may lead to differences in the result from two equivalent queries, which means that the level of determinism is low.

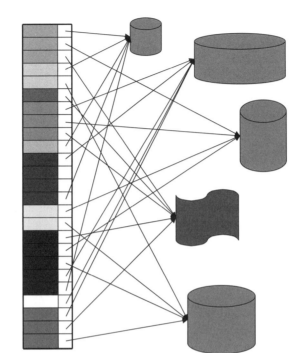

- Timeliness – high
- Currency – high
- Consistency – low
- Coherence – low
- Determinism – low

■ **FIGURE 11.1** Synchronization characteristics of the registry model.

11.5.2 **Repository Data Sharing**

In the repository style, more master attributes are managed within a single conceptual data asset. If the data asset is truly a single data system comprising the entire set of data attributes, the focus of synchronization is the master data service layer's ability to flow data access transactions directly through to the underlying database platform to rely on its means for transaction serialization and so forth.

At the end of the spectrum representing the full-scale single repository, any updates to the master are immediately available to any of the client applications. Correspondingly, the levels of timeliness, currency, and consistency are high, as seen in Figure 11.2. In the case where there is only one underlying data system, there will be no issues with coherence between copies, and therefore the level of coherence is also high. Lastly, all changes will have been serialized according to the underlying data system's protocols, and subsequent queries are extremely likely to return largely similar, if not exactly the same, results; therefore, this approach will have a high degree of determinism.

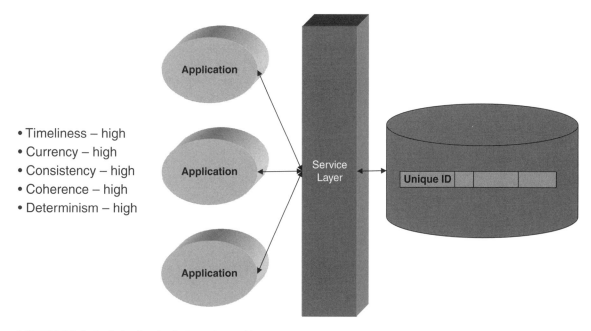

■ **FIGURE 11.2** Synchronization dimensions for the repository model.

11.5.3 **Hybrids and Federated Repositories**

Both ends of the spectrum seem to be covered; it is with the spectrum in between where we start to see issues, because the hybrid model (where some attributes are managed within a master repository and others are managed by the application) and the federated model (in which the conceptually monolithic data master is implemented via data replication and data distribution) are where we see multiple copies of what we believe to be unique instances of data.

In the hybrid approach, the applications are still driving the sequences of transactions, and with data writes needing to traverse multiple underlying database platforms, there is a new level of complexity for the managing record locking and multiple phases for committing transactions. Because the transactions may be broken up into chunks applied to different underlying databases, the transaction semantics may need to be engineered into the master data service layer.

A different issue arises in aspects of a replicated model (shown in Figure 11.3), in which copies of the master data asset are made available to different applications, allowing each to operate on its copy as if

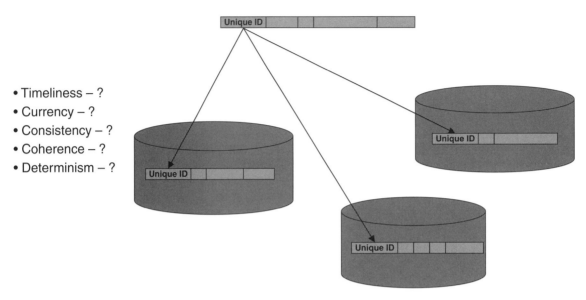

- Timeliness – ?
- Currency – ?
- Consistency – ?
- Coherence – ?
- Determinism – ?

■ FIGURE 11.3 The synchronization characteristics of a hybrid model depend on the implementation.

it were completely under application control. Modifications to a copy of a master object must be propagated back to any other replicated copies that exist across the enterprise.

The different aspects of the underlying implementations mean that without details of how the master data asset is managed, it is difficult to project the determination of levels of our synchronization dimensions. For example, in the replicated model, maintaining coherence across the replicas becomes the critical activity, with all the other characteristics directly dependent on the degree of coherence. On the other hand, if there is not an expectation of a high degree of overlapping master data object accesses, engineering delayed consistency into the framework is an acceptable solution.

11.5.4 **MDM, the Cache Model, and Coherence**

Abstractly, the integrated view of master data begins to mimic a memory hierarchy not unlike the physical cache and memory models employed across most computer hardware systems. The master data repository itself represents the persistent storage, but the data from that asset are accessed and copied into versions both closer to and more easily by the using applications. For example, a replicated model essentially carries three levels of a memory hierarchy: the actual master version, a replica in a local data management asset, and individual records being manipulated directly by the application before commitment back through the local copy into the ultimate master copy.

Luckily, many of the issues regarding consistency and coherence across a cache memory environment have been addressed successfully to ensure that hardware caching and shared memory management will work at the hardware level. Because these are essentially solved problems, we can see the same approaches applied at the conceptual master data service level. In other words, we can apply a cache model to MDM in order to provide a framework for managing coherence across multiple copies. In this approach, there is an assumption that the applications store data to a local copy of the master data (whether that is a full replica or just a selection of attributes), which corresponds to the persistent version managed in the master repository (Figure 11.4).

Whenever a copy of a master record is updated in one of the application replicas, some protocol must be followed to ensure that the update is

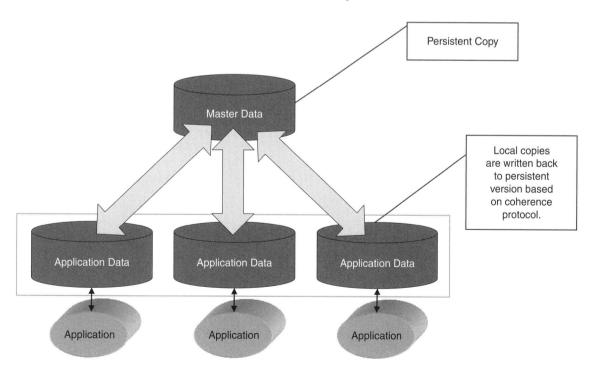

■ **FIGURE 11.4** The virtual cache model shows local copies of master data managed by each application.

PROTOCOLS USED FOR UPDATING

- *Write-through.* This occurs when a modification to a local copy of master data is also written directly at the same time into the master repository. In this case, all the other applications that maintain copies of the same master objects must be notified that their copies are no longer current and that before using the record it must be refreshed from the persistent master.

- *Write-back.* This occurs when a modification to a local copy is written back to the persistent master at some time after the modification was made to local copy. In this case, there is no direct notification to other applications with copies at the time of modification, but there is likely to be at the time of writing back to the persistent master.

- *Refresh notification.* The process by which "stale" copies of mater records are marked as inconsistent or out of date when an application is notified that the master record has been updated. At that point, the application can determine whether or not the copy should be updated immediately.

- *Refresh on read.* A process by which stale copies are reloaded when an application requires reading or modifying the local copy after the persistent master record has been updated.

made consistent with the persistent master as well as the other application replicas. Examples of protocols include the ones shown in the sidebar.

The processes will be handled ultimately within the master data service layer at the component services level. The determination of when local copies are updated becomes a policy management issue, especially with respect to performance. For example, immediately refreshing copies marked as stale may lead to an increase in network interactions, with data moving from a single resource (the persistent master) to the applications' copies, even if the data are not needed at that point, creating a performance bottleneck and increase in bandwidth requirements. On the other hand, delaying updates until the data are read may cause performance issues when generating reports against the local copies if many records are invalid and need to be accessed before the report can be run. The implication is that managing synchronization and coherence within the replicated/distributed/federated approaches to deploying a master repository impacts the performance aspects of the client applications, and, yet again, we see that the decisions regarding implementation of the underlying master data architecture depend on business application requirements for consistency and synchronization.

11.6 **INCREMENTAL ADOPTION**

A different way of considering the synchronization challenge involves the incremental adoption of master data management within the enterprise. There are essentially two aspects to MDM adoption: absorbing new data sources into the master asset and applications adopting the master repository. In this section, we explore some of the issues associated with synchronization when new data sources and applications are integrated into the master data environment.

11.6.1 **Incorporating and Synchronizing New Data Sources**

In Chapter 10 we looked at the challenges of master data consolidation—the process of creating the initial master data repository. Because there is no existing master data asset at the beginning of the program, the initial consolidation does not incur any additional demands for data synchronization. However, as soon as the initial version is moved into production, any subsequent data source incorporated into the master data asset is likely to not be aligned with that master data set.

Incorporating new data sources without intending to "sunset" them will always create the situation of one data silo lagging behind the other in terms of maintaining consistency. Therefore, think twice before considering absorbing data sources that will probably be retained as data stores for applications (such as specialized business tools) that will not be migrating to integrating with the master environment. That being said, there will always be situations in which there are data sets that will be absorbed into the master repository even though they will not be eliminated. Some of the issues that need to be addressed basically focus on coordination between the two data sets (and their client applications).

When there are applications that still use the data source but not the master data asset, that data source must remain in production. In this case, when is the data set synchronized with the master? The best scenario would impose the same level of coherence on that data as the replicated/distributed/federated approach, yet this is unlikely for a few reasons. First, the level of effort necessary for full coherence is probably close to the level of effort necessary for full integration, but maintaining segregation implies constraint on some assets (resource, time, staff), preventing the full integration. Second, isolation of the data and its services may create a barrier that limits the ability to invoke master data services from within the client applications. The alternate suggestion is periodic, one-way synchronization. Similar to the consolidation process, we can apply the integration process in a batch mode applied via the consolidation services within the master data service layer.

The other issue, which may be of lesser concern, is synchronizing the master data back with the segregated data source. The decision to do so should be left to the discretion of the manager/owner of that data source's client applications.

11.6.2 **Application Adoption**

When application managers prepare to adopt the use of the master repository, their production applications may need to run in a dual mode, with modifications being made to the existing source and the master data asset. This introduces yet another synchronization challenge—maintaining consistency between the data set to be retired and the master data asset. However, as we will explore in Chapter 12, the dual operation model should be handled transparently as part of the master data services layer.

11.7 **SUMMARY**

Ultimately, the synchronization requirements feed into the selection process for an underlying architecture style, because we can see that the different choices for implementing a master data management system will support different degrees of synchronization within varying levels of systemic performance. Evaluating the characteristics of the different usage scenarios described in Chapter 9, assessing the number of participating applications, assessing the number of operational/transactional systems as opposed to analytical systems, determining the frequency of modifications, updates, and batch loads, and so on will help in driving the decision as to whether the most appropriate underlying architecture style should be based on a registry, full-scale hub repository or some hybrid version.

12

MDM and the Functional Services Layer

One of the main objectives of a master data management program is to support the enterprise application use of a synchronized shared repository of core information objects relevant to business application success. There are two focuses here: sharing and coordination/synchronization. To maintain the master data environment, proper data governance policies and procedures at the corporate or *organizational* level oversee the quality of the data as the contributing data sets are consolidated.

However, the process does not end when the data sets are first consolidated; the objectives of MDM are not accomplished through the initial integration. Quite the contrary, the value is achieved when the consolidated master data are published back for operational and analytical use by the participating applications to truly provide a single, synchronized view of the customer, product, or other master data entity. This means that integration and consolidation must be performed on a continuous basis, and as applications embrace the use of MDM, it is necessary to support how application-level life cycle events impact the master data system.

This suggests that the data integration layer should be abstracted as it relates to business application development, which exposes two ways that master data are integrated into a services-based framework. Tactically, a services layer can be introduced to facilitate the transition of applications to the use of the master repository, perhaps through the use of message-based interfacing. Strategically, the abstraction of the core master entities at a data integration layer provides the foundation for establishing a hierarchical set of information services to support the rapid and efficient development of business applications in an autonomous fashion. Both of these imperatives are satisfied by a services-oriented architecture (SOA).

217

In essence, there is a symbiotic relationship between MDM and SOA: a services-oriented approach to business solution development relies on the existence of a master data repository, and the success of an MDM program depends on the ability to deploy and use master object access and manipulation services.

12.1 COLLECTING AND USING MASTER DATA

An MDM program that only collects data into a consolidated repository without allowing for the use of that data is essentially worthless, considering that the driving factor for establishing a single point of truth is providing a high-quality asset that can be shared across the enterprise. This means that information must easily be brought into the master repository and in turn must also be easily accessible by enterprise applications *from* the repository.

The first part is actually straightforward, as it mimics the typical extraction, transformation, and loading (ETL) techniques used within the data warehouse environment. However, exposing the master data for use across the different application poses more of a challenge for a number of factors. To enable the consistent sharing of master data, there are a number of issues to consider:

- The insufficiency of extraction/transformation/loading tools
- The replication of functionality across the de facto application framework
- The need for applications to adjust the way they access relevant data
- The need for a level of maturity to be reached for enterprise information models and associated architectures

12.1.1 Insufficiency of ETL

Traditional ETL is insufficient for continuous synchronization. Although the master repository may have initially been populated through an extraction, transformation, and loading process, there is a need to maintain a state of consistency between the master repository and each participating application's views of the master data. Although ETL can support the flow of data out of application data sets into the master repository, its fundamentally batch approach to consolidation is insufficient for flowing data back out from the repository to the applications. This may become less of an issue as real-time warehousing and change data capture facilities mature.

12.1.2 **Replication of Functionality**

There will be slight variances in the data model and component functionality associated with each application. Yet the inclusion of application data as part of a master data object type within the master repository implies that there are similarities in data entity format and use. Clearly, the corresponding data life cycle service functionality (creation, access, modification/update, retirement) is bound to be replicated across different applications as well. Minor differences in the ways these functions are implemented may affect the meaning and use of what will end up as shared data, and those variations expose potential risks to consistency.

12.1.3 **Adjusting Application Dependencies**

The value proposition for application participation in the MDM program includes the benefit of accessing and using the higher quality consolidated data managed via the MDM repository. However, each application may have been originally designed with a specific data model and corresponding functionality, both of which must be adjusted to target the data managed in the core master model.

12.1.4 **Need for Architectural Maturation**

Applications must echo architectural maturation. Architectural approaches to MDM may vary in complexity, and the repository will become more sophisticated, adapt different implementation styles (e.g., registry versus transaction hub), and grow in functionality as the program matures. This introduces a significant system development risk if all the applications must be modified continually in order to use the master data system.

The natural process for application migration is that production applications will be expected to be modified to access the master data repository at the same time as the application's data sets are consolidated within the master. But trying to recode production applications to support a new underlying information infrastructure is both invasive and risky. Therefore, part of the MDM implementation process must accommodate existing application infrastructures in ways that are minimally disruptive yet provide a standardized path for transitioning to the synchronized master.

12.1.5 **Similarity of Functionality**

During the early phases of the MDM program, the similarities of data objects were evaluated to identify candidate master data entities. To support application integration, the analysts must also review the similarities in application use of those master data entities as part of a functional resolution for determining core master data services. In essence, not only must we consolidate the *data*, we must also consider the consolidation of the *functionality* as well.

In addition, as the MDM program matures, new applications can increasingly rely on the abstraction of the conceptual master data objects (and corresponding functionality) to support newer business architecture designs. The use of the standard representations for master data objects reduces the need for application architects to focus on data access and manipulation, security and access control, or policy management; instead they can use the abstracted functionality to develop master data object services.

The ability to consolidate application functionality (e.g., creating a new customer or listing a new product) using a services layer that supplements multiple application approaches will add value to existing and future applications. In turn, MDM services become established as a layer of abstraction that supports an organization's transition to an SOA architecture. MDM allows us to create master data objects that embody behaviors that correctly govern the creation, identification, uniqueness, completeness, relationships with/between, and propagation of these MDOs throughout an ecosystem using defined policies. This goes above and beyond the duplication of functionality present in existing systems. Taking the opportunity to define an "object model" for capturing policy and behavior as part of the representation and service layer enables the creation of reusable master data objects that endure over generations of environmental changes.

12.2 CONCEPTS OF THE SERVICES-BASED APPROACH

The market defines SOA in many ways, but two descriptions best capture the concepts that solidify the value of an MDM initiative. According to Eric Marks and Michael Bell:

> SOA is a conceptual business architecture where business functionality, or application logic, is made available to SOA users, or consumers, as shared, reusable services on an IT network.[1]

---

[1]Marks, Eric A., and Michael Bell, *Service-Oriented Architecture—A Planning and Implementation Guide for Business and Technology*, Wiley, 2006.

The Organization for the Advancement of Structured Information Standards (OASIS) provides this definition:

> *A paradigm for organizing and utilizing distributed capabilities that may be under the control of different ownership domains.*[2]

To paraphrase these descriptions, a major aspect of the services-based approach is that business application requirements drive the need to identify and consolidate the use of *capabilities* managed across an enterprise in a way that can be shared and reused within the boundaries of a governed environment. From the business perspective, SOA abstracts the layers associated with the ways that business processes are deployed in applications. The collection of services that comprises the business functions and processes that can be accessed, executed, and delivered is essentially a catalog of capabilities from which any business solution would want to draw.

This addresses the fundamental opportunity for SOA: The SOA-enabled organization is one that is transitioning from delivering *applications* to delivering *business solutions*. Application development traditionally documents the functional requirements from a vertical support point of view; the workflow is documented, procedures are defined, data objects are modeled to support those procedures, and code is written to execute those procedures within the context of the data model. The resulting product operates sufficiently—it does what it needs to do and nothing more.

Alternatively, the services-based approach looks at the problem from the top down:

- Identifying the business objectives to be achieved
- Determining how those objectives relate to the existing enterprise business architecture
- Defining the service components that are necessary to achieve those goals
- Cataloging the services that are already available within the enterprise
- Designing and implementing those services that are not

Master data lends itself nicely to a services-based approach for a number of reasons (see the following sidebar).

---

[2]OASIS Reference Model for Service Oriented Architecture, *http://www.oasis-open.org/committees/download.php/19679/soa-rm-cs.pdf*

> **REASONS A SERVICES-BASED APPROACH WORKS FOR MASTER DATA**
>
> - The use of master data is intended to address alignment of the way that applications contribute to achieving business objectives, and the services approach complements this alignment through functional abstraction.
> - The inheritance model for core master object types captures common operational methods at the lowest level of use.
> - MDM provides the standardized services and data objects that a services-oriented architecture needs in order to achieve consistency and effective reuse.
> - A commonality of purpose of functionality is associated with master objects at the application level (e.g., different applications might have reasons for modifying aspects of a product description, but it is critical that any modifications be seen by all applications).
> - Similarity of application functionality suggests opportunities for reuse.
> - The services model reflects the master data object life cycle in a way that is independent of any specific implementation decisions.

12.3 IDENTIFYING MASTER DATA SERVICES

Before designing and assembling the service layer for master data, it is a good idea to evaluate how each participating application touches master data objects in order to identify abstract actions that can be conveyed as services at either the core component level or the business level. Of course, this process should be done in concert with a top-down evaluation of the business processes as described in the business process models (see Chapter 2) to validate that what is learned from an assessment is congruent with what the business clients expect from their applications.

12.3.1 Master Data Object Life Cycle

To understand which service components are needed for master data management, it is worthwhile to review the conceptual life cycle of a master data object in relation to the context of the business applications that use it. For example, consider the context of a bank and its customer data objects. A number of applications deal directly with customer data, including branch banking, ATM, Internet banking, telephone banking, wireless banking, mortgages, and so on. Not only that, but the customer service department also requires access to customers' data, as do other collaborative divisions including credit, consumer loans, investments, and even real estate. Each of these applications must deal with some of the following aspects of the data's life cycle.

Establishment. This is the point at which a customer record is established; it includes collecting the data element values to populate that record's attributes as well as populating the record with data from shared resources.

Distribution. This aspect includes the ability to make the data available in a way that allows applications to use it as well as managing that data within the constraints of any imposed information policies derived from business policies (such as security and privacy restrictions).

Access and use. This aspect includes the ability to locate the (hopefully unique) master record associated with the real-world entity and to qualify that record's accuracy and completeness for the specified application usage.

Deactivate and retire. On the one hand, this incorporates the protocols for ensuring that the records are current while they are still active, as well as properly documenting when master records are deactivated and to be considered no longer in use.

Maintain and update. This aspect involves identifying issues that may have been introduced into the master repository, including duplicate data, data element errors, modifying or correcting the data, and ensuring that the proper amount of identifying information is maintained to be able to distinguish any pair of entities.

In other words, every application that deals with customer data is bound to have some functionality associated with the creation, distribution and sharing, accessing, modification, updating, and retirement of customer records. In typical environments where the applications have developed organically, each application will have dealt with this functionality in slightly different ways. In the master data environment, however, we must look at these life cycle functions in terms of their business requirements and how those requirements are mapped to those functions.

In turn, as the business uses of the customer data change over time, we must also look at the contexts in which each customer object is created and used over the customer lifetime. These considerations remain true whether we examine customer, product, or any other generic master data set. As we navigate the process of consolidating multiple data sets into a single master repository, we are necessarily faced not just with the consolidation of life cycle functionality but also with the prospect of maintaining the contexts associated with the master data items over their lifetime as a support for historical assessment and rollback. This necessity suggests the need for a process to both assess the operational service components as well as the analytical service components.

12.3.2 **MDM Service Components**

The service components necessary to support an MDM program directly rely on both the common capabilities expected for object management and the primary business functions associated with each of the participating applications. The service identification process is composed of two aspects: the core services and the business services. Identifying application functionality and categorizing the way to abstract that functionality within a service layer exposes how the applications touch data objects that seem to be related to master object types. This reverse engineering process is used to resolve and ultimately standardize that functionality for simplification and reuse.

The first part of the process relies on the mapping from data object to its application references, which one hopes will have been captured within the metadata repository. Each application reference can be annotated to classify the type of access (create, use, modify, retire). In turn, the different references can be evaluated to ascertain the similarity of access. For example, the contact information associated with a vendor might be modified by two different applications, each of which is updating a specific set of attributes. The analysts can flag the similarity between those actions for more precise review to determine if they actually represent the same (or similar) actions and whether the action sequence is of common enough use for abstraction. By examining how each application reflects the different aspects of the data life cycle, analysts begin to detect patterns that enable them to construct the catalog of service components. The process is to then isolate and characterize the routine services necessary to perform core master data functions.

The next step is to seek out the higher levels of functionality associated with the business applications to understand how the master objects are manipulated to support the applications' primary business functions. The candidate services will focus specifically on business functionality, which will depend on the lower-level life cycle actions already associated with the master data objects.

12.3.3 **More on the Banking Example**

Let's return to our bank example. Whenever an individual attempts to access account features through any of the numerous customer-facing interfaces, there are routine activities (some business-oriented, others purely operational) that any of the applications are expected to perform before any application-specific services are provided:

- Collecting identifying information
- Uniquely identifying the customer
- Retrieving the customer's information
- Verifying customer roles and security characteristics
- Validating customer acceptability against the Office of Foreign Asset Control (OFAC) lists
- Monitoring for suspicious behavior

Whether the individual is banking through the Internet, checking credit card balances, or calling the customer support center, at the operational level the application must be able to determine who the individual is, establish that the individual is a customer, and access that customer's electronic profile. As core customer information changes (contact mechanisms, marital status, etc.), the records must be updated, and profiles must be marked as "retired" as customers eliminate their interaction. At the business level, each application must verify roles and permissions, validate "Know Your Customer" (KYC) characteristics, and monitor for suspicious behavior.

When reviewing these actions, the distinctions become clear. Collecting identifying information, uniquely identifying the customer, and retrieving the customer information are core master data services that any of the applications would use. Verifying roles and access rights for security purposes, validating against OFAC, and suspicious behavior monitoring are business application-level services.

Most application architects will have engineered *functions* performing these services into each application, especially when each application originally maintains an underlying data store for customer information. Consolidating the data into a single repository enables the enterprise architect to establish corresponding services to support both the operational and the business-oriented capabilities. The applications share these services, as Figure 12.1 illustrates.

12.3.4 **Identifying Capabilities**

In practice, the applications are making use of the same set of core capabilities, except that each capability has been implemented multiple times in slightly variant ways. Our goal is to identify these capabilities in relation to how they make use of master data objects and to consolidate them into a set of services. So if every application must collect individual identifying information, uniquely resolve the customer identity, and retrieve customer records, then an application that assembles a set of generic services to collect identifying information,

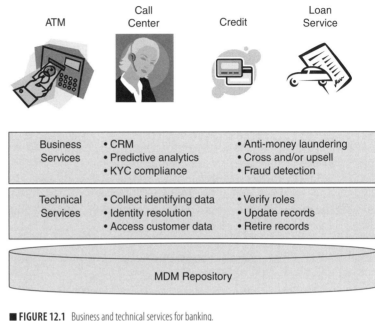

■ **FIGURE 12.1** Business and technical services for banking.

to resolve customer identity, and to retrieve customer records and profiles is recommended.

In retrospect, then, the analyst can review the component services and recast them in terms of the business needs. For example, collecting identifying information and resolving identity are components of the service to access a customer record. On the other hand, when a new customer establishes a relationship with the organization through one of the applications, there will not be an existing customer record in the master repository. At that point, the customer's identifying information must be collected so that a new customer record can be created. This new record is then provided back to the application in a seamless manner. Whether or not the customer record already exists, the result of the search is the materialization of the requested record!

In both of these cases, the core business service is accessing the unique customer record. Alternate business scenarios may require the invocation of different services to supply that record; in the first case, the identifying information is used to find an existing record, whereas in the second case, the absence of an existing record triggers its creation. But the end result is the same—the requesting application gains access to the master customer record.

Building business services on top of core technical services provides flexibility in implementation, yet the shared aspect of the service layer allows the application architect to engineer the necessary master data synchronization constraints into the system while abstracting its complexity from the business applications themselves. Because every application does pretty much the same thing, consolidating those components into services simplifies the application architecture. In essence, considering the business needs enables a collection of individual operational capabilities to be consolidated into a layer of shared services supporting the business objectives.

To isolate the service components, the process of reverse engineering is initiated, as described in Section 12.3.2. This process exposes the capabilities embedded within each application and documents how those capabilities use the master data objects. Each proposed service can be registered within a metadata repository and subjected to the same governance and standards processes we have used for the identifying candidate master data objects. By iterating across the applications that are participating in the MDM program, analysts can assemble a catalog of capabilities. Reviewing and resolving the similarities between the documented capabilities enables the analysts to determine business services and their corresponding technical components.

In turn, these capabilities can be abstracted to support each application's specific needs across the data life cycle. Component services are assembled for the establishment of a master record, distribution of master data in a synchronized manner, access and use of master objects, and validation of role-based access control, as well as to ensure the currency and accuracy of active records and proper process for deactivation. At the same time, service components are introduced to support the consistency and reasonableness of master objects and to identify and remediate issues that may have been introduced into the master repository. Business services can be designed using these core technical component services.

12.4 **TRANSITIONING TO MDM**

Providing the component service layer addresses two of the four issues introduced in Section 12.1. Regarding the fact that traditional ETL is insufficient for continuous synchronization, the challenge changes from enforcing strict synchronization to evaluating business requirements for synchronicity and then developing a service level agreement (SLA) to ensure conformance to those business requirements.

The transaction semantics necessary to maintain consistency can be embedded within the service components that support master data object creation and access, eliminating the concern that using ETL impedes consistency. The consolidation of application capabilities within a component service catalog through the resolution of functionality eliminates functional redundancy, thereby reducing the risks of inconsistency caused by replication.

Yet the challenge of applications transitioning to using the master repository still exists, requiring a migration strategy that minimizes invasiveness, and a reasonable migration strategy will address the other concerns from Section 12.1. To transition to using the master repository, applications must be adjusted to target the master repository instead of their own local data store. This transition can be simplified if an interface to the master repository can be created that mimics each application's own existing interface. Provided that core service components for the master data have been implemented, one method for this transition is to employ the conceptual service layer as a stepping-stone, using a design pattern known as "wrapper façade."

12.4.1 **Transition via Wrappers**

The idea behind using this design pattern is to encapsulate functionality associated with master data objects into a concise, robust, and portable high-level interface. It essentially builds on the use of the developed service layer supporting core functionality for data life cycle actions. After the necessary service components have been identified and isolated, the application architects devise and design the component services. The programmers also create a set of application interfaces that reflect the new services, then they wrap these interfaces around the calls to the existing application capabilities, as is shown in Figure 12.2.

At the same time, the MDM service layer is constructed by developing the components using the same interface as the one used for the wrapper façade. Once the new service layer has been tested and validated, the applications are prepared to migrate by switching from the use of the wrapper façade to the actual MDM service components.

12.4.2 **Maturation via Services**

This philosophy also addresses the fourth concern regarding the growing MDM sophistication as the program matures. MDM projects may initially rely on the simplest registry models for consolidation and data

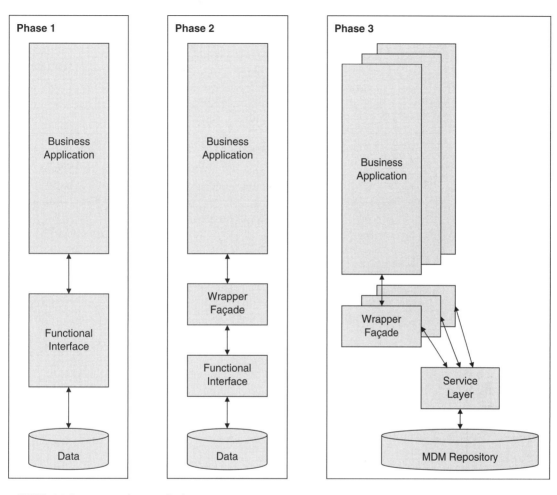

■ **FIGURE 12.2** Transitioning via the wrapper façade.

management, but over time the business needs may suggest moving to a more complex central repository or transaction hub. The complexity of the underlying model and framework has its corresponding needs at the application level, which introduces a significant system development risk if all the applications must be continually modified to use the master data system. In addition, there may be autonomous applications that are tightly coupled with their own data stores and will not be amenable to modification to be dependent on an external data set, which may preclude ever evolving to a full-scale hub deployment.

The services-based approach addresses this concern by encapsulating functionality at the technical layer. The business capabilities remain the same and will continue to be supported by the underlying technical layer. That underlying technical layer, though, can easily be adjusted to support any of the core master data implementation frameworks, with little or no impact at the application level.

12.5 SUPPORTING APPLICATION SERVICES

A services-based approach supports the migration to an MDM environment. The more important concept, though, is how the capability of a centralized view of enterprise master data more fully supports solving business problems through the services-based approach. Once the data and the functional capabilities have been consolidated and the technical service components established, the process of supporting business applications changes from a procedural, functional architecture to a business-directed one. In other words, abstracting out the details associated with common actions related to access, maintenance, or security enables the developers to focus on supporting the business needs.

New services can be built based on business requirements and engineered from the existing service components. Returning to our banking example, consider that regulations change over time, and new business opportunities continue to emerge as technology and lifestyles change. In addition, we may want to adjust certain customer-facing applications by introducing predictive analytics driven off the master customer profiles to help agents identify business opportunities in real time. The master repository makes this possible, but it is SOA that brings it into practice.

With a services-based approach, there is greater nimbleness and flexibility in being able to react to changes in the business environment. Integrating new capabilities at the business service layer enables all applications to take advantage of them, reducing development costs while speeding new capabilities into production.

12.5.1 Master Data Services

What are the master data services? Implementations may vary, but in general, we can characterize services grouped within three layers:[3]

---

[3]Special thanks to Colin White, who directly provided some relevant insight into this topic.

- Core services, which focus on life cycle actions, then the capabilities necessary for supporting general functions applied to master data
- Object services, which focus on actions related to the master data object type or classification (such as customer or product)
- Business application services, which focus on functionality necessary at the business level

In Figure 12.3, we show a sampling of core services, which include life cycle services, access control, integration, consolidation, and workflow/rules management. Of course, every organization is slightly different and each catalog of services may reflect these differences, but this framework is a generic starting point for evaluation and design.

12.5.2 **Life Cycle Services**

At the lowest level, simple services are needed for basic master data actions, providing a "master data service bus" to stream data in from and out to the applications.

■ **FIGURE 12.3** Some examples of core master data services.

Create. The point of establishment of a master record; this level of service presumes that all necessary identifying and auxiliary data element values have been supplied.

Read. The ability to make the data available within the context of any application; this level of service presumes that the desired master entity has been established and the corresponding record can be located and accessed.

Modify. This level of service addresses any maintenance issues that may have been introduced into the master repository, such as eliminating duplicate data, correcting data element errors, modifying the data, and ensuring that the proper amount of identifying information is available.

Retire. This process ensures the currency of active records and documents those master records that are deactivated and no longer in use.

12.5.3 **Access Control**

As part of the governance structure that supplements the application need to access master data, access control and security management services "guard the gateway."

Access control. Actors in different roles are granted different levels of access to specific master data objects. These services manage access control based on the classification of roles assigned to each actor.

Authentication. These services qualify requestors to ensure they are who they say they are.

Security management. These services oversee the management of access control and authentication information, including the management of data for actors (people or applications) authorized to access the master repository.

Audit. Audit services manage access logging as well as analysis and presentation of access history.

12.5.4 **Integration**

The integration layer is where the mechanics of data consolidation are provided.

Metadata management. Metadata management services are consulted within the context of any data element and data entity that would qualify for inclusion in the master repository. The details of what identifying information is necessary for each data entity are managed within the metadata management component.

Data quality. This set of services provides a number of capabilities, including parsing data values, standardizing the preparation for matching and identity resolution and integration, and profiling for analysis and monitoring.

Integration. These services adjust data records to comply with formats for insertion into the master repository and rely on the metadata management and data quality services to determine how and when records are integrated as master data.

12.5.5 **Consolidation**

At a higher level, multiple records may be consolidated from different sources, and there must be a service layer to support the consolidation process. This layer relies on the services in the integration layer (particularly the data quality services).

Modeling. Analysis of the structure of incoming data as it compares to the master model as well as revisions to the rules for matching and identity resolution are handled through a set of modeling and analysis services.

Identity management. For each master object type, a registry of identified entities will be established and managed through the identity management services.

Match/merge. As the core component of the identity resolution process, match and merge services compare supplied identifying information against the registry index to find exact or similar matches to help determine when the candidate information already exists within the registry.

Hierarchy management. These services support two aspects of hierarchy management. The first deals with lineage and tracking the historical decisions made in establishing or breaking connectivity between records drawn from different sources to support adjustments based on discovered false positive/false negatives. The second tracks relationships among entities within one master data set (such as "parent-child relationships"), as well as relationships between entities across different master data sets (such as "customer A prefers product X").

12.5.6 **Workflow/Rules**

At the level closest to the applications, there are services to support the policies and tasks/actions associated with user or application use of master data.

Browsing and editing. A service for direct access into the master repository enables critical data stewardship actions to be performed, such as the administration of master metadata as well as edits to master data to correct discovered data element value errors as well as false positive and false negative links.

Rules manager. Business rules that drive the workflow engine for supporting application use of master data are managed within a repository; services are defined to enable the creation, review, and modification of these rules as external drivers warrant. Conflict resolution directives to differentiate identities can be managed through this set of services, as well as the business classification typing applied to core master objects as needed by the applications.

Workflow manager. Similar to the way that application rules are managed through a service, the work streams, data exchanges, and application workflow is managed through a service as well. The workflows are specifically configured to integrate the master data life cycle events into the corresponding applications within the specific business contexts.

Service level agreements. By formulating SLAs as combinations of rules dictated by management policies and workflows that drive the adherence to an agreed-to level of service, the automation of conformance to information policy can be integrated as an embedded service within the applications themselves.

Propagation and synchronization. As changes are made to master data, dependent applications must be notified based on the synchronization objectives specified through defined SLAs. Depending on the architectural configuration, this may imply pushing data out from the master repository or simply notifying embedded application agents that local copies are no longer in synch with the master, but allowing the application to refresh itself as needed.

12.6 **SUMMARY**

There is a symbiotic relationship between MDM and SOA: a services-oriented approach to business solution development relies on the existence of a master data repository, and the success of an MDM program depends on the ability to deploy and use master object access and manipulation services. But employing a services-based approach serves multiple purposes within a master data management program. As the program is launched and developed, the use of multiple service layers simplifies both the implementation of the capabilities supporting the data object life cycle and the transition from the diffused, distributed application architecture into the consolidated master application infrastructure. But more important, the flexibility provided by a services-oriented architecture triggers the fundamental organizational changes necessary to use the shared information asset in its most effective manner. By driving application development from the perspective of the business instead of as a sequence of procedural operations, the organization can exploit the master data object set in relation to all business operations and ways that those objects drive business performance.

13

Management Guidance for MDM

The approach taken in this book to introduce and provide details about the development of a master data management program is to develop an awareness of the critical concepts of master data management before committing time, resources, or money to technology acquisition or consulting engagements. That being said, readers who have reached this point in the book show a readiness to take on the challenges of MDM, in expectation of the benefits in terms of business productivity improvement, risk management, and cost reduction—all facilitated via the conceptual master repository.

Therefore, this chapter reviews the insights discussed throughout the book and provides a high-level, end-to-end overview of the activities associated with developing the master data management program. This process begins with the initial activities of determining the business justifications for introducing MDM, developing a road map, identifying roles and responsibilities, planning the stages of the MDM development projects, and so on. The process continues through the middle stages of documenting the business process models, developing a metadata management facility, instituting data governance, and analyzing and developing master data models. Finally, it extends to the later stages of development, such as selecting and instantiating MDM architectures, developing master data services, deploying a transition strategy for existing applications, and then maintaining the MDM environment.

In this chapter, we review the key activities covered earlier in the book and provide guidance on the milestones and deliverables from each activity. An experienced project manager will cherry-pick from the list of activities depending on how critical each stage is to achieving the organization's business objectives. However, understanding the scale and scope of justifying, designing, planning, implementing, and maintaining an MDM system can be a large process in its own right. One of the hardest parts of the entire process is knowing where and how to start, and to that end, it is often more cost effective to engage external experts or consultants during the initial stages of the project to expedite producing the early deliverables.

13.1 ESTABLISHING A BUSINESS JUSTIFICATION FOR MASTER DATA INTEGRATION AND MANAGEMENT

As we have seen, master data integration and master data management are not truly the end objectives; rather they are the means by which other objectives are successfully accomplished, such as those promised by customer relationship management systems, product information management systems, Enterprise Resource Planning (ERP) systems, and so on. And while the principles that drive and support MDM reflect sound data management practices, it would be unusual (although not unheard of) that senior management would embrace and fund the MDM effort solely for the sake of establishing good practices.

That being said, the business justification for MDM should be coupled with those programs that will benefit from the availability of the unified view of master data. That means that MDM can be justified in support of a business initiative that relies on any of the following MDM benefits:

Comprehensive customer knowledge. A master data repository for customer data will provide the virtual single source for consolidating all customer activity, which can then be used to support both operational and analytical applications in a consistent manner.

Consistent reporting. Reliance on end-user applications to digest intermittent system data extracts leads to questions regarding inconsistency from one report to another. Reliance on the reports generated from governed processes using master data reduces the inconsistencies experienced.

Improved risk management. The improvement in the quality of enterprise information is the result of master data management; more trustworthy and consistent financial information improves the ability to manage enterprise risk.

Improved decision making. The information consistency that MDM provides across applications reduces data variability, which in turn minimizes organizational data mistrust and allows for faster and more reliable business decisions.

Better spend analysis and planning. Master data associated with product, supplier, and vendor data improves the ability to aggregate purchasing activities, coordinate competitive sourcing, predict future spend, and improve vendor and supplier management.

Regulatory compliance. As one of the major enterprise areas of risk, compliance drives the need for quality data and data governance, and MDM addresses both of these needs. Information auditing is simplified across a consistent master view of enterprise data, enabling more effective information controls that facilitate compliance with regulations.

Increased information quality. Collecting metadata comprising standardized models, value domains, and business rules enables more effective monitoring of conformance to information quality expectations across vertical applications, which reduces information scrap and rework.

Quicker results. A standardized view of the information asset reduces the delays associated with extraction and transformation of data, speeding the implementation of application migrations, modernization projects, and data warehouse/data mart construction.

Improved business productivity. Master data help organizations understand how the same data objects are represented, manipulated, or exchanged across applications within the enterprise and how those objects relate to business process workflows. This understanding allows enterprise architects the opportunity to explore how effective the organization is in automating its business processes by exploiting the information asset.

Simplified application development. The consolidation activities of MDM are not limited to the data; when the multiple master data objects are consolidated into a master repository, there is a corresponding opportunity to consolidate the application functionality associated with the data life cycle. Consolidating many product systems into a single resource allows us to provide a single functional service for the creation of a new product entry to which the different applications can subscribe, thereby supporting the development of a services-oriented architecture (SOA).

Reduction in cross-system reconciliation. The unified view of data reduces the occurrence of inconsistencies across systems, which in turn reduces the effort spent on reconciling data between multiple source systems.

In this context, enterprise applications such as Customer Relationship Management (CRM) and ERP maintain components that apply to instances of the same object type across processing streams (e.g., "Order to Cash"), and maintaining a unified version of each master data object directly supports the enterprise initiative. Therefore, it is reasonable to justify incorporating an MDM initiative as part of these comprehensive projects.

The key deliverables of this stage are the materials for documenting the business case for the stakeholders in the organization, including (not exclusively) the following:

- Identification of key business drivers for master data integration
- Business impacts and risks of not employing an MDM environment
- Cost estimates for implementation
- Success criteria
- Metrics for measuring success
- Expected time to deploy
- Break-even point
- Education, training, and/or messaging material

13.2 DEVELOPING AN MDM ROAD MAP AND ROLLOUT PLAN

The implementation of a complex program, such as MDM, requires strategic planning along with details for its staged deployment. Specifying a road map for the design and development of the infrastructure and processes supporting MDM guides management and staff expectations.

13.2.1 MDM Road Map

Road maps highlight a plan for development and deployment, indicating the activities to be performed, milestones, and a general schedule for when those activities should be performed and when the milestones should be reached. In deference to the planning processes, activity scheduling, resource allocation, and project management strategies that differ at every organization, it would be a challenge to define a road map for MDM that is suitable to everyone. However, there are general stages of development that could be incorporated into a high-level MDM road map.

Evaluate the business goals. This task is to develop an organizational understanding of the benefits of MDM as they reflect the current and future business objectives. This may involve reviewing the lines of business and their related business processes, evaluating where the absence of a synchronized master view impedes or prevents business processes from completing at all or introducing critical inefficiencies, and identifying key business areas that would benefit from moving to an MDM environment.

Evaluate the business needs. This step is to prioritize the business goals and determine which are most critical, then determine which have dependences on MDM as success criteria.

Assess the current state, Here, staff members can use the maturity model to assess the current landscape of available tools, techniques, methods, and organizational readiness for MDM.

Assess the initial gap. By comparing the business needs against the evaluation of the current state, the analysts can determine the degree to which the current state is satisfactory to support business needs, or alternatively determine where there are gaps that can be addressed by implementing additional MDM capabilities.

Envision the desired state. If the current capabilities are not sufficient to support the business needs, the analysts must determine the maturity level that would be satisfactory and set that as the target for the implementation.

Analyze the capability gap. This step is where the analysts determine the gaps between current state and the desired level of maturity and identify which components and capabilities are necessary to fill the gaps.

Perform capability mapping. To achieve interim benefits, the analysts seek ways to map the MDM capabilities to existing application needs to demonstrate tactical returns.

Plan the project. Having identified the capabilities, tools, and methods that need to be implemented, the "bundle" can be handed off to the project management team to assemble a project plan for the appropriate level of requirements analysis, design, development, and implementation.

13.2.2 **Rollout Plan**

Once the road map has been developed, a rollout plan can be designed to execute against the road map; here is an example of a staged plan.

Preparation and adoption. During this initial stage, the information and application environments are reviewed to determine whether there is value in instituting an MDM program, developing the business justification, marketing and compiling educational materials, and other tasks in preparation for initiating a project. Tasks may include metadata assessment, data profiling, identification of selected data sets for consolidation ("mastering"), vendor outreach, training sessions, and the evaluation of solution approaches.

Proof of concept. As a way of demonstrating feasibility, a specific master data object type is selected as an initial target for a consolidation project. There may be an expectation that the result is a throw-away, and the process is intended to identify issues in the overall development process. This may be taken as an assessment opportunity for vendor products, essentially creating a bake-off that allows each vendor to showcase a solution. At the same time, more comprehensive enterprise-wide requirements are determined, documented, and associated within a metadata framework to capture the correlation between business expectations, business rules, and policy management directed by the MDM environment. By the end of this stage, the target MDM architecture will have been determined and the core set of necessary services enumerated.

Initial deployment. Subsequent to the determination of a solution approach and any associated vendor product selection, the lessons learned from the proof of concept stage are incorporated into this development and deployment activity. Master data models are refined to appropriately reflect the organization's needs; data quality expectations are defined in terms of specific dimensions; and identity searching and matching is in place for both batch and inline record linkage and consolidation. A master registry will be produced for each master data object, and both core services and basic application function services will be made available. The master view of data is more likely to be used as reference data. Data governance processes are identified and codified.

Release 1.0. As the developed registries/repositories and services mature, the program reaches a point where it is recognized as suitable for general release. At this point, there are protocols for the migration of business applications to the use of the master data environment, and there are defined policies for all aspects of master data management, including auditing data integration and consolidation, compliance to defined data expectations, and SLAs for ensuring data quality, and the roles and responsibilities for data governance are activated. Modifications to the master data resources are propagated to application clients. New application development can directly use the master data resource.

Transition. At this point, the application migration processes transition legacy applications to the master data resource. As different types of usage scenarios come into play, the directives for synchronization and coherence are employed. Additional value-added services are implemented and integrated into the service layer.

Operations. As the legacy applications are transitioned, the ongoing operations of the master repository are supported and maintained while new requirements or business opportunities drive the introduction of new services.

Figure 13.1 shows a sample template with project milestones that can be used to model an organization's high-level road map. The detailed road map enumerates the specific tasks to be performed in order to reach the defined milestones.

The key deliverable for this stage is a development road map that does the following:

- Delineates the phased implementation of the program
- Specifies high-level deliverables and milestones for each phase
- Maps phased deliverables to success criteria defined as part of the business case

	Data	*Services*	*Policy*	*Integration*
Preparation and Adoption	• Vendor models	• Vendor services	• Metadata management	• Data profiling • Simple identity search and match
Proof of Concept	• Customized models • Data life cycle • Canonical model for exchange	• Core application services • Data quality, matching	• Business rules • Rules engine • Role-based access control	• Complex identity search and match—batch • Master registry
Initial Deployment	• Master relational models • Hierarchy management	• Functional application services	• Workflow management • Policy server	• Complex identity search and match—inline • Master registry
Release 1.0	• Browsing/editing	• Wrappers and façades	• Audit • Compliance • Service level agreements • Data governance	• Batch consolidation • Propagation
Transition	• Retire legacy data	• Value-added services	• Audit • Compliance • Service level agreements	• Synchronization • Coherence
Operational	• Enterprise information management • Data as a service	• Parameterized configuration • Software as a service	• Business policy management	• Interface with all enterprise applications

■ **FIGURE 13.1** A sample template for developing an MDM development road map.

- Estimates time frames
- Estimates resources (capital expenses, staff time)

13.3 ROLES AND RESPONSIBILITIES

Managing the participants and stakeholders associated with an MDM program means clearly articulating each specific role, each participant's needs, the tasks associated with each role, and the accountability associated with the success of the program. A sampling of roles is shown in Figure 13.2.

To ensure that each participant's needs are addressed and that their associated tasks are appropriately performed, there must be some delineation of specific roles, responsibilities, and accountabilities assigned to each person; in Chapter 2 we reviewed using a RACI model, with the acronym RACI referring to the identification of who is *r*esponsible, *a*ccountable, *c*onsulted, and *i*nformed of each activity.

Within the model, the participation types are allocated by role to each task based on whether the role is responsible for deliverables related to completing the task, accountable for the task's deliverables, consulted for advice on completing the task, or is informed of progress or issues associated with the task.

The key deliverables of this stage include the following:

- An enumeration and description of each of the stakeholder or participant roles
- A RACI matrix detailing the degrees of responsibility for each of the participants

■ **FIGURE 13.2** Roles associated with master data management programs.

13.4 **PROJECT PLANNING**

As the road map is refined and the specific roles and responsibilities identified, a detailed project plan can be produced with specific tasks, milestones, and deliverables. For each of the phases specified in the road map, a more detailed list of milestones and deliverables will be listed, as reflected by the responsibilities in the RACI matrix. The list of tasks to accomplish each milestone or deliverable will be detailed, along with resource/staff allocation, estimated timeframes, dependencies, and so on. The project plan will incorporate the activities in the following sections of this chapter. The key deliverable for this stage is a detailed project plan with specific milestones and deliverables.

13.5 **BUSINESS PROCESS MODELS AND USAGE SCENARIOS**

Business operations are guided by defined performance management goals and the approaches to be taken to reach those goals, and applications are developed to support those operations. Applications are driven by business policies, which should be aligned with the organization's strategic direction, and therefore the applications essentially implement business processes that execute those policies.

Although many application architectures emerge organically, they are always intended to implement those business policies through the interaction with persistent data. By documenting the business processes at a relatively granular level, analysts can understand which data entities are touched, determine if those entities reflect master object types, and map those data entities to their corresponding master type. Ultimately, looking at the ways that these applications access apparent master data objects embedded within each data repository helps drive determination of the initial targets for integration into the master environment.

Finally, and most important, one must consider both the existing applications that will be migrated to the new environment and how their operations must evolve, as well as any new business processes for which new applications will be developed targeting the master data environment. Evaluating the usage scenarios shows the way that the participants within each business process will access master data, which will contribute later to the decisions regarding master data models, master data services, and the underlying architectures.

The key deliverables for this activity are as follows:

- A set of business process models for each of the end-client activities that are targeted for inclusion in the master data management program
- A set of usage scenarios for the business applications that will be the clients of the master data asset

13.6 IDENTIFYING INITIAL DATA SETS FOR MASTER INTEGRATION

During this activity, the business process models are reviewed to identify applications and their corresponding data sets that are suitable as initial targets for mastering. The business process models reflect the data interchanges across multiple processing streams. Observing the use of similar abstract types of shared data instances across different processing streams indicates potential master data objects.

Because the business justification will associate master data requirements with achieving business objectives, those requirements should identify the conceptual master data objects that are under consideration, such as customers, products, or employees. In turn, analysts can gauge the suitability of any data set for integration as a function of the business value to be derived (e.g., in reducing cross-system reconciliation or as a by-product of improving customer profiling) and the complexity in "unwinding" the existing data access points into the master view. Therefore, this stage incorporates the development of guidelines for determining the suitability of data sets for master integration and applying those criteria to select the initial data sets to be mastered.

The key deliverable for this phase is a list of the applications that will participate in the MDM program (at least the initial set) and the master data object types that are candidates for mastering. The actual collection of metadata and determination of extraction and transformation processes are fleshed out in later stages.

13.7 DATA GOVERNANCE

As discussed in Chapter 4, data governance essentially focuses on ways that information management is integrated with controls for management oversight along with the verification of organizational observance of information policies. In this context, the aspects of data governance relate to specifying the information policies that reflect business needs and expectations and the processes for monitoring conformance to those information policies. This means introducing both the management processes for data governance and the operational tools to make governance actionable.

The key deliverables of this stage include the following:

- Management guidance for data governance
- Hierarchical management structures for overseeing standards and protocols
- Processes for defining data expectations
- Processes for defining, implementing, and collecting quantifiable measurements
- Definitions of acceptability thresholds for monitored metrics
- Processes for defining and conforming to directives in SLAs
- Processes for operational data governance and stewardship
- Identification and acquisition of tools for monitoring and reporting compliance with governance directives

13.8 METADATA

In Chapter 6, we looked at how the conceptual view of master metadata starts with basic building blocks and grows to maintain comprehensive views of the information that is used to support the achievement of business objectives. Metadata management provides an anchor for all MDM activities, and the metadata repository is used to "control" the development and maintenance of the master data environment by capturing information as necessary to drive the following:

- The analysis of enterprise data for the purpose of structural and semantic discovery
- The correspondence of meanings to data element types
- The determination of master data element types
- The models for master data object types
- The interaction models for applications touching master data
- The information usage scenarios for master data
- The data quality directives
- Access control and management
- The determination of core master services
- The determination of application-level master services
- Business policy capture and correspondence to information policies

Specifying the business requirements for capturing metadata relevant to MDM is the prelude to the evaluation and acquisition of tools that support the ways for resolving business definitions; classify reference data assets; document data elements structures, table layouts, general information architecture; as well as develop higher-order concepts such as data quality business rules, service level agreements, services metadata, and business data such as the business policies driving application design and implementation.

The following are the milestones and deliverables for this stage:

- Business requirements for metadata management tools
- Evaluation and selection of metadata tools
- Processes for gaining consensus on business data definitions
- Processes for documenting data element usage and service usage

13.9 **MASTER OBJECT ANALYSIS**

In Chapter 7, we looked at how the challenges of master data consolidation are not limited to determining what master objects are used but rather incorporate the need to find where master objects are used in preparation for standardizing the consolidated view of the data. This ultimately requires a strategy for standardizing, harmonizing, and consolidating the different representations in their source formats into a master repository or registry. It is important to provide the means for both the consolidation and the integration of master data as well as to facilitate the most effective and appropriate sharing of that master data. This stage takes place simultaneously with the development of the master data models for exchange and persistence. Actual data analytics must be applied to address some fundamental issues, such as the following, regarding the enterprise assets themselves:

- Determining which specific data objects accessed within the business process models are master data objects
- Mapping application data elements to master data elements
- Selecting the data sets that are the best candidates to populate the organization's master data repository
- Locating and isolating master data objects that may be hidden across various applications
- Applying processes for collecting master metadata and developing data standards for sharing and exchange
- Analyzing the variance between the different representations in preparation for developing master data models

The expected results of this stage will be used to configure the data extraction and consolidation processes for migrating data from existing resources into the master environment; they include the following:

- Cross-system data analytic profiles
- Completed metadata profiles
- Business rules
- Source to target mappings
- Extraction and transformation directives

13.10 MASTER OBJECT MODELING

In Chapter 8, we looked at the issues associated with developing models for master data—from extraction, consolidation, persistence, and delivery. This is the stage for developing and refining the models used for extraction, consolidation, persistence, and sharing. It is important to realize that becoming a skilled practitioner of data modeling requires a significant amount of training and experience, so it is critical to engage individuals with the proper skill sets to successfully complete this task.

Every master data modeling exercise must encompass the set of identifying attributes—the data attribute values that are combined to provide a candidate key that is used to distinguish each record from every other. This will rely on the cross-system data analysis and data profiling performed during the master data object analysis stage, and the outputs of that process iteratively inspire the outputs of the modeling processes. It also relies on the documented metadata that have been accumulated from analysis, interviews, and existing documentation.

The following are the expected deliverables from this stage:

- A model for linearized representations of data extracted from original sources in preparation for sharing and exchange
- A model used during the data consolidation process
- A model for persistent storage of selected master data attributes

13.11 DATA QUALITY MANAGEMENT

One of the key value statements related to application use of master data is an increased level of trust in the representative unified view. This implies a level of trustworthiness of the data as it is extracted from the numerous sources and consolidated into the master data asset. At the operational level, business expectations for data quality will have been associated with clearly defined business rules related to ensuring the accuracy of data values and monitoring the completeness and consistency of master data elements. This relies on what has been accumulated within the master metadata repository, including assertions regarding the core definitions, perceptions, formats, and representations of the data elements that compose the model for each master data object.

The data governance guidance developed during earlier phases of the program will be operationalized using metadata management and data quality techniques. Essentially, monitoring and ensuring data quality within the MDM environment is associated with identifying critical data elements, determining which data elements constitute master data, locating and isolating master data objects that exist within the enterprise, and reviewing and resolving the variances between the different representations in order to consolidate instances into a single view. Even after the initial migration of data into a master repository, there will still be a need to instantiate data inspection, monitoring, and controls to identify any potential data quality issues and prevent any material business impacts from occurring.

Tools supporting parsing, standardization, identity resolution, and enterprise integration contribute to aspects of master data consolidation. During this stage, business requirements for tools necessary for assessing, monitoring, and maintaining the correctness of data within the master environment will be used as part of the technology-acquisition process.

The key deliverables for this stage are as follows:

- The determination of business requirements for data quality tools
- The formalization and implementation of operational data quality assurance techniques
- The formalization and implementation of operational data governance procedures
- The acquisition and deployment of data quality tools

13.12 **DATA EXTRACTION, SHARING, CONSOLIDATION, AND POPULATION**

At this point in the program, there should be enough information gathered as a result of the master object analysis and the creation of the data models for exchange and for persistence in order to formulate the processes for data consolidation. The collected information, carefully documented as master metadata, can now be used to create the middleware for extracting data from original sources and marshaling data within a linearized format suitable for data consolidation.

Providing data integration services captures the ability to extract the critical information from different sources and to ensure that a consolidated view is engineered into the target architecture. This stage is the time for developing the data extraction services that will access data in a variety of source applications as well as being able to select and extract data instance sets into a format that is suitable for exchange. Data integration products are designed to seamlessly incorporate the functions shown in the sidebar.

FUNCTIONS OF DATA INTEGRATION PRODUCTS

- *Data extraction and transformation.* After extraction from the sources, data rules may be triggered to transform the data into a format that is acceptable to the target architecture. These rules may be engineered directly within data integration services or may be embedded within supplemental acquired technologies.
- *Data monitoring.* Business rules may be applied at the time of transformation to monitor the conformance of the data to business expectations (such as data quality) as it moves from one location to another. Monitoring enables oversight of business rules discovered and defined during the data profiling phase to validate data as well as single out records that do not conform to defined data quality, feeding the data governance activity.
- *Data consolidation.* As different sources' data instances are brought together, the integration tools use the parsing, standardization, harmonization, and matching capabilities of the data quality technologies to consolidate data into unique records in the master data model.

Developing these capabilities is part of the data consolidation and integration phase. For MDM programs put in place either as a single source of truth for new applications or as a master index for preventing data instance duplication, the extraction, transformation and consolidation can be applied at both an acute level (i.e., at the point that each data source is introduced into the environment) and on an operational level (i.e., on a continuous basis, applied to a feed from the data source).

This stage's key deliverables and milestones include the following:

- Identification of business requirements for data integration tools
- Acquisition of data integration tools

- Acquisition of data consolidation tools
- Identification and business requirements for data consolidation technology, including identity resolution, entity search and match, and data survivorship
- Development of data extraction "connectors" for the candidate source data systems
- Development of rules for consolidation
- Implementation of consolidation services (batch, inline)
- Development of rules for survivorship
- Implementation of rules for survivorship
- Formalization of the components within the master data services layer

13.13 **MDM ARCHITECTURE**

There are different architectural styles along an implementation spectrum, and these styles are aligned in a way that depends on three dimensions:

1. The number of attributes maintained within the master data system
2. The degree of consolidation applied as data is brought into the master repository
3. How tightly coupled applications are to the data persisted in the master data environment

One end of the spectrum employs a registry, limited to maintaining identifying attributes, which is suited to loosely coupled application environments and where the drivers for MDM are based more on the harmonization of unique representation of master objects on demand. The other end of the spectrum is the transaction hub, best suited to environments requiring tight coupling of application interaction and a high degree of data currency and synchronization. Hybrid approaches can lie anywhere between these two ends, and the architecture can be adjusted in relation to the business requirements as necessary.

Other dimensions also contribute to the decision: service layer complexity, access roles and integration needs, security, and performance. Considering the implementation spectrum (as opposed to static designs) within the context of the dependent factors simplifies selection of an underlying architecture. Employing a template like the one shown in Chapter 9 can help score the requirements associated with defined selection criteria. The scores can be weighted based on identified key aspects, and the resulting assessment can be gauged to determine a reasonable point along the implementation spectrum that will support the MDM requirements.

The following are some of the key deliverables and milestones of this phase:

- Evaluation of master data usage scenarios
- Assessment of synchronization requirements
- Evaluation of vendor data models
- Review of the architectural styles along the implementation spectrum
- Selection of a vendor solution

13.14 **MASTER DATA SERVICES**

Master data service implementations may vary, but as discussed in Chapter 12, the services can be characterized within three layers:

- Core services, which focus on data object life cycle actions, along with the capabilities necessary for supporting general functions applied to master data
- Object services, which focus on actions related to the master data object type or classification (such as customer or product)
- Business application services, which focus on the functionality necessary at the business level

Figure 13.3 shows some example core services, such as the object create, update, and retire services, among others; access control; data consolidation; integration; and the components supporting consolidation, business process workflows, rule-directed operations, and so on. Although the differences inherent across many organizations will reflect slight differences in the business's catalog of services, this framework provides a reasonable starting point for evaluation and design.

There is a clearly mutual dependence between the success of applications relying on master data management and those reliant on a services-oriented architecture. A services-oriented approach to application development relies on the existence of a master data repository, and the success of an MDM program depends on the ability to deploy and use master object access and manipulation services. A flexible SOA enables the organizational changes necessary to use the data most efficiently. Driving application development from the business perspective forces a decision regarding harmonizing both the data objects and

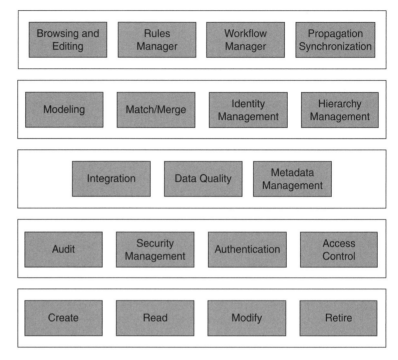

FIGURE 13.3 Core master data services.

the ways those objects are used, and a services-based approach allows the organization to exploit enterprise data in relation to the ways that using enterprise data objects drive business performance.

Access to master data is best achieved when it is made transparent to the application layer, and employing a services-based approach actually serves multiple purposes within the MDM environment. During the initial phases of deploying the master environment, the use of a service layer simplifies the implementation of the master object life cycle and provides a transition path from a distributed application architecture into the consolidated master application infrastructure.

Key milestones and deliverables include the following:

- Qualification of master service layers
- Design of master data services
- Implementation and deployment of master data services
- Application testing

13.15 **TRANSITION PLAN**

Exposing master data for use across existing legacy applications poses a challenge for a number of factors, including the need for customized data extraction and transformation, reduction in the replication of functionality, and adjusting the legacy applications' data access patterns. Providing the component service layer addresses some of these issues; although the traditional extraction, transformation, and loading (ETL) method is insufficient for continuous synchronization, master data services support the data exchange that will use data integration tools in the appropriate manner. In essence, the transaction semantics necessary to maintain consistency can be embedded within the service components that support master data object creation and access, eliminating the concern that using ETL impedes consistency. The consolidation of application capabilities within a component service catalog through the resolution of functionality eliminates functional redundancy, thereby reducing the risks of inconsistency as a result of replication.

Yet the challenge of applications transitioning to using the master repository still exists, requiring a migration strategy that minimizes invasiveness. To transition to using the master repository, applications must be adjusted to target the master repository instead of their own local data store. Planning this transition involves developing an interface to the master repository that mimics each application's own existing interface, and the method discussed in Chapter 12 for this transition is developing a conceptual service layer as a stepping-stone in preparation for the migration using a design pattern known as "wrapper façades."

During the transition stage, the data consolidation processes are iterated and tested to ensure that the right information is migrated from the source data systems into the master data asset. At the same time, any adjustments or changes to the master service layer are made to enable a cutover from dependence on the original source to dependence on the services layer (even if that services layer still accesses the original data). The application transition should be staged to minimize confusion with respect to identifying the source of migration problems. Therefore, instituting a migration and transition process and piloting that process with one application is a prelude to instituting that process on an ongoing basis.

Key milestones and deliverables include the following:

- Development of a migration/transition process
- Design and implementation of wrapper services
- Pilot transition for migration/transition process
- Institutionalization of migration/transition process

13.16 ONGOING MAINTENANCE

At this point, the fundamental architecture has been established, along with the policies, procedures, and processes for master data management, including the following:

- Identifying master data objects
- Creating a master data model
- Assessing candidate data sources for suitability
- Assessing requirements for synchronization and consistency
- Assessing requirements for continuous data quality monitoring
- Overseeing the governance of master data
- Developing master data services
- Transitioning and migrating legacy applications to the master environment

Having the major components of the master data strategy in place enables two maintenance activities: the continued migration of existing applications to the master environment and ensuring the proper performance and suitability of the existing master data system. The former is a by-product of the pieces put together so far; the latter involves ongoing analysis of performance against agreed-to service levels.

At the same time, the system should be reviewed to ensure the quality of record linkage and identity resolution. In addition, MDM program managers should oversee the continued refinement of master data services to support new parameterized capabilities or to support newly migrated applications.

The following are the expectations of this phase:

- Establishing minimum levels of service for data quality
- Establishing minimum levels of service for application performance
- Establishing minimum levels of service for synchronization
- Implementing service-level monitoring and reporting
- Enhancing governance programs to support MDM issue reporting, tracking, and resolution
- Reviewing ongoing vendor product performance

13.17 **SUMMARY: EXCELSIOR!**

Master data management can provide significant value to growing enterprise information management initiatives, especially when MDM improves interapplication information sharing, simplifies application development, reduces complexity in the enterprise information infrastructure, and lowers overall information management costs. In this chapter, we have provided a high-level road map, yet your mileage may vary, depending on your organization's readiness to adopt this emerging technology.

As this technology continues to mature, there will be, by necessity, an evolution in the way we consider the topics discussed here. Therefore, to maintain that view, consult this book's associated website (*www. mdmbook.com*) for updates, new information, and further insights.

That being said, there is great value in engaging others who have the experience of assessing readiness, developing a business case, developing a road map, developing a strategy, designing, and implementing a master data management program. Please do not hesitate to contact us directly (loshin@knowledge-integrity.com) for advice. We are always happy to provide recommendations and suggestions to move your MDM program forward!

Bibliography and Suggested Reading

Bibliography

Dreibelbisawdreibe, Allen, Eberhard Hechler, Bill Mathews, Martin Oberhofer, and Dr. Guenter Sauter, "Information Service Patterns, Part 4: Master Data Management Architecture Patterns," downloaded from *www.ibm.com/developerworks/db2/library/techarticle/dm-0703sauter/index.html*.

Dyche, Jill, and Evan Levy, *Customer Data Integration: Reaching a Single Version of the Truth*, Wiley, 2006.

Inmon, William H., Bonnie O'Neil, and Lowell Fryman, *Business Metadata: Capturing Enterprise Knowledge*, Morgan Kaufmann, 2007.

Loshin David, *Enterprise Knowledge Management: The Data Quality Approach*, Morgan Kaufmann, 2001.

Marks Eric A., and Michael Bell, *Service-Oriented Architecture: A Planning and Implementation Guide for Business and Technology*, Wiley, 2006.

"OASIS Reference Model for Service-Oriented Architecture," downloaded from *www.oasis-open.org/committees/download.php/19679/soa-rm-cs.pdf*.

Silverston, Len, *The Data Model Resource Book*, Volumes 1 and 2, Wiley, 2001.

Suggested Reading

There are many good websites with information about master data management; here is a list of a few that I have browsed in the past to gain insight. We will maintain an updated set of links at the book website, *www.mdmbook.com*.

The Business Intelligence Network: *www.b-eye-network.com*

Intelligent Enterprise: *www.intelligententerprise.com*

DM Review: *www.dmreview.com*

The following are research companies providing coverage of MDM:

Gartner: *www.gartner.com*

Forrester: *www.forrester.com/rb/research*

Ventana: *www.ventanaresearch.com*

The MDM Institute: *www.tcdii.com/home.html*

The Data Warehousing Institute hosts material about aspects of MDM: *www.tdwi.org*

Index